D1520354

"Greed Is Good" and Other Fables

"Greed Is Good" and Other Fables

Office Life in Popular Culture

Tony Osborne

PRAEGER

AN IMPRINT OF ABC-CLIO, LLC
Santa Barbara, California • Denver, Colorado • Oxford, England

Library of Congress Cataloging-in-Publication Data

Osborne, Tony.
   Greed is good and other fables : office life in popular culture / Tony Osborne.
      p. cm.
   Includes bibliographical references and index.
      ISBN 978–0–313–38575–9 (hardback) — ISBN 978–0–313–38576–6 (ebook)
1. Office management—History. 2. Organizations—United States—History. 3. Popular culture—United States—History. I. Title.
HF5547.O73   2012
306.3—dc23   2012002310

ISBN: 978–0–313–38575–9
EISBN: 978–0–313–38576–6

16 15 14 13 12   1 2 3 4 5

This book is also available on the World Wide Web as an eBook.
Visit www.abc-clio.com for details.

Praeger
An Imprint of ABC-CLIO, LLC

ABC-CLIO, LLC
130 Cremona Drive, P.O. Box 1911
Santa Barbara, California 93116-1911

This book is printed on acid-free paper ∞

Manufactured in the United States of America

For Diana, Teddy,
and Tommy

And with everlasting gratitude to
Cheryl Straker

a research professional
of extraordinary ability

Contents

Chapter 1

The Great American Dilemma: Conformity or Rebellion?

An indistinct yet clearly grasped place called "the office" occupies a vast space in popular culture. In truth and in fiction, the office is a site of primal struggle, a battlefield of competing personalities and desires; and on a higher plane, the office is the stage upon which old and new values clash, the ground under which tradition is churned—or into which it extends its roots. Beyond any passing entertainment value, the march of office-themed stories throughout popular culture contains something of the mores of their eras.

Some titles or names personify their eras so vividly they become historical markers or cultural icons. Take, for example, Sloan Wilson's novel *The Man in the Gray Flannel Suit* (1955), whose title is now lodged in American folklore as a metonym for faceless conformity (even though the gray-flannelled man, Tom Rath, was a quietly seething—think "wrath"—nonconformist who struggled against sycophancy; not all '50s rebels wore jeans and t-shirts or berets and goatees). Or take the scene in Oliver Stone's film *Wall Street* (1985) during which in a green-carpeted office (to symbolize greenbacks), the corporate raider Gordon Gekko stands behind his desk, hooked up to a blood pressure monitor while inhaling a cigarette, and barks orders into his headset: "Rip their . . . throats out Ollie and stuff 'em in your garbage compactor. I want every orifice in their body bleeding red." He pauses long enough to declare,

"Lunch is for wimps." Then cut to Gekko's speech to the shareholders of a company he covets: "The point is, ladies and gentlemen, that greed—for lack of a better word—is good. Greed is right. Greed works. Greed clarifies. . . . And greed—you mark my words—will not only save Teldar Paper, but that other malfunctioning corporation called the U.S.A."[1]

"Greed is good" encapsulates the mid-1980s of junk bonds, poison pills, white knights, and golden parachutes. But the intervening years of cultural upheaval have drained the phrase of all irony. Today, it describes and justifies the policy and legal machinations of a system once extolled as a government for the people by the people.

RECASTING THE WILD WEST

Along with the towering, singular characters of office life, stock characters from all forms of popular entertainment shuffle through our minds. There is the pencil-thin clerk with wire rims and green eyeshades, familiar in Westerns as the cowering bank teller, telegraph operator, or ticket agent. In the obscure but prolific filmmaker Jam Handy's (1886–1983) dramatized history of the Coca-Cola company—*Always Tomorrow: The Portrait of an American Business* (1941)—the clerk type resurfaces as a worrywart accountant called Larry. "Oh dear, oh dear . . . makes you want to go out and bury your head like an ostrich,"[2] he frets on cue when blaring headlines announce war or financial panic as the film flits through the horse-and-buggy days to the dawn of World War II. Larry is a comedic foil to his boss Jim, another archetype: the rugged pioneer visionary who settled the West now transplanted into business—the field into which his physical prowess has been sublimated or rechanneled into a more civilized form of aggression. In typical heroic fashion, Jim made it to the top—"won"—by ridiculing risk and calamity. As a small bottler who made it big, Jim typifies the unbreakable spirit of free enterprise while embodying that defining American trait celebrated in myth and legend, undaunted courage. The Great Depression? A mere "bank holiday" that Jim "licks," like he did the "panics" of 1893 and 1907, not by hunkering down, but by expanding, jettisoning horse and wagon for a new truck, hiring more salesmen, and increasing advertising. Like the tall, square-jawed Hollywood heroes he resembles, Jim hits the canvas a time or two but never stays down for the count. As in Horatio Alger's (1832–1899) rags-to-riches stories and other seminal fables of American enterprise, faith, optimism, industry, and honesty are ironclad traits of success—especially when coupled with an unwavering belief in the rightness and goodness of *the* "cause": the product. And Jim is a true believer. Coca-Cola, he tells us, is "healthful, palatable and uniform" and costs only a nickel. Jim isn't so much a salesman as a missionary who spreads happiness by bringing Coca-Cola to the people. As the story's narrator, he appears as a graying, dapper executive who testifies to the sanctity of American enterprise; his youthful tribulations impart moral instruction. For business heroes like Jim, the new frontiersmen, success is a byproduct of courage and risk taking. The thrill of entrepreneurship is in the *doing* rather than in the accumulation of accolades and markers of status. The goal of success isn't a life of ease, isn't freedom from "work," a sentence imposed on most of humanity whose aversion to and evasion of work seems innate and natural. (Who would chose the cloistered tedium of an office—an extension of prison—over free play in the sun?) There is a pronounced Teutonic strain in the American "virtue" of eschewing rest. As Nietzsche said, the genius of the Church was to devise such lengthy and boring services as to make the working man long for the workweek. Or perhaps refusing to hang up one's guns is simply an attempt to clutch at fleeing youth. But Jim derives vigor from work. Thus, his Puritan disdain of easing up. (Retirement, of course, isn't remotely a possibility.) "Every man is a pioneer in his youth, it's natural," says Jim. "I want to be one until they carry me off some place and plant sod on top of me. . . . I'm ten times the pioneer I was twenty years ago. I'm ten times the man. My business has grown and I've grown with it. And I want to keep growing."[3]

SHORT, FAT, AND NASTY

The antipode of the tall, handsome, charismatic leader is the portly and balding tyrant, such as Cosmo Spacely of *The Jetsons*, the animated sitcom set 100 years in the future. Spacely yells and threatens but isn't all bad under the gruffness. *The Jetsons'* debut episode (1962) is based on a ritual of office life, having the boss over for dinner.

"Fine dinner, Jetson. Fine family," says Spacely, lighting a postprandial cigar. George Jetson has apparently passed muster. But when Rosie the Robot brings out Spacely's favorite dessert, pineapple upside down cake, he fires George on the spot: "How can you afford a maid on what I'm overpaying you? . . . You're moonlighting!"[4] George swallows it; the rent-a-maid doesn't. Rosie lights into "shorty" for berating such good people, hectoring him out the door. As Spacely pilots his flying saucer home, Rosie's sting starts to smart. Spacely pulls over to a public vision-phone and apologizes for his "big mouth." He wants George back at a better salary, better hours, *and* a bonus—so the family can keep Rosie.

Be back tomorrow, says Spacely—and "on time." (In an episode in which George fitfully beseeches Spacely for a raise, the big man feigns to know neither Jetson's name nor his department.) But Spacely knows George and his indolent proclivities all too well. If Spacely and the affably unambitious George seem familiar, it's because *The Jetsons'* co-creator, Joe Barbera (with William Hanna) "borrowed" the characters from *Blondie*, the comic strip Chic Young launched in 1930. George Jetson is Dagwood Bumstead, and Cosmo Spacely is Julius (Caesar) Dithers.

SITCOM OFFICES

Comedies tend to portray the office as an extension of the home, a comfortable setting with room for quirky personalities and plenty of time for highjinks and romance. In the sitcom *Bewitched* (1964–1972), a charming young witch (Samantha) married to an ad man (Darin) waltzes in and out of her husband's Madison Avenue office at will, which always delights Darin's boss, Larry Tate. In the program's third episode ("It Shouldn't Happen to a Dog"), a boorish, hung-over client avails himself of the bar in Darin's office, which is appointed with crystal decanters and a silver ice bucket. Typically, Samantha is milling about the office during business hours. The boor makes a play for her, and Darin decks him with a right to the chin, barroom style. Tate seems no more concerned than if Darin had broken a cheap ashtray but reprimands him nonetheless. Why couldn't Darin have used a little diplomacy? His punch just cost the company half a million dollars. What will Tate tell the stockholders?

"Somebody insults my wife that's as diplomatic as I get," says Darin.[5] And furthermore, Tate can tell the stockholders that Darin—the best in the business—has quit. With Sam clutching his arm and beaming proudly, Darin, rather pleased with himself, walks out. But the rupture isn't serious. Firings, resignations, and rehirings are recurring events in sitcom offices. Thus, when Darin is satisfied that his honor has been restored, he, star that he is, deigns to take his job back. (The client had driven to Darin's home, no less, and apologized for having been an ass.)

BUSINESSMEN AND EXECUTIVES ON THE RADIO

There are, of course, a variety of stock types tied to specific jobs, such as the sex bomb secretary who can't type or take shorthand, exemplified by characters like Miss Hedy LaRue in the film *How to Succeed in Business*

Without Really Trying (1967). But popular culture also weighs in on generalized types such as "businessman" and "executive." An early episode of the ABC radio program *This is Your FBI* titled "Extortion," broadcast August 3, 1945, contains an exchange between a "real" man and a man of business, one Paul Martin. Martin receives a late-night phone call at home demanding $20,000 or his life. The "mark" calls the FBI, and an agent called Simmons is dispatched to Martin's home to coach him through a "war of nerves" that will trap the blackmailers. The days pass as cloistered agent and businessman wait out the extortion ring's next move. Predictably, the pressure gets to Martin, who paces incessantly: "Three days feels like three years!" he bleats.

Agent Simmons is stern: "Please sit down! You've walked about one hundred miles!" His voice drips disgust. The program's "voice-of-god" narrator ensures this judgment isn't lost on young listeners: "[No matter what trials he faces] a man who works with his hands can get through the next day. But not a man who sits behind a desk." Japan would surrender two weeks after "Extortion" aired, Germany having surrendered in May. With all the fanfare and parades for the returning soldiers, how many impressionable listeners would have thought: "Risk? Adventure? Heroism? Not for me. *I* want to sit behind a desk and quake." (In dismissing office work, the narrator presumably excluded the FBI, which employs about two paper pushers, such as J. Edgar Hoover was, for every field agent.)[6]

Thus does popular entertainment shape and enforce ideas and values. But popular culture is a carnival of contradictions, inconsistencies, distortions, myths, fabrications, and fables. Like business culture or any other sphere designated "culture," popular culture is wildly factious.

Less than a year before "Extortion" aired, ABC radio served up a very different characterization of office work in an episode of *The Life of Riley*. William Bendix starred in this comedy about an aircraft riveter in California. In the episode called "Night School," which aired on December 10, 1944, Riley takes night classes to learn algebra so he can move off the assembly line and get an "office job."

"Then," Riley tells his teenage son, Junior, "I'll put my feet up on my desk all day. Maybe I'll become an executive. Then I'll get two desks, one for each foot."

Junior: "Hey Pop, that'd be great if you become an executive. Then I can go to college, and after I graduate you can make me a vice president."

Riley: "Oh no Junior, none of that. You're going to start at the bottom of the ladder—just like I did."[7]

Alas, poor Riley didn't have much of a head for numbers and stayed put. But in daydreaming about the upper reaches of office life—a region as familiar to him as ancient Mesopotamia—he voiced a popular notion: "executives" are potentates who do just what they like, which isn't much of anything. Drudge work, the manual labor so valorized on *This is Your FBI*, is what befalls the uneducated. A desk job is more prestigious than dulling your mind and wearing out your body performing manual labor. This is hardly a new insight.

Based on archaeological evidence discovered in Egypt, the prototypical desk job, "scribe," dates at least to 3000 or 2950 BC (the I–II Dynasties in Abydos): scribes are explicitly mentioned as an "official" class in the records (names, titles, inventories) of the period. The Australian archaeologist V. Gordon Childe notes that writing was a "profession that enjoyed a privileged position and offered prospects of advancement to office, power, and wealth . . . a stepping stone to prosperity and social rank."[8] This wasn't lost on ancient Egyptian fathers. A batch of documents dating from 1600 to 1100 BC (the New Kingdom) uncannily presages the conversation between Riley and Junior. The following bits of advice have a distinct, universal parental tone:

Put writing in your heart that you may protect yourself from hard labor of any kind. . . . The scribe is released from manual tasks; it is he who commands. . . . [the scribe's palette] is what makes the difference between you and the man who handles an oar.

I have seen the metal-worker at his task at the mouth of his furnace with fingers like a crocodile's. He stank worse than fish-spawn. Every workman who holds a chisel suffers more than the men who hack the ground. . . . The stonecutter . . . when he has done the great part of his labor his arms are exhausted, he is tired out. . . . The weaver in a workshop is worse off than a woman; [squatting] with knees to his belly [he] does not taste (fresh) air.[9]

In other words, don't be a fool; stay in school.

STUCK IN AN OFFICE

The history of human labor encompasses a crude bifurcation between physical and mental toil. This division between the hands and mind carries over into the office with a qualitative twist. In the office, the semiskilled stroke typewriter keys and lift files rather than stoke blast furnaces and carry hods. Semiskilled office work is such a systemized routine that it's as mind numbing as an assembly line. While office equipment has evolved, the essential nature of office work remains unchanged. Some variation of copying documents, keeping records, and figuring sums, the legal detritus of trade and barter, generates the incessant hum—and tedium—of office life.

The boredom of office life is axiomatic in popular culture. In *How to Stop Worrying and Start Living* (1944), Dale Carnegie postulated that fatigue and worry were more symptomatic of boredom than physical exertion. He illustrated this by describing the work a stenographer did for an oil company in Tulsa as "one of the dullest jobs imaginable: filling out printed forms for oil leases, inserting figures and statistics." The poor woman kept up her spirits by inventing games such as tallying the number of forms she processed and trying to top her output the next day. Soon she restored her vitality and became the most efficient stenographer in her division. Presumably, this is how one works his or her way up from the bottom. So how did the oil company respond to this leap in productivity? A promotion? A raise? A pat on the back? No. Nothing. She quit and married a best-selling author—Dale Carnegie.[10]

Humdrum office work is a life sentence that untold millions must serve. Naturally, resentment against pampered celebrities who don't appreciate their blessings or who throw it all away is a common storyline in the popular press. Here is how *Washington Post* columnist Tracee Hamilton put it in a 2010 diatribe against the Washington Redskins' defensive tackle Albert Haynesworth, then in the second year of a $100 million, seven-year contract (Haynesworth had refused to attend offseason conditioning camps because they cut into his free time): "a lot of these guys have never held a real job before . . . maybe they had a 'no-work' or 'no-show' job when they were in college. But most have never dragged themselves into a cubicle, day after day, and performed soul-sucking work and attended mind-numbing meetings and in-services and all the other dross that most Americans endure every day."[11]

Not everybody goes quietly or willingly into office life. A central narrative thread running throughout popular culture might be called the great American dilemma: the choice between conformity or adventure, security or risk, the office or the road. Even if it's not explicitly present or otherwise mentioned, "the office" is always present as a ghost note. Adventure takes its flavor from its implied antithesis: the safety and tedium of a desk job. The following passage from Ernest Hemingway's short story, "Big Two-Hearted River: Part I" (1925), presents a stark contrast to the harried regimentation of office life:

Nick walked back up the ties to where his pack lay in the cinders beside the railway track. He was happy. He adjusted the pack harness around the bundle, pulling straps tight, slung the pack on his back, got his arms through the shoulder straps and took some of the pull off his shoulders by leaning his forehead against the wide band of the tump-line. Still, it was too heavy. It was much too heavy. He had his leather rod-case in his hand and leaning forward to keep the weight of the pack high on his shoulders he walked along the road that paralleled the railway track, leaving the burned town behind in the heat, and then turned off around a hill with a high, fire-scarred hill on either side onto a road that went back into the country. He walked along the road feeling the ache from the pull of the heavy pack. The road climbed steadily. It was hard work walking up-hill. His muscles ached and the day was hot, but Nick felt happy. He felt he had left everything behind, the need for thinking, the need to write, other needs. It was all back of him.[12]

Unlike the stenographer who needs to play mental tricks to feel more alive than dead, Nick has no need to think at all. In fact, he has no needs. He lives in the moment, at one with nature. Nick's day isn't ordered by clocks, by mindless tasks, by superiors. He does what he likes, when he likes. And most important, Nick is happy. Admittedly, "freedom" is an unwieldy abstraction, impossible to pin down. After wrestling with it for some 600 pages in *Being and Nothingness* (1943), Jean-Paul Sartre pronounced freedom an empty philosophical category. But in everyday life, if freedom, however fleeting, looks or feels like anything, it might look and feel like Nick Adams.

Like Hemingway's most memorable characters, many of the characters that animate Tennessee Williams's plays also flee the straight life. In *Sweet Bird of Youth* (1959), Chance Wayne, played by Paul Newman in the movie version (1962), rebels against small-town Southern life and hits the road looking for fame and fortune. Chance finds neither. Nevertheless, he returns to his hometown, which treats him as an untouchable, wearing the air of a big man. Chance tries to justify his choices by taunting a young man he grew up with. It's a pathetic attempt to validate his life. However, Williams uncorks a put-down for the ages that transcends the context and neatly sums up office life: "You still work down at the bank? You sit on your can all day countin' century notes and once every week they let you slip one in your pockets? That's a fine set-up, Scotty, if you're satisfied with it but it's starting to give you a little pot and a can."[13]

You sit on your butt all day getting fat and counting hundred-dollar bills, and at the end of the week, they let you pocket one. Williams himself could never abide the nine-to-five routine and had a near nervous breakdown trying. Later in life, whenever Williams was asked his age, he always deducted three years, saying the time he spent working for the International Shoe Company in St. Louis "didn't count."

THE ROAD

The history of popular culture is rich in colorful adventurers who chose the road: Huckleberry Finn, Hemingway's existential heroes, Woody Guthrie and his boxcar companions, Jack Kerouac and the Beats, Ken Kesey and the Merry Pranksters—"you're either on the bus or off the bus." However, that was then. Hitting the road in search of adventure isn't the same in our age of standardization and homogenization and superhighways. The same motels, diners, and filling stations are in every city and state—and now Europe, Asia, and Russia, too.

Walter Kirn cleverly makes this point in *Up in the Air* (2002), a novel about a new type of peripatetic office creature called a "career transitions counselor" (CTC)—corporate-speak for a person who attempts to soothe fired employees. CTCs parachute into offices throughout the United States to tell employees that they've been fired, which, of course, is couched as a great opportunity. As Kirn's protagonist, Ryan Bingham, says, the job was presented to him as "an ethical revolution in American business practices . . . [that] served the downsizing employer by minimizing potential legal blowback from the parties dismissed."[14] Before he became a corporate "turk"—football slang for the man who tells players they've been cut—Bingham and a girlfriend loaded a Subaru station wagon with beer and sleeping bags and set out to discover the America of folklore and legend. They flipped coins to pick the day's route. His girlfriend hungered for roadside stands and "wicked stares from old-timers in greasy spoons." As they drove, she read *On the Road*, "declaimed the thing." Bingham knew he was being used as a "native guide." Just the same, he "wanted to show her something she hadn't seen." But he failed:

Nothing there. That America was finished. Too many movies had turned the deserts to sets. The all-night coffee shops served Egg Beaters. And everywhere, from dustiest Nebraska to swampiest Louisiana, folks were expecting us, the road-trip pilgrims. They sold us Route 66 T-shirts, and they took credit cards. The hitchhikers didn't tell stories, they just slept, and the gas stations were self-service, no toothless grease monkeys. In Kansas, my girlfriend threw away [*On the Road*] at a truckstop Dunkin' Donuts stand and called her father for a ticket home. . . . I doubt that she's thought twice in fifteen years about our hoboing. No reason to. The real America had left the ground and we'd spent the summer circling a ruin. Not even that. An imitation ruin.[15]

For Bingham, airline hubs now constitute the "road." The way to see America is by flying. It's all in the sky now, "not down there, where the show is almost over." Contemporary America is structured in "spokes, not lines." And as "long as you're aimed at a city with an airport, you can get anywhere from anywhere and there's no such thing as a wrong turn. . . . Just find a hub."[16]

A STATE OF MIND

The office is both a physical place and a state of mind. Certainly, office life doesn't preclude well-being; offices aren't inherently dreadful, excepting those vast catacombs systemized into bureaucracies. Nonetheless, the office represents something akin to a gray purgatory (preferable to the hell of unemployment): a type of holding-cell where drives, desires, dreams— all the things that point to self-fulfillment, to that elusive and imaginary state of happiness called "the future"—are arrested or veer off course. "Kafkaesque" has entered the popular lexicon as a description of bureaucratic red tape. More specifically, it captures the frustration of attempting to negotiate a tangle of absurd procedures and regulations, a fragmented journey through a warren of offices whose inhabitants lack empathy and seem programmed to say such things as "your document is not valid" or "you are in the wrong office" or "no . . . that's not possible"—and hundreds of other convoluted ways to say "no." Such ludicrous difficulties plague K., the protagonist of Franz Kafka's unfinished novel *The Castle* (1926). But more telling of the deeper ravages of office life is Kafka's novella *The Metamorphosis* (1915), a parable of bureaucratic contingencies infiltrating the psyche. Gregor Samsa, a young salesman, awakens one morning to find himself transformed into a giant insect. He's frantic. Yet Gregor's corporal catastrophe isn't the source of his anxiety. Rather, it's the clock the sets him off. It's late. Gregor panics. His alarm didn't go off. Now there's no time to pack his samples. Gregor will miss his train. His boss will fire him. So completely has office regimentation colonized the innermost recesses of Gregor's mind, a sanctuary that should be inviolate, that he's lost his selfhood.[17] He can't help experiencing—or measuring—life through clocks and timetables. Gregor sees *everything* only from the company's perspective. He's lost the ability to mourn his own tragedy. It's no longer his. It belongs to the company.

THE DOMINANT IDEOLOGY

Beyond rows of mahogany desks, gray file cabinets, ringing telephones, and clacking typewriters, "the office" is an ideology, a way of viewing and structuring life. Office culture governs and structures society. Customs such as "business hours" and "business days" set the tempo and regulate the flow of social intercourse. Not long ago, "business attire" and "business English" set the standards of dress and discourse. But there is also a toxic strain of business culture: a voracious and shameless drive for obscene levels of profiteering untethered to social utility and virulent to the nation's well-being.

Today, America no longer manufactures much of anything; rather, our debt-riddled economy rides on the tottering haunches of usury, called the "finance industry" in the popular press. Congress, the courts, the president—regardless of party—all behave like corporate servants. (A central facet of pop culture today is politics, a celebrity freak show that provides equal parts mirth and despair.) In recent years, the government "of the people" has aided and abetted an assault on democratic safeguards under the name of "deregulation," a lawlessness that permits the manipulation of markets and the plunder of public funds. Deregulation is the crowning achievement of office culture. With impunity, Wall Street now "manufactures" and sells worthless paper—the same bits over and over and over.

The culture of acquisition dominates America today. (Indeed, mainstream American culture *is* business culture.) To this way of thinking, "getting more" is the supreme value. Everything is for sale: national parks, museums, college athletics. University presidents speak of "revenue-generating" buildings with junk-food stalls and coffee bars. Every conceivable public space is branded, littered with signage.

But business culture is neither monolithic nor static, and it's easy to forget that notions of public service once tempered voraciousness. Naked accumulation was once considered unseemly, if not immoral, and checked by social censure. Proud, working Americans didn't grovel before wealth; they regarded the likes of John D. Rockefeller and J. P. Morgan with suspicion and scorn, as though they and their money stank. There was a time when American presidents—Grover Cleveland, both Theodore and Franklin Roosevelt, and Woodrow Wilson come to mind—used soaring rhetoric to eviscerate buccaneer monopolists and financiers.

In sum, things weren't always as they are today. Nor need they be. Depictions of office life in popular culture include untold normative threads and pictures, as utopian as old high school civics texts, belied by reality. But this dissonance contains a critical impetus. An idealized business world is also an indictment of the way things are. Thus, a 1950s corporate film on office etiquette that seems hopelessly passé at first glance also contains a critical dimension: it pictures a model office, the way things should be in a just world—an ideal to strive for and a means of measuring present shortcomings. Hence the value of examining office life in all facets of popular culture. The most ostensibly innocuous portrayals may bite the deepest.

Chapter 2

My Approach and Some Reflections on Pop Culture and Such

This book looks at how office life has been portrayed in popular culture through a mix of both mainstream and submerged voices. I've lifted narrative threads and images about office life from the mass media's main channels, beginning with nineteenth-century fiction and running through contemporary film and television. First, a word about language. Because many of the older business stories I draw from portray an exclusive world of men, it would be inaccurate (and cumbersome) to adhere to the current practice of gender-inclusive terminology. If I write *salesman* instead of *salesperson*, it's not to make a political statement or to offend; rather, it's because the salesmen in some stories—the Bible salesmen in *Salesman*, the real estate salesmen in *Glengarry Glen Ross*, the bond traders in *Liar's Poker*, for example—were all men, with nary a woman in sight. My purpose is to document popular culture as it was and is, not to purge the past. Also, for ease of expression, I use the terms *mass*, *pop*, and *low* culture interchangeably; likewise, *office life*, *business*, and *corporate* culture. Of course, business culture and mainstream culture are intertwined and overlap. Just as pop culture shapes beliefs about office life, business culture influences the form (the medium) and content of popular culture. This is still true, but it doesn't quite recognize the recent bare-knuckled upheaval in American society: corporate culture's dominance—that is, stopping at *nothing*, no matter how base or blasphemous, to make a killing. ("Killing" doesn't quite describe the scale of today's untethered rapaciousness; "financial extermination" is more accurate.) Today, corporate culture *is* mainstream American culture: gluttony in all shapes and forms is the supreme American value. It's unavoidable that corporate culture's ascendancy is one of the tales that emerges in my treatment of popular culture and entertainment: it's woven into the fabric of office life. However, it's a nuanced story and not as subject to easy moralizing as one might imagine.

I recount stories, vignettes, fragments, and images about office life that span three centuries. The oldest is from 1837: Charles Dickens's description of musty offices and grimy lawyers in the *Pickwick Papers* (whose chapters originally appeared in 24- and 32-page illustrated monthly installments that sold for a shilling, about a quarter in U.S. currency). A sense of how business culture has progressed is contained in the magazine fiction of Herman Melville, Mark Twain, O. Henry, Willa Cather, Rudyard Kipling, Edna Ferber, and Edwin Lefevre and also in Arnold Bennett's reportage and a number of essays from *Harper's Monthly*, including a 1902 business-corruption piece by four-term president Grover Cleveland.

In addition to commercial movies and television, I've drawn from narrower channels. These include speeches, documentaries, newsletters, blogs, and message boards. In particular, I highlight so-called "orphan" films, a category that includes corporate training and promotional films (also called sponsored films). Orphan films fall outside the mainstream. As the National Film Preservation Foundation explains,

These are not Hollywood sound features belonging to the major motion picture studios, but "orphans" that fall outside the scope of commercial preservation programs. Orphan films often exist as one-of-a-kind copies. Because they document subjects and viewpoints not captured in the mainstream media of their period, the works can take on special historical and cultural value today.[1]

The oldest orphan film I cite is an uncredited silent motivational film, *How to Succeed* (1926), a melodrama about a salesman stuck in a dead-end job who rises to the top.

The examples I have collected constitute the main threads of our collective wisdom and accepted truths about office life or business culture.

MY APPROACH

My approach is impressionistic and idiosyncratic rather than comprehensive or encyclopedic. Generally, the examples unfold in a loose chronology, which is freely broken or interspersed thematically. In selecting examples, I was initially guided by memory and thus hostage to likes, dislikes, and various contingencies (such as time and place of birth and upbringing). I sought TV programs, movies, and writings that had left imprints. That many of these were deemed disposable entertainment, by myself included, only speaks to the strange and unpredictable power of pop. (Since then, such fare as *The Jetsons* and *Bewitched* have been resurrected on DVD replete with commentary and elevated to the status of "artifact," enabling them to enter the university curriculum.) To plug gaps, I conducted a quasimethodical "objective" search for interesting and representative stories about office life. I also drew on my firsthand experience with office life at AT&T Communications in marketing, in newspaper journalism, and in training and consulting.

Globally, the office is the hub of civilization. Laws and economic policies are products of office culture, as is government, which is driven and shaped by business ambitions. (Critics of the banking system would say the confluence between business and government is complete: oligarchy has strangled democracy.) Ostensibly, this book is about the confluence between business and popular culture, but the deeper subject is human nature.

POP AND/OR ELITE CULTURE

Pop and *low culture* are fluid terms that can mean anything. Popular culture is a mongrel, a patchwork, to which anything may be added, excised, reranked. To treat "high" and "low" cultures as live, separate "entities" is to mystify reality. In actuality, the terms reify individual desires and tastes. In reality, there is just culture, which is itself a labyrinthine abstraction. To label artifacts "high" or "low" is an *ex post facto* designation. Both spheres treat the same subjects and themes—the human condition—while lobbing grenades at the imagined Other's bailiwick: mass culture is dumb, shoddy, and shamelessly commercial; elite culture is pretentious, boring, and sterile. But these caricatures are easily reversible.

More accurately, the designations *high* and *low* point to audiences, to marketing strategies based on the preconception that the hoi polloi are less educated—whatever that means—and therefore must appreciate *less*. But this is specious thinking; the reverse is equally true, such as the music snob who can't "hear" folk music. (A musicologist once told me he couldn't "relate" to his colleagues because they spun Burt Bacharach records at parties, while *he* was into Karlheinz Stockhausen. Well, fine and dandy, but perhaps a bit ungenerous: the German composer's

Helicopter String Quartet isn't exactly party music—although after a few drinks, the atonal whirring of rotor blades might gain converts.) But likes and dislikes are individual, and typecasting people by their tastes complicates things by adding an extra layer of abstraction.

HIGHBROW/LOWBROW

As Lawrence W. Levine shows in *Highbrow/Lowbrow* (1988), the bifurcation of culture into high and low spheres is a nineteenth-century conception. Levine's splendid study merits an extended summary. In the 1850s, the meaning of *culture* began to shift from the cultivation of crops—*culture* derives from *agriculture*—to the refinement of people. High-minded social and art critics advocated inculcation, that is, the introjection of values through art, as a means of harmonizing the lower classes and new waves of immigrants. Here is how the critic Frederick Nast put it in 1881: "the present discordant elements [must be] merged into a homogeneous people."[2] Matthew Arnold's (1822–1888) definition of culture became definitive: "the best that has been thought and known in the world . . . the study and pursuit of perfection."[3]

The means of inculcation are many, including literature—especially myths, fables, histories—music, art, and even public parks. Frederick Law Olmsted designed Central Park as a sanctuary from commerce. Nature cleansed the soul; commerce polluted it. To mitigate contact with the foul city, Olmsted sank the Park's four thoroughfares, which connect the city's east and west sides, beneath ground level. Olmsted said he built the 843-acre park, which opened in 1857, not for pleasure, but for edification: to provide "a distinctly harmonizing and refining influence upon the most unfortunate and most lawless classes of the city—an influence favorable to courtesy, self-control, and temperance," and "we want . . . to completely shut out the city from our landscapes."[4] The Olmsted doctrine caught on in other cities. An orator in Boston (1876) reckoned there would be "less gambling, drinking, and quarreling [once the city's] inhabitants shall be allowed to partake of the blessing and beauty of a public park."[5] And in San Francisco, a report published in 1890 claimed that under the spell of Golden Gate Park, "the rudest boy forgets his jack-knife."[6]

Not everybody accepted Arnold's view of culture or Olmsted's vision of immaculate landscapes. Editorials that objected to Central Park's many rules argued the people would be better served with looser restrictions and the addition of playing fields, chestnut trees (for boys to climb), a parade ground, organized footraces, and such. Olmsted and his associates were ridiculed as overly delicate and effete. In 1877, the *New York Evening Express* characterized Olmsted's supporters as "Miss Nancies [who] babble in the papers and in Society Circles, about aesthetics and architecture, vistas and landscapes, the quiver of a leaf and the proper blendings of light and shade."[7]

Theodore Roosevelt thought cultural refinement was a decidedly decadent European notion that threatened to smother the growth of a distinct, robust American culture. In 1894, he criticized those he called "over-civilized, over-sensitive, over-refined [who] still retain their spirit of colonial dependence [in] exaggerated deference to . . . European opinion."[8] In the same vein, Walt Whitman complained that Matthew Arnold had unleashed a tide of "delicacy, refinement, elegance, prettiness, propriety, criticism, analysis: all of them things which threaten to overwhelm us."[9]

Prior to the Civil War, there was simply all-encompassing culture. Fine music and drama were popular entertainments. Shakespeare, Beethoven, and Italian opera, for example, belonged to everybody—no pedigree, license, or expert commentary required. The finest drama infiltrated even the swamps of civilization: some 150 performances of Shakespeare, featuring the greatest British and American actors, such as Junius Brutus Booth and Edwin Forrest, were held in the Mississippi towns of Natchez and Vicksburg between 1814 and 1861. Shakespeare accompanied the California Gold Rush on makeshift stages in Red Dog, Rattlesnake, Mad Springs, Hangtown, and numerous other mining camps.[10] Symphonic concerts lacked the reverent behavior later attached to "high" art. Audiences hooted, hollered and stomped; shouts of "Do it again!" followed favored theatrical scenes. With vociferous urging, Europe's finest singers freely interspersed popular folk songs, such as "Home Sweet Home," between arias. Programs were often a prevaudevillian pastiche, as evidenced in this 1854 *New York Times* announcement of a performance by an outfit called Perham's Troupe: The Laughable Operatic Extravaganza of *Don Giovanni*; or, The Spectre On Horseback with An Unequaled Programme of Ethiopian Songs, Choruses, solos, Duets, Jigs, Fancy Dances, and more.[11] Ethiopian indeed!

By the century's turn, conspicuous consumption had claimed the higher reaches of art. Cultural consumption became a mark of distinction. Despite their allegiance to democratic ideals in principle, in practice, the leisure class insisted on demonstrating superiority through exclusion. The appreciation of "art" became a status game. Certain cognoscenti set themselves up as arbiters of taste and claimed the "best" of popular culture as "theirs." Shakespeare, Mozart, Beethoven, Wagner, and the like became the preserve of self-appointed guardians of ornate temples governed by formal dress, decorum, and hush-hush reverence.

THE CPI

The divorce from mass culture perpetrated by high culture's acolytes was a backlash against democracy. By the end of World War I, many intellectuals were arguing that the "voice" of the people contained no inherent wisdom and was too easily manipulated. This had been proven during the war. Woodrow Wilson won the election of 1916 as the "peace" candidate on the slogan "He Kept Us Out Of War." But once elected, Wilson did an about-face. Thus, to tilt a staunchly isolationist America toward war, Wilson created a vast propaganda apparatus that utilized every possible communication channel. Headed by a former muckraking editor, George Creel of the *Denver Post*, the Committee for Public Information (CPI) enlisted journalists, advertising executives, commercial artists, cartoonists, Hollywood scriptwriters, the foreign language press, and even a speakers' bureau with divisions for black and white audiences and children.[12]

The CPI demonstrated how ideas could be sold like soap. The lessons learned on the home front during World War I spawned modern advertising and public relations, corporate tools used to propagate a new dominant ideology, the culture of consumption. Walter Lippmann, who worked for the CPI, learned that public opinion is inchoate; before it can be manipulated, it first must be formed. Another CPI veteran, Edward Berynays, called the "father" of public relations—he also happened to be Sigmund Freud's nephew—applied his uncle's theory of dreams and subconscious censorship to shaping "the group mind's" dreams and aspirations.

COLLECTIVE MEMORY

All of the images and narratives about office life, whether freely floating in the ether, individual consciousnesses, or lying dormant in libraries and archives, may be said to reside in our collective memory, a nebulous term that designates an aggregation of millions of memories, or potential memories. Like popular culture, popular memory is an imaginary sphere. It is a fluid concept, impossible to map. Ultimately, a person can explore only his or her own memory (with any degree of thoroughness), deducing, "If this work affects me, it's probable others may also have been amused, revolted, moved, and so forth."

However, bunching into a totality all of the ideas and beliefs that presumably inform cultural practices—that is, positing a "superstructure"—is overreaching. There is no accounting for all of the individual existential and cognitive variables that shape attitudes. (It's curious that the public's perception—and "the public" is yet another abstraction or imaginary entity—is always spoken of as if it were clearly defined and easily manipulated, while social critics who are wont to "totalize" *always* see clearly, even clairvoyantly. Gibing aside, Karl Marx's coinage "false consciousness" is rhetorically brilliant!) But again, it's not so much about elites looking down upon the masses as it is a matter of human nature. Any person, no matter what his or her station, is *always* right, is always smarter than others. And the amount of scorn, contempt, and ridicule heaped upon intellectuals by anti-intellectuals, for want of a better word, is magnitudes higher that what the former visit upon the latter.

But no one can truly get inside another person's head, let alone a million heads posited as interconnected and treated as a single entity. As an explanation of the workings of the group mind, the "data" produced through Likert scales, panel groups, and surveys are laughable. Can anyone even claim to understand his or her own attitudes and motivations?

But whatever the origins of our attitudes and ideas, pop culture is a formative influence. Pop culture is always "on," if only as background noise. Pop culture is the horizon, the stage set against which contemporary life unfolds. Any aspect of it, the high, the low, the good, the bad—even the milliseconds of unwanted intrusion—is capable of tunneling into consciousness. There is no way to predict where and when submerged images and sounds will resurface in transmogrified form, such as in dreams that synthesize and distort elements of fact and fiction.

A good analogy of how pop culture impinges itself upon consciousness may be found in Aravind Adiga's Booker Prize-winning novel *The White Tiger* (2008), in which Adiga lists the ideas and beliefs that constitute his protagonist's working memory. Adiga's hero is Balram Halwai, an uneducated Indian villager who claws his way up from serfdom to owning a taxi service. Excepting Balram's scant schooling, the sources of the following inventory of ideas—the pandemonium of thoughts that circulate inside his "half-baked" mind—are all forms of pop culture. Balram's mind, like all other minds, has been predominantly and haphazardly filled by a smattering of the mass media—and who can tell what will stick or why:

Open our skulls, look in with a penlight, and you'll find an odd museum of ideas: sentences of history or mathematics remembered from school textbooks . . . sentences about politics read in a newspaper while waiting for someone to come to an office, triangles and pyramids seen on the torn pages of the old geometry textbooks which every tea shop in this country uses to wrap its snacks in, bits of All India radio news bulletins, things that drop into your mind, like lizards from the ceiling, in the half hour before falling asleep—all these ideas, half formed and half digested and half correct, mix up with other half-cooked ideas in your head, and I guess these half-formed ideas bugger one another and make more half-formed ideas, and this is what you act on and live with.[13]

To this litany, add one more "fact" rattling Balram's skull: cell phones are a Japanese plot to take down the white man by corroding his brains, shrinking his testicles, and drying up his semen.[14] One quibble I have is with Adiga's term *half-formed.* Is there truly such a thing as a fully formed idea? How would one know? Also, in this instance, pop culture and the mass media are not quite synonymous because pop culture's bandwidth is considerably more elastic, encompassing now dormant or extinct forms of communication and artifacts whose eras have long passed. Nonetheless, Adiga's description may be used to postulate the role that the mass media or pop culture plays in implanting the images and ideas that congeal into beliefs and attitudes. No two minds are formed in quite the same way, that is, are subject to the same forces. And of central import, truth or fact or science—whatever you like—has little or no bearing upon the strength of people's beliefs.

ORAL CULTURES

Pop culture is about the *now,* a fickle state of flux with an accelerated life cycle driven by a commercial calculus that valorizes the "new." In oral cultures, what ceases to be repeated is lost. This was the case in pop culture, especially with live radio and TV. But with innovations in media storage, oldies are now continually dredged up and repackaged. Yesteryear's dreck may resurface rebranded as a cult favorite.

Today, the past lives forever in the present, becomes part of the present, but without its *aura,* or original context, which is nonrecoverable. Semiotically, signs and artifacts derive their meanings from their historical or social contexts. Because context is fluid, meaning is always changing or growing in complexity or ambiguity. Every era's cultural horizon functions as a type of context for its art, imbuing it with "meaning." Leonardo da Vinci's portrait *Ginevra de' Benci* (1474–1478) may have been *meant* as a bridal gift, but today, encased in glass in Washington's National Gallery, it's a metonym for the Florentine Renaissance, a symbol of humanity's flowering, and so on—or, more crudely, an *objet d'art* worth a hell of a lot, that is, a great "investment."

There is something honest about even the worst, most blatantly commercial pop artifact. An artifact's existence says something truthful about the society that spawned it, about the process and conditions of its creation, about what living culture is and the needs it fulfills. In other words, artifacts testify as to where people's heads were at. Exhibit A: the plastic model Revell brought out in 1963 of Ed "Big Daddy" Roth's Rat Fink.

From a higher vantage, pop is barometer about how far we've sunk, how corrupted we've become. In the twentieth century, runaway commercialization and mass culture replaced superstition and dogma as the reactionary forces besieging reason and science. In the early days of radio and television, progressives saw mechanisms that would fulfill the Enlightenment's ideals while extending the reach of participatory democracy (whose boundaries Plato had posited as the range of the human voice). However, commercial forces appropriated and co-opted the airwaves. In short order, this new would-be "public sphere" was barraged with low-brow programming incessantly interrupted by the din of barkers. In 1961, the new FCC chairman, Newton Minow, chided television executives for creating a "vast wasteland."

Minow's speech "Television and the Public Interest" is a classic in American rhetoric. As guardians of "the most powerful voice in America," Minow said, broadcasters have "an inescapable duty to make that voice ring with intelligence and with leadership." He said, "I urge you to put the people's airwaves to the service of the people and the cause of freedom. You must help prepare a generation for great decisions. You must help a great nation fulfill its future."[15] Nothing is worse, Minow declaimed, than bad television:

a procession of game shows, violence, audience participation shows, formula comedies about totally unbelievable families, blood and thunder, mayhem, violence, sadism, murder, western bad men, western good men, private eyes, gangsters, more violence, and cartoons. And, endlessly, commercials—many screaming, cajoling, and offending.[16]

And those were television's "golden years!" I don't wish to disparage Mr. Minow's noble and civic-minded concerns, which, in all fairness, did spur the three major networks into an unparalleled era of television documentaries in the early 1960s. However, in hindsight, I believe he hideously distorted television programming—tilted it totally to one side for maximum sensationalism. If you're going to uphold public service and the "cause of freedom," at least lose the sophistry.

As an antidote, I offer my own brief and distorted picture of 1950s television fare: *The Bell Telephone Hour* (which featured ballet and opera); *Leonard Bernstein's Omnibus*—hosted by Alistair Cooke!—and later, *Leonard Bernstein's Young People's Concerts*; *The Hallmark Hall of Fame* (which presented Shakespeare and Broadway plays); there was *Alfred Hitchcock Presents*; Rod Serling's *The Twilight Zone*; *Gunsmoke*, especially the episodes written by John Meston, some of which raised pressing social issues—a pregnant American Indian woman is refused lodging because of her color, for example. And as to civil rights, how about the *Jack Benny Show* episode that featured Nat King Cole at a time when black entertainers where banned from performing in many of the top venues: Jack bantered and spoofed with Nat—as a human being, not a "black" man—unselfconsciously, as if to show it were the most natural thing in the world. Then there were the documentaries and news programs, particularly those produced by Fred Friendly on CBS, such as Edward R. Murrow's *See It Now*.

Certainly Minow was right to castigate television programming. That was his job as head of the FCC. But if you're going to mount the pulpit to save American youth from "bad" entertainment, humor might help. (Of course, it never seemed to occur to Mr. Minow that *he* could learn something from teenagers.) Today, the venerable Mr. Minow functions as something called the Honorary General Counsel of the Republic of Singapore (based in Chicago). Should he be so inclined, I can think of no greater public service he could render than to turn his critical powers to *Jersey Shore* and its so-called "Guido" culture, and other such "lowbrow" programming. Doubtless, our nation's broadcasters would profit from his sage advice. I can't vouch for the veracity of this tidbit: among those not taken with Minow's "Wasteland" speech were the creators of *Gilligan's Island* (1964–1967), who named the program's unseaworthy vessel the *S.S. Minnow*.

I have set down a heterogeneous conception of popular culture that includes both mainstream and nonconventional channels of communication. My examples include blatantly commercial forms of entertainment and works that aspired to that kingdom called art—not that mass appeal or commercial success preclude fine craftsmanship or enduring value. My purpose, however, isn't to pass judgment on artistic merit; it's to document the pervasiveness—and, in some cases, the origins—of the main narratives that have shaped today's attitudes and beliefs about office life. For example, *The Man in the Gray Flannel Suit* and *The Jetsons* may seem an incongruous grouping; however, they share a narrative thread: the underling enjoys a better home life and is more carefree (usually without realizing it) than the unhappily married boss.

Into variegated pictures of office life, I have blended more oblique or purely ideological examples. I attend to this lofty plane of business culture because it tempers office life and the behaviors therein. Business (or corporate) culture and office life are reciprocal: each reflects the other. Thus, along with the portraiture of different eras, I trace the genealogy and propagation of the ideas and values central to corporate culture today. To understand where we are today, we must understand where we came from. Fundamentally, "the office" is less a physical setting than an ideology or a way of life. Thus, I treat popular culture as an amalgam of high and low, concrete and abstract.

My approach is to let the examples speak for themselves.

Chapter 3

Early Mass Culture: Print from the Victorian Era to the Roaring Twenties

CHARLES DICKENS AND MASS ENTERTAINMENT: OFFICE LIFE AND DIRTY TRICKS

Charles Dickens sought, above all, to improve or educate his audiences by weaving moral instruction into an *entertaining* tale. Detesting the dry, stern pedagogy inflicted upon England's youth, he championed the need for uplifting entertainment. Dickens thought learning should be fun—as Jam Handy too would discover a century later. Dickens argued that bad or morally vapid entertainment hurt England's national character. His first novel, *The Pickwick Papers* (1837), contains passages that document the centrality of a parasitic type of office creature—the lawyer—in shaping the odious and rapacious nature of modern urban life. *The Pickwick Papers* was written during an embryonic stage of transformation in Western culture: the eruption of mass circulation newspapers, particularly the penny press in the United States. Dickens is also a good place to begin a survey of office life in popular culture because his writings exemplify how time transforms one era's mass entertainment into a future era's classics. (In his own day—and beyond—Dickens drew much scorn as a purveyor of sentimental, mass entertainment.)

The stories by Dickens, Melville, Twain, Kipling, and others that I draw from all originally appeared in cheap newspapers or more or less widely circulated magazines.

LAW OFFICES IN CHARLES DICKENS'S LONDON

The Pickwick Papers is a loose-fitting compilation of 20 monthly illustrated installments that sold for a shilling each. Dickens began the series in April 1836. The principal character, Samuel Pickwick, is a kind, older, well-to-do gentleman. Pickwick's unfortunate entanglement with the legal profession gives us a glimpse of office life during the dawning of the Victorian era, which began with Queen Victoria's coronation in 1837 and ended with her death in 1901. Dickens said he set Pickwick's adventures in 1827 and 1828.

Dickens's depictions of the ways and means of law offices give justification for the widespread opprobrium visited upon lawyers. The breed not only feed on misfortune, but their "art" consists in exacerbating or manufacturing misery—the greater the suffering, the greater the profit. Also, the grave, important air that successful Victorian lawyers adopted reminds us that much of today's "consulting" profession is bluff and bluster—a pound of arcane "knowledge" and a ton of desk-side manner. Of course, none of this is news to anyone. Nonetheless, folk wisdom says, "if you ever get into a jam, get yourself a *smart* lawyer." The emphasis on *smart* plays into the common belief that the system can be gamed through cunning.

Pickwick becomes caught in the legal profession's snares when his widowed landlady sues him on a ludicrous trumped-up charge of "breach of matrimonial promise." Although the wholly imaginary breach originated from a comical misunderstanding, two crooked lawyers step in and instigate a lawsuit. (The shysters had agreed to take the poor widow's case for free, taking payment only from the damages sought: the preposterous amount of £1500—about $8,000!) Repulsed by the odious legal team directing the scam, one Dodson and Fogg—whom Dickens labels "men of business"—Pickwick vows not to pay even a single penny. He is thus forced to hire a lawyer.

Leaving aside the changes in office accouterments wrought by technological advances, the structure of office life, by which I mean the web of human interaction, remains intact. We see this in the following interplay, which features two timeless social roles, that of buyer and seller.

Consider the following universal type, the person in need. This down-and-out soul desperately believes that some person exists somewhere who has the power to vanquish his troubles. This powerful fixer, of course, resides in an office, and all manner of distress in human form fastens itself outside that chamber. Whether in London, New York, or Des Moines, what most likely greets the destitute is the inevitable brush-off. Thus, when Pickwick calls at his lawyer's offices, he finds a clerk screening a man in toeless boots and fingerless gloves. Their exchange is all too familiar: When do you think he'll be back? Couldn't say for sure. How about if I wait for him? No, that wouldn't do, he won't be back this week, and maybe not even next week.

Uninitiated in the routine mendacity that is the currency of London's law offices, Pickwick takes the dialogue at its face, thinks the man he seeks is out, and Pickwick himself becomes dispirited. But the clerk gives Pickwick a sly wink and beckons him enter the office under the ruse that a letter awaits him. As Pickwick enters the office, the poor man left hanging beseeches the clerk not to forget to convey his message. "I won't forget," says the clerk. How many distraught legions across time have nourished their last hopes upon such false promises and the attendant belief that some "fixer" would vanquish their worries if they were just permitted to plead the righteousness of their cause?

This, then, is the essential, recurring drama of law offices. Psychologically or emotionally, Pickwick's needs are identical to the destitute man's. The difference between the two is not in the nature or the sanctity of their grievances, it's that Pickwick has money: he is admitted, the mendicant is not. Pickwick is thus duly presented to a Mr. Perker, who, it turns out, is merely the go-between, called a "solicitor" in English jurisprudence, who selects and hires the "barrister," who will argue the case in court. Perker, however, is not only indifferent to the outcome of Pickwick's case, he openly admires Pickwick's tormentors, Dodson and Fogg. Perkins's clerk Lowten had earlier expressed the same sentiment to Pickwick during their meeting in a tavern to set the appointment with Perkins: "Dodson and Fogg—sharp practice theirs—capital men of business is Dobson and Fogg, Sir."[1] And now, for his part, Perkins calls the pair "very smart fellows." They are "great scoundrels," retorts Pickwick. Perkins offers no comfort: "that's a mere matter of opinion, you know, and we won't dispute about terms; because of course you can't be expected to view these subjects with a professional eye."[2]

Nevertheless, he tells Pickwick that he's done everything necessary on his behalf by retaining one Sergeant Snubbin. (In English law, a qualified barrister earns the degree of "sergeant," the highest grade of legal practitioner.) Perker assures Pickwick that Snubbin is at the top of the legal game, and here's the proof: Snubbin draws triple the business of any other barrister. Perker, in effect, serves to distance laymen like Pickwick from the next echelon, thereby imbuing barristers with an aura of power and mystery—and, more important, augmenting legal fees at every level. But Pickwick wants to see Snubbin, wants to use his fevered voice of innocence to better impress upon Snubbin the sanctity of his case. Pickwick wants somebody to care. The snuff-taking Perker smells opportunity. He feigns to take Pickwick's request as a joke: Impossible. Unheard of. Simply can't be done . . . unless a "consultation fee" were paid—in advance. Within 10 minutes Pickwick finds himself in the great Snubbin's outer office, which Dickens describes as an

uncarpeted room of tolerable dimensions, with a large writing-table drawn up near the fire, the baize top of which had long since lost all claim to its original hue of green, and had gradually grown grey with dust and age, except where all traces of its natural colour were obliterated by ink-stains. Upon the table were numerous little bundles of papers tied with red tape; and behind it, sat an elderly clerk, whose sleek appearance and heavy gold watch-chain presented imposing indications of the extensive and lucrative practice of Mr. Sergeant Snubbin.[3]

Here, already in use at this early date, is one of the great twentieth-century metonyms for the absurd horrors of entanglement in bureaucratic procedure: "red tape." Also, the clerk's heavy gold watch-chain as a symbol for the high price of counsel draws an implicit distinction between two basic types of remuneration: a set price for the entire job, such as building a house, versus a bottomless fee structure—set by the hour—whereby the client is forced to take the "expert" at his word as to time worked. (In the late twentieth century, some lawyers and consultants billed clients upward of $1,000 an hour for the time they spent in transit on airplanes. They justified this as time spent thinking.)

The gold-chained clerk, one Mr. Mallard, is yet another snuff-pinching, fee-extracting gatekeeper. It seems Mallard, a scrivener, is the only person who can read Snubbin's hand-writing. Pointing to a pile of Snubbin's opinions that he has yet to copy and for which clients have paid an "expedition fee," Mallard gloats over his power to control the legal machinery. He directs a smile at his confrere, Perker, who has reeled in a fish they will both feed upon—although they're both too low in the chain to taste the choicest morsels.

The prey wants to see the Sergeant, says Perker. Mallard, playing his part, pretends the request is a joke: See the Sergeant? That's a good one —what an absurdity. However, after a whispered exchange between Mallard and Perker, outside of Pickwick's earshot, Mallard disappears into the "legal luminary's sanctum." Returning on tiptoe, he reports that in contravention to all of the Sergeant's "established rules and customs," he has consented to see Pickwick. Sergeant Snubbin's face and dress describe the ravages of a life spent at a desk. Fiftyish, sallow-complexioned and extremely nearsighted, Snubbin had a "dull-looking boiled eye" and thin, weak hair owing to 25 years of wearing a forensic wig; the wig's powder blemished Snubbin's coat-collar, and around his neck he wore a badly tied and ill-washed white neckerchief.

As to Snubbin's lair,

Books of practice, heaps of papers and opened letters, were scattered over the table without any attempt at order or arrangement; the furniture of the room was old and rickety; the doors of the book-case were rotting in their hinges; the dust flew out from the carpet in little clouds at every step; the blinds were yellow with age and dirt; and the state of every thing in the room showed, with a clearness not to be mistaken, that Mr. Sergeant Snubbin was far too much occupied with his professional pursuits to take any great heed or regard of his personal comforts.[4]

Thus, a portrait of a prominent office dweller in the days when the Industrial Revolution began picking up steam. Eye glass scrunched in place, hunched over a sheet of paper with pen in hand, Snubbin resembles a mole: oblivious to his dusty, dilapidated quarters, and myopic in his pursuits, he clearly lives to lose himself in the intellectual challenge of the legal game and the ritual drama of the courtroom. He can smell that Pickwick's case—truth be damned—will doubtless be twisted into a melodrama lapped up by the jury: heartless cad reneges on promise to marry poor, innocent widow.

Pickwick's case is months away from being heard and isn't worthy of Snubbin's time. So Snubbin dumps Pickwick upon his inexperienced assistant, a lawyer called Mr. Phunky, whom Snubbin had neither met nor heard of until then. (The choice to substitute Phunky was Perkins's.) Promptly, Phunky is sent for. He is an "infant barrister," of nervous manner and painfully hesitant in speech. So callow is Phunky that he doesn't know how to play the game: rather than enact his profession's ritual of concealing ignorance by dissembling and bluffing, he tips his hand. Here, Dickens is instructive in the art of legal pantomime. Snubbin had put two questions to Phunky: Are you working with me on this case, and, have you read the briefs? In answer to the first, Phunky reddens and bows in subservience; in answer to the second, he turns a deeper red and bows again.

Had Phunky been a *rich* lawyer, says Dickens, he would have answered the first by instantly sending for his clerk to remind him; had he been *wise*, he might have placed a forefinger to his forehead "and endeavoured to recollect whether in the multiplicity of his engagements he had undertaken" this one. But Phunky is neither rich nor wise. As to the second question, Phunky "should have professed to have forgotten all about" the case's merits, yet claim that he had read all pertinent papers and had "thought of nothing else, waking or sleeping, throughout the two months during which he had been retained as Mr. Sergeant Snubbin's junior."[5]

With a wave of his pen, Snubbin introduces Pickwick to Phunky. It turns out that Pickwick is Phunky's first client! Snubbin suggests that Phunky take Pickwick away and listen to anything the client wishes to say. For Pickwick's benefit, Snubbin adds that he and Phunky will naturally have a consultation. Sure they will.

It doesn't end well for Pickwick at the trial. He gets his arse royally kicked by Sergeant Buzfuz, the silver-tongued barrister Dodson and Fogg have partnered with. (As a matter of principle, Pickwick chooses debtor's prison rather than pay damages, which the jury had reduced to £750.) Thus did the gleeful instigators of this extortion, Dodson and Fogg, prove that they were indeed "capital men of business." In Dickens's realist picture of London, "business" means a clever swindle. In preying on the weak and the unsuspecting, Dodson and Fogg displayed such hard-heartedness and originality in transgressing moral and legal boundaries that their legal brethren conferred upon them the honorific of "capital" men of business.

Here's an example of what capital businessmen do. The court ordered a working man called Ramsey to pay Fogg a £5 settlement. The very morning after his hearing, Ramsey called on Fogg to pay. Not enough, says Fogg because he, Fogg, has since filed something called a "declaration," which "increases the costs materially." Ramsey is incredulous. The hearing was just last night; there wouldn't have been time to file papers. This is true.

But Fogg lies: he has already dispatched a clerk on that very mission, he tells Ramsey. (The clerk will file after Ramsey leaves.) Thus Ramsey, who had scraped together everything he had, will now teeter on penury; Fogg's take will be peanuts, but no prey is too small. It all adds up. But more than that, it pleases Fogg to take food off of Ramsey's table. Inflicting pain keeps his claws sharp and allows him to show off in front of his scurvy clerks. Fogg tells a clerk that picking Ramsey clean was a "Christian act ... for with his large family and small income, he'll be all the better for a good lesson against getting into debt." The admiring clerk, recounting this episode, said it was a delight to watch Fogg operate, adding, "He is a capital man of business ... capital isn't he?"[6]

Dickens's description of Fogg in his office is worth recounting:

an elderly pimply-faced, vegetable-diet sort of man in a black coat, dark mixture trowsers, and small black gaiters; a kind of being who seemed to be an essential of the desk at which he was writing, and to have about as much thought or feeling.[7]

The description of the clerks' office at Dodson and Fogg also enriches our understanding of office life. To visit Dodson and Fogg, clients or supplicants such as Pickwick had to first pass through the clerks' office:

a dark, mouldy, earthy-smelling room, with a high wainscoted partition to screen the clerks from the vulgar gaze: a couple of old wooden chairs, a very loud-ticking clock, an almanac, an umbrella-stand, a row of hat pegs, and a few shelves, on which were deposited several ticketed bundles of dirty papers, some old deal boxes with paper labels, and sundry decayed stone ink bottles of various shapes and sizes.[8]

MELVILLE'S NEW YORK: "I WOULD PREFER NOT TO," SAID BARTLEBY TO HIS BOSS

In the mid-nineteenth century, there was a close correspondence, despite inherent differences, between English and American juristic and office life. Without clerks, both countries' legal machinery would cease to move. So central was their role that Dickens saw fit to offer a typology of clerks, a genus whose varieties, he said, were too numerous to mention. But Dickens did identify four main grades of legal clerks: the articled clerk, the salaried clerk, the copying clerk, and the office boys. The articled clerk is the aristocrat of clerks. He acts and dresses like the solicitor to whom he has apprenticed himself for five years. In the interim, he runs up tailor's bills, buys and sells "innumerable" horses, receives invitations to parties, consorts with well-heeled families, and vacations out of town. The salaried clerk spends much of his 30 shillings a week (about $7) on pleasure and clothes. This "dirty caricature" of last season's fashion attends the theatre at least thrice weekly (on half-price tickets) and afterward "dissipates majestically at the cider cellars." As to the "copying clerk," Dickens pegs him as shabby, often drunk and with a large family. Finally come the office lads. Proudly wearing their first overcoats, they stop at the pub on their way home at night and wash down pork sausages with dark beer. Drunk on independence, on living "life," office boys feel superior to boys their age who remain in day school.[9]

Two representatives of Dickens's clerical typology, the copyist and the office boy, appear in Herman Melville's short story, "Bartleby the Scrivener: A Tale of Wall Street," which is set sometime prior to 1848. As John

Updike wrote, "No anthology of classic American short stories can do without a Melville entry, usually 'Bartleby, the Scrivener.' "[10] "Bartleby" first appeared in a rising form of mass entertainment, magazines, which Melville called "the most salable of all books nowadays." This was about the time *Putnam's Monthly Magazine* began paying him $5 a page—very good money!—for his short fiction. ("Bartleby" ran in two parts, in the November and December 1853 issues.) Unlike *Harper's*, which had a circulation of 100,000 and serialized English authors such as Dickens and Thackeray, *Putnam's* was devoted specifically to the work of American writers. Along with most of Melville's short pieces, it published works by Thoreau, Cooper, Longfellow, Lowell, and two of America's most storied newspaper editors, Charles A. Dana and Horace Greeley. (Greeley is best remembered for the slogan "Go west, young man." And before Benjamin Day succeeded with the New York *Sun* in 1833, Greely had tried and failed to start a penny paper in Philadelphia.) *Putnam's* was founded in 1852 to target "an educated, politically liberal (that is, anti-slavery) readership that never exceeded twenty thousand."[11] Although a readership of 20,000 seems small, when individual penny papers finally hit the circulation mark of 10,000, it was a very big deal.

Before typewriters changed the atmosphere of office life by speeding up the routine and adding that rhythmic clacking associated with productivity, scriveners were employed to make pen-and-ink copies of documents. (Christopher Latham Sholes patented the first typewriter in 1867; the gun manufacturer Remington & Sons bought his patent and began marketing the first typewriters in 1874.) Bartleby is one of three scriveners employed by the tale's narrator, who is "somewhere not far from sixty," and who further says of himself: "I am one of those unambitious lawyers who never address a jury, or in any way draw down public applause; but, in the cool tranquility of a snug retreat, do a snug business among rich men's bonds, and mortgages, and title-deeds."[12] Compared to Dickens's cold, conniving lawyers, Melville's unnamed attorney is saintly: he seems incapable of cheating and lying. As to his clerks, far from ordering them about, he gives in to their bizarre habits and failings; and, as much as Bartleby's brazen insubordination rankles him, he can never quite fire him. In this office, human regard, however attenuated by business actively, is never completely submerged. And in extreme contrast to modern office life, the inhabitants of Melville's office never repress their personalities; their work doesn't form or give rise to a second self, to an office persona. Far from the office shaping its inhabitants, just the opposite occurred: the push and pull of idiosyncratic characters created the office climate to an extent impossible to imagine happening today, save within the smallest shops engaged in creative work.

Working alongside Bartleby are two other scriveners, Turkey and Nippers, and a 12-year-old office boy, Ginger Nut. (As a point of historical interest, the scriveners are paid four cents per one hundred words, which, in legal parlance, constitutes a standard measure called a "folio.") The singularity and cheekiness of these clerks evidence a workplace individuality now sadly extinct. Take Turkey, a "short, pursy Englishman," whose face is florid in the morning but blazes "like a grate full of Christmas coals" from noon to six. This inflammation signaled an impairment of his "business capacities" for the remainder of the day. While gripped in this fit of "flighty recklessness," Turkey would carelessly dip his pen into his inkstand, causing blots on the legal documents, make an "unpleasant racket" with his chair, split his pens to pieces, and passionately throw them on the floor. Any remonstrances by the boss were met with insolence. Point out the blots, yes, he'd say, but look at my gray hair: "Old age—even if it blot the page—is honorable."[13] Then there is Nippers, a sallow, "piratical-looking" 25-year-old who was victimized by twin evils, ambition and indigestion. He apparently did a little side business at the law courts and carried on like a ward boss, receiving a stream of seedily attired "clients" during business hours. Nippers wrote in a steady, neat hand. However, he was forever making adjustments to his writing table; never able to fix it at a satisfactory height, Nippers was wont to seize the entire desk and commence jerking and grinding it into the floor. Throughout the day, the scriveners wolfed down small, flat and spicy ginger nut cakes—eight for a penny—after whom the office boy, who procured these, was named. Besides running errands, Ginger Nut also swept the office to earn one dollar for a six-day week (Saturday was a workday back then).

And finally, there was Bartleby, who immortalized one of the great lines in popular culture, "I would prefer not to," which still amuses today. Doubtless, Bartleby is an allegorical character; what he or this tale means is open to conjecture. However, Bartleby's spirit is worth reviving as the antithesis of the modern "yes man"—a spirit also shared by Turkey and Nippers. Bartleby, was a sedate, motionless young man who ceaselessly copied documents—by sunlight and candlelight—never pausing to take sustenance. However, when first called upon—and forever after—to perform the dullest, most wearisome part of his duties, proofreading, Bartleby always replied with "I would prefer not to." Badgered on the point, What? What does this mean? Why do you refuse? Speak? Answer me! Bartleby would utter the same dispassionate refrain, "I would prefer not to." And it wasn't only mind-numbing proofreading that Bartleby met thus, but any order or question: How about stepping round to the post office, a mere three minutes' walk? "I would prefer not to." OK, how about just stepping into the *next room* and calling Nippers? "I would prefer not to." Would Bartleby be kind enough to tell his employer where he was born? He "would prefer not to." (Any employee today wishing to make a lasting—or last—impression may use Bartleby's line to that effect.)

In "Bartleby," the office atmosphere has the significance of a character: when all the people spill out onto the street at day's end, the place becomes a tomb. (Looking at historical photographs of Wall Street interiors, heavy in wood and leather, I was struck by the familiar feeling they evoked: I'd felt the same sort of creepy mustiness while looking at thousands of antique wood and leather crutches that lined the walls of a "miracle-cure" basilica I'd once visited in Montreal.) But during the day, the hustle and bustle drowns out the eerie office silence, so different from the uplifting serenity of nature. One of Bartleby's quirks is that while the other clerks clear out at sundown, he alone is willing to work by candlelight. Most striking in this milieu is that the duration of the workday is governed by the sun rather than by clocks, which didn't become a fixture of office life until the end of the nineteenth century. (The aesthetically pleasing big windows and cathedral ceilings in lower Manhattan's old buildings were decidedly utilitarian.)

SMALL-TOWN OFFICE LIFE

The contrast between the look and tempo of big-city law offices and those in the hinterlands is pronounced. Here is what the office of an up-and-coming lawyer looked like in Springfield, Illinois, in 1844. Abraham Lincoln and his partner, William Herndon, set up shop in a plain room above the post office.

It contained a small number of the standard legal books and some odds and ends of furniture. . . . An old leather office couch became Lincoln's favorite place to read, his feet extending far out, propped on chairs above a floor that seemed always dirty. Stretched out on the couch, he spent many workdays reading newspapers and books, handling legal papers, walking to the courthouses or the legislature.[14]

The laid-back rhythm of inland office life attracted all kinds of hangers-on and deadbeats, intruders that no clerk or watchman would dream of screening. Such human distractions were simply tolerated as a part of office life. Mark Twain showed this in *The Office Bore*, a sketch about a newspaper office he wrote around 1870.

Ironically, Twain's deadbeat bore arrives bright and early, often beating the editor in. This causes the porter to drop his work to unlock the editor-in-chief's office, within which the bore is allowed to loll about unattended. He might begin by puffing on one of the chief's pipes, unaware "that the editor may be one of those 'stuck-up' people who would as soon have a stranger defile his tooth-brush as his pipe-stem." The bore enjoys stretching out on the office sofa, and as the various editors file in, so do more bores, as many as four are "on hand, day and night." They intrude into the business conversations between editors and visitors or loudly swap tall tales among themselves or hold forth on politics. Sometimes bores turn silent and pensive; they stare and listen to the scratching of an editor's pen, which is nearly as irritating as peering over a person's shoulder. Such relentless boorishness, "to feel always the fetters of his clogging presence," saps good cheer: "spirits begin to sink as [the bore's] footstep sounds on the stair, and utterly vanish away as his tiresome form enters the door"; one suffers "through his anecdotes and [dies] slowly to his reminiscences."[15]

Through the foil of the bore, Twain offers a glimpse of an enjoyable type of office life, creative work involving a steady stream of public interaction. The normal, inherent mood in the newspaper office is cheerfulness; dread and anxiety are external, unnatural elements, the results of mindless insensitivity, uninvited guests tracking mud on the rug. Yet the humanity of these newspapermen prevents them from brusquely turning out their tormentors; by definition, bores are impervious to tact. Although the editors attempt to seek relief by daydreaming of casting the bores into various hells, they can never bring themselves to hurt the bores' feelings by revealing theirs. Far better to suffer the bores' presence than resort to any manner of cruelty. Kindness is a trait Twain's editors share with Melville's lawyer, who always loses his resolve when it comes to turning Bartleby out on the streets.

UNREQUITED KINDNESS IN A BANK: (A PRECURSOR OF HOW-TO-GET-AHEAD BOOKS)

Bankers, moneylenders, don't fare well in popular culture. Hard-hearted, they profit by trampling the little guy—witness Mr. Potter in Frank Capra's *It's a Wonderful Life* (1946). Rudyard Kipling's short story "A Bank Fraud," set in colonial India, reverses the usual cardboard caricature of bankers by portraying one of unusual magnanimity. Reggie Burke confers extreme kindness upon a terribly conceited subordinate who openly despises him. Kipling's banker is all the more unusual because he performs these kind acts unbeknownst to the underling and with no expectation of reciprocity—not even a nod of recognition. Like many professional people of his era, Burke lived both a public and a private life—a distinction that has long since collapsed, particularly in our smart-phone world. Between 10 a.m. and 4 p.m.—classic "banker's hours"—Burke managed an upcountry branch of a bank headquartered in Calcutta; but between 4 and 10 p.m., Burke was "ready for anything," particularly activities requiring equestrian skill. So distinct were Burke's public and private selves that you could play polo and converse with him one afternoon, presumably getting to know him, but when you called on him for a loan the next morning, "He would recognise you, but you would have some trouble in recognising him."[16] While Burke partitioned business and leisure, he succeeded as a lender because he took the trouble to go out among his clients and know something about their affairs. Thus, the directors of the bank "trusted him just as much as Directors ever trust Managers."[17] (A good observation, that: trust between levels of management is always an unbalanced feeling, never pure, always allayed with suspicion.)

Another universal truism about office life is that it's not so much the work that's deplorable but the close-quartered hell of malicious or wacky people. "A Bank Fraud" shows that the tormentors aren't always the bosses. Owing to political machinations in England, a very bad and very big-headed accountant called Silas Riley is foisted upon the bank, and, in turn, Reggie. Riley is sickly. Actually, he doesn't know he's terminally ill. Nor does Riley know that he landed this job only because a member of Parliament pulled some strings to curry favor with his powerful father. In his ignorance, Riley grows delusional with self-importance. Somehow or other, he "had construed the ordinarily polite terms of his letter of engagement into a belief that the Directors had chosen him on account of his special and brilliant talents, and that they set great store by him." This notion grows and crystallizes. In his crazy conceit, Riley thinks Reggie "a wild, feather-headed idiot" completely unfit "for the serious and solemn vocation of banking." Riley is always telling Reggie how he ought to do his job. When Reggie would remind Riley that his limited experience in rural England didn't qualify him "to steer a big up-country business" in India, Riley would sulk and refer to "himself as a pillar of the Bank and a cherished friend of the Directors, and Reggie tore his hair."[18]

Riley alternates stretches of sickness—weeks at a time—"with restless, persistent, meddling irritation of Reggie, and all the hundred ways in which conceit in a subordinate situation can find play." Even though it means more work thrown at him, Reggie prefers Riley's absences to the unbroken friction of his presence, which causes Reggie to blow off steam in an identical manner to the editors tormented by the bores in Twain's story—by fantasizing about telling him off. Thus, Reggie called Riley "striking and hair-curling names behind his back," but never to his face, because he feared for Riley's frailty (he suffers from consumption). In fact, in generosity of spirit, Reggie tells himself that "half of [Riley's] loathsome conceit is due to pains in the chest."[19]

Riley takes a turn for the worse. The doctor tells Reggie that the bedridden Riley has but three months to live and if he cares about him, to keep him cheerful. Reggie conceals the truth from Riley. This doesn't much matter to the bank's Directors; business is business, and they, through Reggie, order Riley to resign in one month. Reggie hides this from Riley and lets him believe that he's on an approved leave and his return is eagerly awaited by the Directors. Throughout the sweltering summer— 116 degrees in the shade is a typical day—Reggie visits Riley, bringing him the bank's books to show him what's been going on. Riley wants to know if the Directors have noted his absence. Oh yes, says Reggie, they've been hoping he will soon be able to "resume his valuable services," and Reggie showed the invalid their sympathetic letters stating so—letters which Reggie had forged. Through it all, Riley remains as ungracious as ever, never giving a thought to the extra work his illness has heaped upon Reggie. Rather, Riley thinks "solely of the damage to his own prospects of advancement."[20] At the end of the first month of his "leave," Riley tells Reggie he wants his salary sent to his mother. Reggie duly sends her Riley's salary. The second month's salary comes out of Reggie's own pocket, as does a bogus 25 percent raise Reggie concocts to keep Riley's spirits up. Without, of course, mentioning anything to Riley, Reggie had dropped his dinners, polo, tennis—everything—to attend to him. The strain wears on Reggie's nerves; his billiards game goes to hell. His reward? During Reggie's visits, Riley was wont to lecture him "on his evil ways: his horses and his bad friends. 'Of course lying here, on my back, Mr. Burke, I can't keep you straight; but when I'm well, I do hope you'll pay some heed to my words.'" Or Riley would ask Reggie to read from the Bible and grim Methodist tracts, whose morals he always pointed back at Reggie.

Reggie's visits and forged letters succeed in keeping Riley alive for an additional month. But only death stops Riley's carping. Reggie is present when Riley expires. In his last words, Riley thanks the deity for saving him from the "grosser" forms of sin—yet another blatant dig at Reggie —and adds how he would have put the bank to rights—by undoing all of Reggie's "mistaken" policies—had his life been extended. As Reggie stepped out onto the verandah, he lamented his tardiness. Ten minutes sooner, he thought, and he might have bought the poor beggar another day with his last, unused forgery—a sympathy letter from the Directors.

These antithetical characters transcend the world of business. Pitted against the quietly intelligent and decent *bon vivant* is the brash know-it-all, whose grossly inflated sense of self-worth is fed and sustained by lashing others with a punitive brand of piety. Why Reggie behaved so magnanimously—at such physical and emotional cost—to such a badgering incompetent is a mystery. Perhaps he was guided by some Victorian code of gentlemanly behavior or moved by simple pity.

However, such questions aside, Reggie's behavior might well serve as an exemplar for the "new" type of office behavior promulgated by corporate guru Mr. Tom Peters, best known for his 1982 best-seller *In Search of Excellence*, whose methodology and underlying data have since been suspect. Peters's latest bible is called *The Little Big Things: 163 Ways to Pursue Excellence* (2010). In the chapter "Kindness is Free!," Peters strings together snippets on kindness from a variety of sources: Plato, "Be kind, for everyone you meet is fighting a great battle." Henry James, "Three things in human life are important. The first is to be kind. The second is to be kind. And the third is to be kind." George Washington, "Speak not injurious words neither in jest nor earnest; scoff at none although they give occasion." Dale Carnegie, "You can make more friends in two months by becoming interested in other people than you can in two years by trying to get other people interested in you." And from the late Ann Richards, the former governor of Texas, who offered advice on how to deal with the "most loathsome of all creatures imaginable, a live airline employee." Says Richards, "Take two deep breaths, smile with the smile you'd use if you were meeting Queen Elizabeth II, and say to yourself, 'This woman/man is the only human being on earth who at this moment in time can help me with my most pressing problem.' Then act accordingly." Peters says he tried this and it worked—always. "Behave decently," he says, "because it's the decent thing to do. Behave decently because it works." Peters reports that he has elevated kindness into a routine he uses in every situation he faces. Although he can't prove it, he believes kindness has led to better business decisions and the sense that he's become a better human being—well "maybe, just a little." His parting advice: "Before going into a meeting or making an important call, or most any call: Be kind, for everyone is fighting a great battle. I think it at least ups the awareness ante a notch or two."[21]

Thus do the sophists called consultants (their wisdom will set you free, for a fee) hawk the next new thing, which, in this case, is disembodied and repackaged quotations from great historical figures—and some not so great. These quotes are sold as business techniques, secrets to success and happiness. So in 2010, one of the great business breakthroughs is . . . kindness. (Hey, did you hear the one about the consultant who . . .)

THE MODERN BROKER: TOO BUSY TO NOTICE

O. Henry's "The Romance of a Busy Broker" originally appeared in the *New York Sunday World Magazine* (March 13, 1904). The *World's* storied place in popular culture—not to speak of American history—is worth recalling. Joseph Pulitzer bought the money-losing newspaper (established in 1860) for $346,000 in 1883. He returned the *World* to profitability through sensationalistic feature stories that beckoned readers with huge, screaming headlines. In a publicity stunt indicative of Pulitzer's salesmanship, his star reporter, Nellie Bly, attempted to beat the fictional record for circumnavigating the globe set by the hero of Jules Verne's *Around the World in Eighty Days* (1873). More than one million people entered the *World's* contest to guess the duration of Bly's journey. (She did it in 72 days, 6 hours, 11 minutes and 14 seconds—brilliant showmanship, pinning it down to the minutes and seconds.) The censorious term "yellow journalism" came from one of Pulitzer's many innovations. In 1895, the *World* began publishing a color supplement that included a comic strip called *Hogan's Alley* (drawn by Richard F. Outcault), whose main character was a gap-toothed street urchin called the Yellow Kid.

In O. Henry's story, the office is vastly different—both psychologically and physically—than those in the preceding examples. Ticker tapes and telephones signal the emergence of a new age of sped-up activity that imbues minutes and even seconds with deal-breaking significance. The modern business era has arrived and Manhattan is king. Frenzied trading on the New York Stock Exchange dictates the reactive pace in Harvey Maxwell's office, where success depends on the broker's ability to inhale information and make decisions in a blink. Currents of information flow into Maxwell's office from a variety of conduits old and new: messenger boys, visitors, letters, telegrams, the telephone, the ticker tape. As Maxwell begins his day by plunging into the mounds of paper waiting for him, he becomes curt, impatient. All that matters is business. Sitting at his desk, Maxwell is "no longer a man," but a machine animated by "buzzing wheels and uncoiling springs." On a busy day, this is the scene in Maxwell's office:

The ticker began to reel out jerkily its fitful coils of tape, the desk telephone had a chronic attack of buzzing. Men began to throng into the office and call at him over the railing, jovially, sharply, viciously, excitedly. Messenger boys ran in and out with messages and telegrams. The clerks in the office jumped about like sailors during a storm.[22]

As the day progresses, the stock exchange grows frenetic. Its current amps up Maxwell's office:

The rush and pace of business grew fiercer and faster. On the floor [of the Exchange] they were pounding half a dozen stocks in which Maxwell's customers were heavy investors. Orders to buy and sell were coming and going as swift as the flight of swallows. Some of his own holdings were imperiled, and the man was working like some high-geared, delicate, strong machine—strung to full tension, going at full speed, accurate, never hesitating, with the proper word and decision and act [,] ready and prompt as clockwork. Stocks and bonds, loans and mortgages, margins and securities—here was a world of finance, and there was no room in it for the human world or the world of nature.[23]

The lunch hour brings a slight respite that returns Maxwell to humanity. He notices an attractive stenographer, a Miss Leslie. A waft of her perfume reduces the world of finance to "a speck." Maxwell charges to her desk and tells her he has but a moment to spare, but wants to say something: "Will you be my wife? . . . Talk quick, please—those fellows are clubbing the stuffing out of Union Pacific." Miss Leslie is bewildered. Maxwell believes he hasn't been understood: "I love you Miss Leslie. I wanted to tell you, and I snatched a minute when things had slackened up a bit." Miss Leslie sheds tears. Not the joyous sort. She is frightened but composes herself when the light of understanding comes on and she grasps that business has driven everything out of Maxwell's mind.

"Don't you remember, Harvey? We were married last evening at 8 o'clock in the Little Church Around the Corner."[24]

O. Henry's point is clear. The machine age's arrival has accelerated the rhythms of office life and turned men into machines. This transformation threatens to squeeze the humanity out of office life, at least in the world of finance, where, observes O. Henry, there is no room "for the human world or the world of nature."

"SKYSCRAPER"

By the turn of the century, mechanical and structural innovations had changed the look and feel of offices. These included steel-framed skyscrapers (1885) and electric elevators (1880); as noted earlier, typewriters were invented in 1867 (Remington's debuted in 1874); and telephones (1876).

Carl Sandburg's poem "Skyscraper," published in 1912, remarks the eruption of 20-story towers across the prairies. The skyscraper is an enormous living thing upon which thousands feed. Like a huge metronome, it beats out the rhythms of the business day: presto during the morning until it disgorges its occupants at noon and finally begins to slacken its tempo as the day winds down.

The skyscraper is a monument to American business. However, Sandburg's poem isn't as much a tribute to the captains of industry as it is to the laborers—hod carriers, masons, carpenters, welders, and electricians—the people who actually erect the edifices. Sandburg evokes images of muscular, single-minded laborers building America. Work is important, noble. Sandburg's anonymous men and women anticipate the idealized worker heroes depicted in Soviet propaganda posters during Stalin's era.

Sandburg's workers may be as heroic as soldiers, but military bearing or not, they stumble. They take the wrong roads.

> Men who sunk the pilings and mixed the mortar are laid
> in graves where the wind whistles a wild song
> without words
> And so are men who strung the wires and fixed the pipes
> and tubes and those who saw it rise floor by floor.
> Souls of them all are here, even the hod carrier begging
> at back doors hundreds of miles away and the brick-
> layer who went to state's prison for shooting another
> man while drunk.
> (One man fell from a girder and broke his neck at the
> end of a straight plunge—he is here—his soul has
> gone into the stones of the building.)[25]

"Skyscraper" recalls Walt Whitman's "Song of Myself" in its celebration of the American spirit as it pushes forever onward in its rugged New World fashion. These buildings are the future. They represent a new, brisk ordering of life. The city's streets "pour people into [the skyscraper] and they mingle among its twenty floors and are poured out again back to the streets, prairies and valleys." They mingle, but in a tight-lipped and ordered fashion:

> Behind the signs on the doors they work and the walls
> tell nothing from room to room.
> Ten-dollar-a-week stenographers take letters from
> corporation officers, lawyers, efficiency engineers,
> and tons of letters go bundled from the building to all
> ends of the earth.

Smiles and tears of each office girl go into the soul of
the building just the same as the master-men who
rule the building.[26]

Furthermore, routine based on business contingencies—repetition
based on the clock—is imposed—more or less successfully—on the
body's natural rhythms:

Hands of clocks turn to noon hours and each floor
empties its men and women who go away and eat
and come back to work.
Toward the end of the afternoon all work slackens and
all jobs go slower as the people feel day closing on
them.
One by one the floors are emptied . . . the uniformed
elevator men are gone. Pails clang . . . Scrubbers
work, talking in foreign tongues. Broom and water
and mop clean from the floors human dust and spit,
and machine grime of the day.
Spelled in electric fire on the roof are words telling
miles of houses and people where to buy a thing for
money. The sign speaks till midnight.[27]

After midnight, darkness descends and silence reigns. But the skyscraper
isn't quite empty. The whole point of ordering life in this fashion, of
streamlining work, is to increase profits. In "Skyscraper," money was still
tactile, bundled and piled into massive steel safes. Watchmen, revolvers
bulging from their hips, made their rounds, walking slowly from floor
to floor, trying each door.

THE TELEPHONE

"The efficiency and fearful universality of the telephone" impressed and
alarmed the English novelist Arnold Bennett upon his first visit to the
United States. The European telephone was a clumsy "toy" compared to
the "serious" American instrument, he noted in *Your United States:
Impressions of a First Visit* (1912). Bennett saw the telephone—the visible
end of a network composed of millions upon millions of live filaments—
as a dreadful invasion of privacy, even capable of shattering a hotel room's
inviolate serenity. Bennett sensed something different in the American air.
Today it's easy to articulate his premonition: a mania for efficiency. Bennett puts his finger on it when he talks about "people whose passion is to
'get results,'" and how irresistible the telephone's efficiency must be to

them: "the instancy with which the communication is given, and the clear loudness of the telephone's voice in reply to yours."[28]

The telephone was the ideal business instrument. It defined the modern office and gave rise to a new position, the switchboard operator. Bennett knew that business reveals its true nature on the ground floor, in the demeanor and behavior of the employees, not in elevated mission statements, organizational charts, and sanitized reports. Thus, he visited a telephone exchange in New York. In a dimly lit room, in a long row, young women were seated on stools before a "long apparatus of holes and pegs and elastic cord." They seemed connected to the switchboard, seemed part of the machine. Bennett saw by their movements and intent faces that they hadn't a moment to spare. Thousands of tiny lights continually went on and off and caused the women to plug and unplug colored cords, which crisscrossed in "fantastic patterns." When their supervisors—who were "less-young women"—watched them, the operators were silent, but their "delicate shoulders" spoke:

Here come these tyrants and taskmasters again, who have invented this exercise which nearly but not quite cracks our little brains for us! They know exactly how much they can get out of us, and they get it. They are cleverer than us and more powerful than us; and we have to submit to their discipline.[29]

Bennett wonders if the operators are happy:

As a professional reader of faces, I glanced as well as I could sideways at those bent girls' faces to see if they were happy. An absurd inquiry! Do *I* look happy when I'm at work, I wonder! Did they then look reasonably content? Well, I came to the conclusion that they looked like most other faces—neither one thing nor the other. Still, in a great establishment, I would sooner search for sociological information in the faces of the employed than in the managerial rules.[30]

The entry-level salary for an operator is $5 a week (which is what Bennett was paying for one night in a grand hotel). The salary rose

To six, seven, eight, eleven, and even fourteen dollars for supervisors, who, however, had to stand on their feet seven and a half hours a day, as shopgirls do for ten hours a day; and that in general the girls had thirty minutes for lunch; and a day off every week, and that the company supplied them gratuitously with tea, coffee, sugar, couches, newspapers, arm-chairs, and fresh air.[31]

However, for such good money—hotel work paid $4 a week, for example—the women were subjected to strict discipline. Supervisors kept a record of every call and could time call length. (Even then, just as in today's service centers, operators were encouraged to close the call as soon as possible.) That telephone operators, on average, stayed on the job for 30 months attests to the limited opportunities for unskilled women.

OFFICE POLITICS AND CHANGING FASHIONS

Willa Cather's short story "Ardessa"[32] is about superannuated people and outmoded office norms—lingering Gilded Age manners. On a more basic level, "Ardessa" is about the age-old conflict between cunning and industriousness, the great curse of office life. Set in the offices of a trendy magazine, "Ardessa" is also a prescient comment on the mass media and celebrity at a critical cultural juncture in two respects: images began to supersede the word; and, the emergence of a new phenomenon, the celebrity—creatures of fleeting fame that are entirely the creation of the mass media, which in Ardessa's day consisted of newspapers, magazines, moving pictures, and sound recordings. Appropriately, "Ardessa" appeared in the May 1918 issue of *The Century Illustrated Monthly Magazine.* The magazine (which was founded in 1881 and folded in 1930) left its imprint on American culture by publishing the country's best writers, including Mark Twain, Henry James, Jack London, Stephen Crane, and Walt Whitman. At its apogee during the 1890s, *The Century*'s circulation topped 200,000. Today, the five illustrations that embellish Cather's story are more notable for their portrayal of ethnic stereotypes—Ardessa's foil is a young Jewish woman—than for what they convey about office dress and décor.

Ardessa Devine, an aging office bully, is surpassed by a fledgling she'd taken under her wing, Becky. Ardessa personifies sloth and deceit, Becky, persistence and industry. Officially, Ardessa bears the title of executive stenographer (to the publisher of a magazine). However, through force of personality, she has managed to cut a brazen swath through the office by manipulating her boss, Marcus O'Mally, and everyone else—at least Ardessa presumes no one sees through her, or if they do, they're powerless, like the time clerk. Before employees punched time clocks, clerks recorded their punctuality in ledgers in pen and ink. As is typical of Ardessa, she breezes in at 10 past 10 on a morning the boss is out of town. She condescendingly greets the old gentleman who keeps the time-book. "It's banker's hours she keeps," he mutters to himself. Her boss she handles by being "insinuatingly feminine." Ardessa shudders "at the cold candor of the new business woman." Although she thinks herself indispensible, she knows her position hinges entirely on O'Mally. She shivers at the thought that he might die and she would be "thrust out into the world to work in competition with the brazen, competent young women she saw about her everywhere."[33]

Marcus O'Mally owns and edits *The Outcry*, a magazine of social protest that the people had "howled for." Readers wanted a publication that presented "their real tastes and interests" in the manner of "a moving-picture film." O'Mally had tired of being a rich nobody in Nevada (he owned a silver mine in South Dakota). He'd come to New York to make "the East take notice of him," figuring "the quickest way to cut into the known world was through the printing press." O'Mally was looking to make a stir, not a career. However, he found himself thrust into the public eye and into politics. He'd built an organization that left him both bored and fearful. In his rise to social prominence, O'Mally seems to have stumbled upon the correlation between publicity and "success," as measured by name recognition. O'Mally is an unwitting pioneer in a new industry that would change social life, the culture industry. He discovered the formula to manufacture celebrities. This he preceded to do with five of his staff writers, *making* each "famous." In detailing O'Mally's process, Cather could be describing any number of modern celebrities found in every social sphere today:

He found he could take an average reporter from the daily press, give him a "line" to follow, a trust to fight, a vice to expose,—this was all in that good time when people were eager to read about their own wickedness,—and in two years the reporter would be recognized as an authority. Other people—Napoleon, Disraeli, Sarah Bernhardt—had discovered that advertising would go a long way; but Marcus O'Mally discovered that in America it would go all the way—as far as you wished to pay its passage. Any human countenance, plastered in three-sheet posters from sea to sea, would be revered by the American people. The strangest thing was that the owners of these grave countenances, staring at their own faces on newsstands and billboards, fell to venerating themselves; and even he, O'Mally, was more or less constrained by these reputations that he had created out of cheap paper and cheap ink.[34]

So bewitching is celebrity that even those like O'Mally, the king-makers who fabricate identities for public consumption, are not entirely free of its spell. However, O'Mally never succumbed to his own public image. He didn't believe the hype about himself. No amount of recognition could turn him into someone full of himself. Although he was celebrated as a "great medicine-man" across the nation, O'Mally knew what he was: a gambler and a mercenary. O'Mally is also rare because he doesn't live tied or wired to the office. Unlike today's institutional neurotics, who never really leave the office even when physically absent, O'Mally simply viewed business as the means to an end, and a boring means at that. (What healthy animal would willingly choose to spend its days indoors, trussed up in a monkey suit fussing with all things tedious?) For many months of the year, O'Mally let the office run itself while he gallivanted out West, giving balls—as a "great man" from the East—in cities that once knew him only as a big spender.

In *The Outcry*'s early days, Ardessa functioned much like a social secretary. She had been steeped in the editorial traditions of the '80s and the '90s and knew everybody's place in the social order. She could tell O'Mally who absolutely had to be seen, who had to be made welcome, and who could safely be dismissed. Ardessa could give O'Mally a sense of a "man's connections, of the price his work commanded, and insinuate whether he ought to be met with the old punctiliousness or with the new joviality." (Ardessa's former boss, a scholarly editor of "the old school," had retired because he felt "out of place in the world of brighter, breezier magazines that had been flowering since the new century came in.")

O'Mally is quick to take up people and quick to drop them when they've served their purpose. With him, relationships are never genuine, they are only business. Ardessa was skillful in assuaging those whom O'Mally dropped. She answered their letters and used gentle lies to soothe great authors whom O'Mally had courted just the month prior and who now suddenly found themselves cooling their heels in the reception room. In discarding a writer, O'Mally might declare privately that he'd never read another line they wrote. However, Ardessa, feeding her own vanity, would ply the cast-outs with false hopes, letting them spill out story ideas and promising to bring these to O'Mally's attention.

Ruthlessness and phoniness are not normally listed among the timeless virtues. However, they are essential pillars of success in commerce. (In O'Mally's case, phoniness is perhaps a wrong characterization, as it's likely he is truly excited by and even fond of each of his new finds—at least until the shine wears off.) Adages such as "business is business," or "it's not personal, it's just business," express the business virtues of this new age. O'Mally's product is *new* information. Media organizations package novelty, even if what they tout is a formulaic recasting of old forms. Thus, O'Mally must cast aside any story not glistening in "newness," even if it is still attached to a human being. After all, it's just business. Like hospital patients known to doctors only by their afflictions— "the gall bladder in 330," "the pancreas in 204"—O'Mally's cast-offs lack names (which might betray some sort of lingering affection and which, of course, would be anathema to business). Why is "the prison-reform guy" loafing around here? he thunders at Ardessa. And he threatens to turn violent if he ever sees "that causes-of-blindness-in-babies woman" in the office again.

In spite of his propensity to trample on the feelings of people no longer useful to him, O'Mally can't quite bring himself to deal with Ardessa in such a brutal manner. He knows she loafs in his absence and that handling his correspondence isn't enough to keep her busy. So as recompense, he makes her type his "breezy" editorials and various articles by his staff writers. As Cather remarks, "Transcribing editorial copy is always laborious." Unbeknownst to O'Mally, Ardessa evades this labor by dumping it on others. This is easy. Ardessa preys on the neophyte Becky. Becky's $8 weekly salary—excellent money for a working girl—helps her parents and eight younger siblings. And she's eager to please Ardessa, who got her hired. "This seems to be very smeary copy again, Becky. You don't keep your mind on your work, and so you have to erase continually." This is untrue. The fault lies entirely with the writer, who is notorious for his illegible hand and bizarre abbreviations and inserts. Becky defends herself. But Ardessa browbeats Becky and twists everything Becky says into a personal failing. Her ultimate threat is "it would be terrible if Mr. O'Mally saw" such work. But that would be most unlikely. Ardessa keeps O'Mally well insulated from her machinations and the petty injustices she inflicts on others. He has no idea that Becky actually does the work he assigns Ardessa. Ardessa's hold on Becky is such that Becky even asks her permission to purchase white shoes. Becky is dying to shed her frumpy shoes.

"No," answers Ardessa. "With only one pair, you could not keep them properly clean; and black shoes are much less conspicuous. Tan, if you prefer."

As though speaking to a parent, Becky pleads: "Nearly all the girls I know wear white shoes to business."

Ardessa parries: "They are probably little girls who work in factories or department stores, and that is quite another matter. Since you raise the question, Becky, I ought to speak to you about your new waist. Don't wear it to the office again, please. Those cheap open-work waists are not appropriate in an office like this. They are all very well for little chorus girls."

Becky counterattacks, "But Miss Kalski wears expensive waists to business more open than this, and jewelry—"[35]

But Ardessa has the last word. Miss Kalski doesn't count because she works in the *business* side of the house, which a long corridor separates from the editorial offices where Becky works. Ardessa goes on to explain the difference in status between those who handle the dirty end of things—the nitty-gritty of monetary exchange—and those who work with the great and important people who write *The Outcry*'s copy or otherwise confer in its offices. (Ardessa is blind to Miss Kalski's enormous contempt for her "prima donna" airs.)

Becky believed her job depended on Ardessa. Becky's father was a tailor who pressed Ardessa's skirts and kept her wardrobe in good repair. Two years prior, he'd pressed himself on Ardessa, beseeching her to find an office job for his bright daughter, who'd just graduated from a commercial high school. Ardessa prevailed upon O'Mally and soon begin training Becky, who she said "was as ignorant as a young savage" and knew as much about the English language as a "Kafir girl."

HARD WORK BEGETS SUCCESS

"Ardessa" articulates the formula for success embedded in America's reputation as "the land of opportunity"—particularly resonant with the turn-of-the-century Ellis Island immigrants. Becky, trained in typing and shorthand, aspires to become a real "business woman," which for her means becoming a "high-priced stenographer." With indefatigable zeal, she sets about improving herself. She nearly wears out her dictionary. At night, she studies grammar. At work, she covets all the work Ardessa piles upon her, seeing it as a way to practice and test her efficiency. She increasingly makes short work of anything Ardessa throws at her. Becky's confidence grows. She also learns deportment from Ardessa: how to walk quietly, when to efface herself, when to hold her tongue, and not to chew gum.

As Becky takes on more of Ardessa's work, she grows stronger while her mentor slacks. And, of course, virtue is rewarded and vice punished. In much the same way that many an egotistical CEO has attempted to cement a legacy by picking a weakling as his or her successor, Ardessa arranges for a gratingly poor steno, one Miss Milligan, to do O'Mally's work during her vacation. She's grown so ungrateful and sure of herself that, in a pout, she actually refuses O'Mally's request for dictation. No, she couldn't possibly stay the Saturday afternoon before her vacation. She has shopping to do. Why not ask the Tietelbaum girl (Becky)? Accepting Ardessa's goldbricking pace as an honest benchmark, after an hour of dictation, the mellow O'Mally merely asks Becky to type as many letters as she can. O'Mally is incredulous when Becky soon returns to report she has typed *all* the letters. They must, of course, be filled with errors. After all, he knows Becky only through Ardessa's smear: the girl who makes so many mistakes. Becky sets him right. The problem is the illegible scrawl of certain writers. She never errs with articles written in a neat hand, such as those from O'Mally himself. This proves revelatory. This lowly steno types *articles* and his own editorials—work he had assigned to Ardessa! O'Mally soon replaces the ineffectual Miss Milligan with Becky. He now sees how Ardessa has played him. Yes, Ardessa makes his life difficult, but O'Mally realizes he bears some responsibility for having pampered her. Rather than fire Ardessa, O'Mally dreams up a rehabilitation plan. Ardessa returns from vacation to find she's been transferred to the business office. O'Mally tells the business manager Henderson that Ardessa "needs regular exercise. She owes it to her complexion." O'Mally admits that he's incapable of disciplining people, but perhaps Henderson can be firm with her. Henderson knows just the person, the brash and thoroughly modern Miss Kalski, whom Ardessa had held up to Becky as an example of how not to dress.

Ardessa protests the change: "I've not been accustomed to commercial work, Mr. O'Mally. I've no interest in it, and I don't care to brush up in it." O'Mally is sure footed. He's going to brush *everybody* up and "brush a few people out." But, of course, he wants Ardessa to stay: "Don't be hasty now. Go to your room and think it over." Never was an ultimatum framed as the employee's choice delivered so sweetly.

Ardessa is miserable in the business office but can't quit. She thinks about all the offices she knows and realizes "she could never meet their inexorable standards of efficiency." O'Mally is still a bit nervous about Ardessa. He isn't oblivious to her feelings. Six years of service—spotty as they may have been—does count for something. He does the brave thing. He speaks with Ardessa honestly and masterfully. He doesn't want Henderson, he tells her, to form the impression that all of his editorial people are

stuck up and think the business department are old shoes. That's where we get our money from, as [Henderson] often reminds me. You'll be the best-paid girl over there; no reduction, of course. You don't want to go wandering off to some new office where personality doesn't count for anything. . . . Do you, now, Miss Devine?

Personality is Ardessa's only card. She plays it: "Becky is not the sort of girl to meet people for you when you are away."

But times have changed. Ardessa's personality, her way with people, is obsolete. Her manner is a liability. "You're too soft-handed with the has-beens and the never-was-ers," O'Mally tells her, "You're too much of a lady for this rough game. Nearly everybody who comes in here wants to sell us a gold-brick, and you treat them as if they were bringing in wedding presents. Becky is as rough as sandpaper, and she'll clear out a lot of dead wood."

The office in "Ardessa" is a microcosm of the great transition in American business that swept away the antiquated manners of the Gilded Age in favor of a new type of professionalism. Spurred by the belief that there was only one best way, which could be determined "scientifically"—a doctrine brilliantly marketed by Frederick Taylor (1856–1915)—business managers now looked to the twin deities of efficiency and professionalism. People entering the salaried work force increasingly came from two-year business colleges. (I will say more about these later.) O'Mally's office still has a foot in the past, when strength of personality, more than "professional" know-how, dominated office relationships. But the new professionalism, rational and impersonal, began to loosen the emotional bonds, the manners and niceties, that previously colored hiring and office relationships. Efficiency and sentiment don't mix. Ardessa knows her social skills and wiles count for nothing in the new business world. The thought of competing against the young, competent women she sees everywhere terrifies her. But O'Mally's office still has a human face, still provides sanctuary. And it even turns out that Miss Kalski doesn't bear grudges. She good-naturedly goes out of her way to break Ardessa's fall. So too does Henderson, Ardessa's new boss. Rather than cast her in a bad light, Henderson blames the bad atmosphere in the editorial offices, where people get "moldy."

THE INDEPENDENT WOMAN'S GUIDE TO SUCCESS

"Ardessa" set down a type of status order for working women: at the bottom, factories; next, department stores; then offices. Office work meant the prestige of a *salary*, being called a professional rather than a wage earner. It also represented independence. Women needn't depend on the servitude of marriage for sustenance, a life only marginally better than sewing in a Lower East Side sweatshop. To the woman who applied herself, anything was possible. So said Elizabeth Sears, an early feminist in word and deed. Sears is a radical analogue to Willa Cather's $6-a-week stenographer, Becky Tietelbaum. Much of what Sears says echoes her coeval, the anarchist Emma Goldman (whose brilliantly reasoned oratory on emancipation so terrified the United States government that she was deported in 1919). Sears's 1917 article in *Harper's Monthly Magazine*, "Business Women and Women in Business," is both a manifesto of emancipation and a woman's guide to success, whose lessons Sears derives from her own career and the successes and failures of others.[36] Sears's rules are variations of the same adages and beliefs uttered today. They constitute one of the great myths sustained by American business:

any person with the right stuff can start at the bottom and make it to the top: the Horatio Alger "rags-to-riches" myth. I use the term *myth* not to denigrate the rules of success, which are true and timeless. But crooked offices skew everything. Sears presumes a straight and narrow business world, a just place indifferent to everything but merit. That's how it should be but isn't always. Hence, we enter the realm of myth.

Women who don't succeed, says Sears, have no excuse but themselves. Advancement comes through persistence and industry. Sears serves notice that pulling your weight doesn't apply only to men. There is something of the rugged individualism of America's westward expansion in this. When Sears writes, "In that Middle West town no girl dreamed of remaining at home as a burden to the family support," she implies that Eastern women are averse to work. Blame lazy women for all the doubts about women's suitability for prominent positions. There are two types of women, says Sears, those who earn their own bread and those who don't. Sears went to work right after finishing "that condensed form of instruction known as the business college." It never occurred to her "to apologize for the fact that I worked for my living." Sears says that housework is also work, and work that should be paid for. But, she notes, "A man is usually more willing to pay any woman outside his family money which he is sure she does not earn than to pay to the women folks of his own family the money he knows they earn." The reality is that women must depend on husbands or the men in their families. About matrimony, Sears is as unromantic as Emma Goldman, who advocated free love. Even if women manage to shake free of men by earning their own money, they don't escape servitude. They become slaves to their occupations. "We love to be slaves to something," she says.

"BUSINESS WOMEN" AND "WOMEN IN BUSINESS"

For Sears, *job* is a dirty word. Hearing the word in a speech, she called it a "crude" remark because it presumes inferiority. The connotative distinctions between *job* and *position* and their correlates, *wages* and *salary*, mark social status. The lecturer had said, "When the business girl is trained to know the meaning of economic independence, she has made herself the boss of her job." Sears said, "I always spoke of my work as a 'position.' To have a position carried with it a dignity that savored of importance. It was only the girls who earned wages, rather than a salary, who had 'jobs.'" The concern with dignity reflects the semantic nuances that explain the title of Sears's article: not every woman in business has the right to the honorific "business woman." Just as there are women "parasites" in the home, there are parasites in business, whom Sears terms "women in business." Unlike the business woman who likes her work, the parasite exudes "a sullen resentment against the world in general and her job in particular because of it"—that is, she would prefer to live off of a man. This type, does, however, find at least one solace about office work: it puts her in striking distance of her prey: the "man-hunter" stalks her quarry in the habitat where he is most abundant.

Another species of the women-in-business genus is the "six-dollar-a-week girl" (the universal starting salary for entry-level office work). Sears derives a truism from the $6 girl, repeated *ad nauseam* by motivational speakers and such: you are paid what you are worth. This is accepted as a fundamental law of business, as valid as Newton's laws, and is used to justify both underpay and exorbitant salaries. Just as in the natural world, reason and order reign in the business world, which is indifferent but just. The $6 girl is worth exactly that, says Sears. It would be wrong to pay her more. But, "When she is worth more than that to herself as well as her employer, she will demand it and get it." But not as long as "she is a slave to her job." As long as her attitude is poor, she will stay poor. These are the tenets of the new professionalism, whose ascendancy alarmed some as unfair and remorseless. Only merit counts; personal contingencies, or sob stories, don't matter. Back in 1911, Sears says, during a "stringency in business," a corporation advertised to fill an $8 a week job. Forty applicants were winnowed to two "girls." The one hired was letter-perfect. The one passed over "made considerable fuss" about how the other one lived at home and didn't need the money. This moved the superintendent into making a spot for the cry-baby. The outcome, however, was predictable. The whiner and the complainer simply couldn't do the work and was fired within a week. The lesson is clear. Success is predicated on *attitude*. Sears finds most employers impervious to tales of woe; they hire solely on competence. However, old attitudes still abound. From old habit, some employers still view women's entry into the ranks of business as nothing more than a means of earning "extra pin money." (The expression comes from an extra allowance given to a wife by her husband for small household items, such as pins, which were dear in days past.)

By Sears's reckoning, 85 percent of business women work because they must support themselves or other family members. The other 15 percent are "human fluffs," a term Sears borrows from housekeeping. Anyone who lives on hardwood floors, Sears says, knows what a fluff is. Floor fluffs are unpredictable sources of embarrassment. They hide in dark corners and appear only when company arrives. Just as floor fluffs cause guests to question a woman's housekeeping, office fluffs cast doubt about the suitability of women in offices. A human fluff is in an office for one or both of these reasons: she finds home life boring or seeks a husband. "She exploits her sex in the office, consciously or unconsciously. She works cheaper because she is a woman." And she acts like the weaker sex:

She wants the window continually up or down; she hints for candy and flowers and theater tickets; she embroils the entire office in petty politics; and she clouds the record for the business woman who tackles her work like any other employee in the office and who fails to see why there should be any question of personal privilege in office routine.

As in nature, there is no personal privilege in office life. You get what you earn. The law is simple and just. Salary is a function of responsibility. The more you carry, the more you earn. Six-dollar-a-week women shun responsibility. They get through the day, close their desks, and gaily skip home free of worry. Sears equates large salaries with creative ability: nothing is as mentally taxing as the responsibility of creative work. Sears's employer is an example. He goes to lunch in a limousine and his "tip alone would buy me a good dinner." But Sears isn't envious because she doesn't "have to lie awake nights to wonder how the shortage in paper will affect the business, or whether or not [she] can meet the obligations that will fall due next month, as he must. The lunch and the limousine are merely a part of the job."

GUMPTION

There is no sentiment in the business world, says Sears. For true business women, this is liberating. Half of the business women Sears knows are married but retain their maiden names, the names by which they made good. They refuse to relinquish "what Bobby Burns [the Scottish poet (1759–1796)] has called the 'blessed privilege of being independent.' " Looking back over her own climb, Sears extracts one essential ingredient, "gumption." Don't be taken in by the sob stories of poor working girls subsisting on tea and crackers. Put their failures down to a lack of gumption. Before the health advocates of the day, whom Sears calls "food sharps," had "expatiated upon the delights of proteins and carbohydrates," she and her roommate had discovered that brown bread and cheese contained all the nutrients they needed.

We made cocoa over a gas-plate, and a bottle of milk is food in itself. We hunted for the cheap little places where you could buy for a dime a beef stew, and first take the soup and then eat the beef and potatoes. We ate plenty of whole-wheat bread, and bought bananas and oranges when they were plentiful and cheap.

And as to clothing,

We made our suits last a long time, and we wore cotton hose and cheap shoes; but we lived on that six a week and had a lot of fun out of it. We looked upon it as a temporary phase of development and a not as a permanent bogging-down place.

Today, that's called a winning attitude: confidence that you will achieve your goal. All it takes is gumption. But humor helps. The roommates called their bed, apparently some sort of fold-out sofa bed, a "sanitary grouch." The formula for success works. Here is Sears's testimony:

My room-mate in those days is bossing a four-thousand-dollar job now, and it took those two years of six-a-week responsibilities to develop her for the bigger job. She knew she had to get up at six in the morning to get to the office on time, but she did not waste any time in moaning over her fate; she got up and went to work. And she never allowed either of us to slight the washbasin.

To blame discrimination for failure to advance is illogical. There is no sentiment in the business world. How then can there be feelings against women? Yes, antagonism and resentment against women are facts of office life, as is unequal pay. But, says Sears, women themselves must bear the blame for these things. Women who complain of lesser pay only confirm their inefficiency. When women entered into competition with men, they were forced to play by the existing rules. But that was then. Now, "in almost every office," Sears believes women are accepted as equals. Office life has been emotionally bracing for women, teaching them to shed their "petty" outlook and contemplate bigger things than their "neighbor's affairs." Successful women have learned to master their emotions. Sears met a business woman who closed a big deal only to be told by the man on the other end that no woman should be allowed to hold such a position of responsibility. Naturally, the remark stung. But she dismissed it with a smile, knowing that getting emotional was giving way to "pettiness"—the bane of success. "She was right," concludes Sears, "no business woman can afford to allow personal worries to interfere with her office work."

Here is more on emotional restraint. A friend of Sears began to "take her despondency to the office with her. Her depression began to affect the office staff unconsciously." (How quickly was Freud absorbed and made a part of everyday culture!) Fortunately, her employer was wise. He believed in a cheerful office. His handling of the problem employee reads like something out of a modern-day management text. The implied threat, knock it off or else, is instantly recognizable to anyone versed in smiley, even-voiced corporate-speak:

"I am tremendously sorry for you," he said, kindly. "I know things are breaking badly for you at home just now. But I employ you to do a certain amount of work here for me, and one of the requirements of the place is that you bring a reasonable amount of cheerfulness to bear upon your work. You may not realize it, but your state of mind is actually affecting the work in the office."

Of course she took his meaning. The effective business woman is serene. Nerves have no place in the modern business office. She was forced to choose between "being a half-way business girl and a half-way home girl. I put my family on its own resources and bent every bit of my time and energy to climbing the ladder in my own office." And it did "the family good, for they learned to get along by themselves." When you're right with the business world, it's right with you.

A DRAWER OF ONE'S OWN

A woman must sacrifice a lot to advance, but she doesn't need to lose her femininity. Sears recalls one of her friends, a woman who

would be pretty if she gave herself a chance; but she is deadly conscientious. She is not only a slave to her job, but to her duty. She wears flat-heeled shoes and plain hats and unbecoming gowns, not because she really likes them or feels more comfortable in them, but because it is a matter of principle with her. She believes that business women must sacrifice feminine fripperies to the exigencies of the occasion.

At issue was a woman in her department who paid $10 for a pair of tan shoes. This the frump thought "wicked." Sears disagreed. The purchase was a step upward: the woman wanted the shoes so badly that she asked for a raise—and got it. Desire spurred ambition. And Sears predicts the woman will one day wear $14 shoes—all because "she dared to have an ambition for ten-dollar shoes."

Professionalism. Quieting nerves. Suppressing petty resentments. Putting one's family on notice. These are driven by gumption and character-ize the newly emerging business woman, who is also emancipated. A decade before Virginia Woolf's metaphoric cry for freedom—"a room of one's own"—Sears wrote about "a drawer of one's own." Efficiency (playing a role) is an office expedient. But that's where it stays. Once out the door, the business woman drops the mask. At home, she is herself. She trims her personality at the office, but not at home. Not all women are naturally neat and tidy. And that's fine. Take the upper drawer of Sears's bureau, "like that of every other woman, [it] is generally mingling with its own contents in the most sociable manner. I would not like to live with a woman who kept her upper bureau drawer neat and tidy. I would be afraid of her."

Having won their "economic independence," Sears and the new league of women professionals have earned their "right to keep our upper bureau drawer as we please, we business women."

SUCCESS AND THE BUSINESS COLLEGE

Elizabeth Sears graduated from a business college or technical school, which she called "a condensed form of education." Presuming the Michigan Business & Normal College (MBNC in Battle Creek) typical, its 1922 course catalogue gives an idea of what Sears learned, or the skills needed to crack an entry-level position. The catalogue also documents a phase in the evolution of office work. MBNC's curriculum included courses in typewriting, shorthand, bookkeeping, business English, business letter writing, punctuation, mimeographing, and a variety of accounting classes—corporate, wholesale, and railroad. Office work was primarily clerical, writing and keeping books: except for the tools (typewriters and mimeographs), the work's essence remained unchanged from Bartleby the Scrivener's era. Indeed, the college trained modern-day scriveners, even offering a course in penmanship.

More significant than its vocational offerings, however, MBNC propagated an ideology of success. It's a safe bet that Sears was inculcated in the same way at her college. Regardless of the source, the rules of success that pervade—or even define—American culture (up to the present day) are of a piece. The line runs through Ben Franklin's *Autobiography*, Russell Conwell's nineteenth-century oratory, and Bruce Barton's magazine articles and books in the 1920s. Indeed, Sears's anecdotes might have run in MBNC's publication *Success: A Magazine for Future Executives—Both Young Men and Women*. Above its masthead is an oval of Abraham Lincoln and words attributed to him: "I will study and prepare myself and some day my chance will come." Essentially an advertisement for the college, the magazine's articles and ads reinforce the tenets of success through personal testimony and such. (All copy in *Success* resembles newspaper articles, even the ads, and most stories carry bylines and head shots of their subjects.) The March 1922 issue of *Success* gives an idea of how firmly the ideology of success had become entrenched in American culture. As Ben Franklin discovered in sustaining his vigor and perfecting his social skills, the key is persistent self-improvement. The business world holds out the promise that it rewards diligence, even temperament, and initiative. The business world, like sports, is rational, impersonal, and just. Success is a personal decision, a function of discipline. Failure's causes are located entirely within. Blaming outside factors shows lack of character: sloth and toxic thought.

Success magazine claims that MBNC prepares its students to reach the first step: "We Increase Your Worth," claims an ad showing a vacant desk with a candlestick telephone and the nameplate "Office Mgr."[37] To one day sit behind that desk, one must first learn to write in a neat, legible hand, a requisite to efficient bookkeeping:

Before you leave here you "take" in shorthand and transcribe on the typewriter, real business letters—hundreds of them. You are taught how to serve your employer and thus increase your own worth to him. You keep real books. You are taught how to open and close a set of books—for manufacturers, wholesalers, retailers, banks. And we teach the methods used now, not the methods of twenty years ago.

Beyond the college itself, *Success* sells the idea of office work. Unskilled factory work pays well and is more "manly," while business school delays entry into the labor force *and* charges tuition. J. W. Roth's article, "The Lesson Today's Unemployment Teaches," addresses these objections. The labor market peaked directly after the Armistice (November 11, 1918): jobs requiring muscle couldn't fill their vacancies and wages soared; there seemed no end in sight. The younger generation trusted their future "to muscle power alone." With the blessing of their parents, they jumped from high school to factory. Commanding excellent wages, "any other course seemed folly." But within 18 months, an "ill wind" swept away all the post–Armistice inflation, and those who chose factories over offices lost their jobs. For some, it's too late. They're tied down by home and family and must ride out the storm. But millions of others can start anew. "They see the plight into which they may be thrown at any time if they place their whole trust on muscle-power." In contrast, office work is steady. Its payrolls aren't cut to the bone at the first hint of depression because American business needs its offices intact, its "brainworkers" at the ready, when industry's wheels begin turning again. Accompanying the article is a teaser box titled "The Land of *Manana*" (the future). Everyone knows that business college leads to success. But even so, enrollment is put off until *manana*, which means "never getting it done." And ominously, "If you are postponing taking up a business training, you are simply giving other young people an opportunity some day to dominate you."[38]

Following are several *Success* stories about those who didn't wait. Clyde L. Bush began his special courses in accounting and business administration right out of high school. Immediately upon graduation, he was "placed" as a "personal secretary and assistant" to a branch auditor at Republic Motor Truck Company. Clyde's desk is in "one of those offices with a thick rug on the floor, mahogany furniture and a sign of the door which reads: 'Branch and General Auditors—PRIVATE—Next Door for Information.' " Enjoying the serenity of an office screened from information seekers and other riffraff, Clyde is "in the direct line of promotion and has every opportunity to learn the details connected with the job."[39]

Jessie B. Edwards landed a "Big Job Half Way 'Round the World." Before the war, Jessie was "just an errand girl in a big department store."[40] It was hard work, but the best she could do without office skills. But Jessie didn't lack gumption. She taught herself secretarial skills in her spare time and quadrupled her salary when she landed the job of private secretary to the president of the company. She soon saved enough for business school. Jessie's efficiency was in great demand, and today, the former errand girl is business manager of the Magaw Hospital in Fuchau, China.

Lurtin R. Ginn began as a humble clerk. Today, his old job pays $25 a week, but he made much, much less. But rather than dwell on his poor salary, Lurtin turned his thoughts to self-improvement. He hungrily mastered his job. His supervisors noticed and increased his responsibilities. Promotions followed. Today, Lurtin associates with "big people." He is the assistant controller general of the United States. His climb in "power and influence"—all through "sheer ability"—was possible because "Uncle Sam believes in giving every young man or young woman in his employ an opportunity for higher service." Even while holding down a lowly government job like Lurtin did at the beginning, a person can attend any of the numerous colleges in his or her vicinity.[41]

Success magazine is full of homilies. Ambition alone might propel a person to a promising start but won't "attract the favorable attention of the men higher up who have promotions to give." In addition to ambition, promotion demands three things: speed, accuracy, and personality. Merna B. Holmes heads MBNC's Shorthand Department. Like all faculty, Merna gives special attention to "the development of character and personality." MBNC graduate Gertrude Wilkins attested that, "No real business office has room for the untrained, and they will not make room to convenience you, no matter who you are. Your pay is based on what you KNOW." *Success* quotes Charles M. Schwab: the captains of industry are not hunting money. America is "heavy" with money. They seek "brains—and faithful, loyal service. I have found that when 'stars' drop out, successors are merely men who have learned by application and self-discipline to get full production from an average normal brain."[42] An illustrated sidebar sets down the laws of advancement:

Every office is divided into two groups—those who direct the business—the sales and accounting—and those who carry out these directions. Those who direct are the high salaried department heads and managers. Those who carry out the directions are assistant executives—stenographers, secretaries, accountants, bookkeepers, confidential assistants. As changes take place or as the business expands, these assistant executives inherit or grow into higher executive and administrative positions. This is the history of practically every big organization. The executives of today are the assistant executives of yesterday—the stenographers, bookkeepers, etc. And the executives of today are the owners of tomorrow.[43]

The rules of succession are clear and just. Work fast and accurately—with personality—as you master your job and you will advance.

FANNY HERSELF

Edna Ferber is perhaps best known for two novels, *Show Boat* (1926), the basis for the Broadway musical, and *Giant* (1952), the basis of the 1956 movie starring James Dean, Elizabeth Taylor, and Rock Hudson. Her novel *Fanny Herself* (1917) is about a bright, ambitious young lady, Fanny Brandeis, making her way in the new world of business. The story is set in a giant wholesale operation called Haynes-Cooper, led by a charismatic general manager called Michael Fenger, a visionary. He, long before the German nation forced the term into the American vocabulary, had made "efficiency" a plant slogan. As Ferber notes, "Michael Fenger was System," meaning he had a scientific approach to management, a proven method of doing things that never failed, even with marginal workers.[44]

As Fanny waits for an interview with Fenger, a picture of the modern executive's office emerges. Naturally, Fenger has an outer office that employs three assistants: a "spare, middle-aged, anxious-looking" bespectacled secretary; a young, blond male stenographer, "also spectacled and anxious," and a stern office-boy in knickers "who bore no relation to the slangy, gum-chewing, red-headed office boy of the comic sections."

[Even back then, popular or low-brow entertainment, the funny papers—a newspaper innovation not more than 20 years old—presumably shaped the public's understanding of office life.]

Another feature of the modern executive office brings the outer office to attention—the buzzer, the sound of a potentate summoning his underlings, "who jumped like puppets on a string." Fenger didn't use the cheap theatrical tricks that managers used to convey their importance: when visitors entered, he wasn't writing or telephoning.

Fanny is a candidate to become an assistant to the buyer for infants' wear. The candor of both parties in this interview would be impossible today with candidates who are coached to death in what to say: "People tell me I'm a perfectionist, and I've been criticized for staying late and coming in on weekends." The net effect is that all these plastic MBA-types look and sound alike. And today, no one in management would ask any but the most banal impersonal questions for fear of violating the tangle of antidiscrimination laws. Fenger, for example, tells Fanny that as a rule, he never hires a woman when he could hire a man. In his vast company, there is only one woman who occupies an important position, and she happens to be a "genius." And when he tells Fanny that he supposes she knows little about buying and selling infants' clothing, instead of finessing one of those "well-actually-I've-been-studying" answers and letting drop some memorized number about the main competitor's market share, she answers, "Less than about almost any other article in the world."

This isn't to say the candidate was above gamesmanship or lying. After all, the point is to present yourself in the most favorable light. Too much candor is foolish.

> "Jew?" Fenger asks her.
> "No," she replies. But immediately wishes she could take it back.

However, the enormously intelligent Fenger sees where she's coming from:

> "Now I begin to understand you. . . . You've decided to lop off all the excrescences, eh? Well, I can't say that I blame you. A woman in business is handicapped enough by the very fact of her sex. . . . Too bad you're so pretty."[45]

There it is. Fanny possesses unlimited ambition and imagination—rare qualities. Yet, through no fault of her own, these are negated by three "handicaps," serious detriments to success in business: she is female, Jewish, and pretty. Fenger is brutally honest in his assessment. He approves of her excising all "excrescences," as if her heritage was some sort of disfigurement that could be veiled in lies. Fenger tells Fanny that her immediate supervisor, a Mr. Slosson, is going to resent her.

Fenger seems to have stepped out of one of those case studies used in managerial school, something like the irreverent, nonhierarchical corporate culture Herb Kelleher supposedly introduced at Southwest Airlines. Fenger tells Fanny that he's going to let her grope around and bump her head a few times rather than bog her down with directions or advice. And he tells her that he welcomes suggestions from anyone in the plant, even the elevator boy.

Fenger had made it clear to Fanny that he was gambling by hiring her. It might be a year before she gets results—or maybe never. But she proves her worth even before the interview ends, repaying Fenger in the currency he most values, increased efficiency. Fanny had noticed that his stock boys and girls walk miles each day on every floor of the 15-story building, "Filling up bins, carrying orders, covering those enormous distances from one bin to another, up one aisle and down the next, to the office, back again. Your floors are concrete, or cement, or some such mixture, aren't they? I just happened to think of the boy who used to deliver our paper [in Winnebago, Wisconsin]. He covered his route on roller skates. It saved him an hour." Two days later, every stock clerk in the plant wore "lightweight" roller skates. They were much amused and tended to tumble around corners. But the wackiness of the novelty wore off. By the third week, they treated their roller skates as natural appendages. In true scientific management style, the increased efficiency was quantified and reported to Fenger: owing to a 55 percent savings in time and energy [that energy is a part of this equation is highly suspect], 33 percent of the stock staff was "decreased." Plain talk like "fired" has no place in the pseudoscientific jargon that would become the language of efficiency.

Fenger is one of the new breed of professional managers whose mantra is *efficiency*. But the person who started the modest enterprise that Fenger turned into an empire was a "plumpish, kindly-faced man; a bewildered, gentle, unimaginative and somewhat frightened man, fresh-cheeked and eye-glassed." Here is a description of the executive suite that Nathan Hayes now sat in, with marble and oak everywhere. "Two-toned rugs, and leather upholstery, with dim, rich, brown-toned Dutch masterpieces on the walls." Not reproductions; the real things, mind you. But unlike the tycoons that came after him, Hayes never intended to be buried beneath an avalanche of money—an unexpected and unwanted side effect of doing something he loved and believed in. To remedy this, Hayes "began giving away huge sums, incredible sums. It piled up faster than he could give it away."[46]

Chapter 4

Sponsored Films: Quaintness with a Radical Bite

To the uninitiated, musty industrial and educational films must seem improbable progenitors of a cult following. But some of these "sponsored" films, such as those made for General Motors by the Jam Handy Organization, are as riveting and well made as the Hollywood fare of their era. In the United States alone, approximately 400,000 industrial films exist; add corporate video and the number of so-called "orphan," or non–Hollywood, films numbers in the millions, says Rick Prelinger, an innovative archivist and advocate for the preservation of these films.[1] Sponsored films are typically anonymous: they credit neither directors, writers, nor actors. However, some uncredited works evidence a distinguishable voice or "house style," says Prelinger.[2]

Audience size for sponsored films varied wildly. "Some of the Jam Handy films were made for just one person to see," Prelinger said. "Maybe you're trying to sell a vice president on making a big equipment purchase."[3] Other sponsored films reached upward of twenty million viewers *both* in business settings and in movie theatres, where they ran with newsreels and cartoons prior to the featured attraction.[4]

The films that I draw upon are among popular (or everyday) culture's submerged or forgotten voices. Scattered far and wide, lying hidden in boxes and cabinets in corporate storage vaults and warehouses, it's probable that thousands upon thousands of these films have never been viewed by anyone living today. Only a relative handful of sponsored films have been catalogued by preservationists. Each of those that I treat has a quaint aesthetic charm, but more significant is their unimagined latent critical power. Sponsored films portray a business world as far removed from current conditions as fantasy from reality. In this gulf lies their radical potential: in portraying business practices and relationships as they *should* be, sponsored films indict many current practices. Sponsored films are the antithesis of factual and fictive accounts of offices as deplorable places filled with ruthless, greedy people.

Regardless of their parentage, orphan films owe a debt to Jam Handy, whose philosophy I will sketch before proceeding.

JAM HANDY

Jam Handy (1886–1983) was an innovative filmmaker and storyteller, an iconoclast who pioneered the use of still and moving pictures in education and sales. Although unknown to the public, Handy is one of those great American originals who had one foot in each century. He belongs in the same pantheon as Thomas Edison, Mother Jones, Eugene V. Debs, and Henry Ford. Handy worked as a stringer for the *Chicago Tribune* while attending the University of Michigan. In 1903, he filed a story about a speech professor getting down on one knee to demonstrate how to propose marriage. An artist at the *Chicago Record Herald* ridiculed the professor in a cartoon based on Handy's story. Suspended from the University for sullying its reputation, Handy quit school and worked in advertising and sales (at the *Tribune*, National Cash Register Company [NCR], and International Harvester). At NCR, he used matchstick men on glass slides to close sales. Inspired by a set of Chinese characters containing thousands of pictograms and ideograms, Handy set out to catalogue all possible types of human interaction on slides. He eventually created a 25,000-slide library.

Handy made training films and visual materials to help the Home Front during both World Wars. Illiteracy rendered military and industrial instruction manuals ineffective. In World War I, one million men—one-quarter of those drafted—couldn't even read newspaper headlines; during World War II, one-and-one-half million—11 percent of all service personnel—could not read at the fourth-grade level. Basic written instructions were beyond their ken. Thus the primacy of pictures.

"What goes in one eye doesn't go out the other," said Handy, who said he loved to learn but hated to study. He described the work of his production company, the Jam Handy Organization, as making learning a pleasure. Handy said he believed in "putting the hay where the horse can reach it."[5]

Thomas Edison told Handy he had envisioned moving pictures as an educational medium that would transform American schools and education but suffered the disappointment of seeing his invention used for entertainment. Handy told Edison: "Let me save this daughter of yours from the life of shame to which the motion picture industry has led her."

Over the course of nearly 70 years, the Jam Handy Organization produced some 70,000 motion pictures. "Few if any production units in or out of Hollywood can boast of having produced so many films over such a long period of time under the supervision of just one person," said Prelinger.[6] Handy's films reached an estimated 20 to 30 million viewers: they were featured at the New York World's Fairs of 1939 and 1964; and the 115 films he made for Chevrolet (from 1935 to 1941) were made expressly for theaters, giving mass audiences a taste of Handy's blend of entertainment and education.

For Handy, implanting images in the mind was crucial to learning and could be accomplished through any medium: by "motion pictures," he simply meant the effects of good storytelling. In 1961, he told a Detroit public TV station that Jesus made "motion pictures of the mind" because his parables spoke visually—spoke with the eye. Although a prodigious filmmaker, Handy never eschewed the plain word. The Handy Organization's productions included a great many that used only words, or words accompanied by still pictures. (Film was just one mode of embedding images in minds and accounted for only one-third of Handy's work.) Like Winston Churchill, whom he admired, Handy found short, simple words the best means of connecting "pictorially" and thus emotionally.[7] (Handy's approach instantly summons Ernest Hemingway, who, influenced by Paul Cezanne's proto-cubism, attempted to distill experiential truth into the purest, simplest words possible.)

Jam Handy is the hidden conscience of business. A voice that once dwelt deep in the heart of corporate America is now submerged. Handy was a pitchman for upright conduct. Like Charles Dickens, he believed that learning and entertainment were reciprocal. For Handy, that meant "visual" stories, regardless of channel.

FOREMAN JIM BAXTER

Orphan films are historically invaluable: they freeze the words and images that reflect the values and beliefs that shape and reshape office culture. While business culture has evolved outwardly, changing the look and feel of office life, certain core values have remained constant. These values, as idealized in popular culture, sustain American culture's central, defining myth: anyone with the right stuff can "make it" from the bottom up. (Such variations of the Horatio Alger myth show the fluidity between the nebulous concepts of business culture and culture at large.) While from the 1980s onward, the right stuff came to mean rapacious ambition and avarice, it once meant the virtues and traits tied to honesty and industry. This still obtains in some quarters today despite Wall Street's pernicious influence.

A stellar example of idealized business values is the anti-union film the Handy Organization made for General Motors, *The Open Door: The Story of Foreman Jim Baxter His Family and His Job* (1945).[8] *The Open Door* reinforces the idea that anyone who has "it" is entitled to a shot at the top, even an assembly line worker. The operative ideas in this story are two of the most esteemed notions in business culture, "executive" and "leadership."

Unlike many sponsored films, *The Open Door* is as fully credited as any Hollywood feature and rivals Hollywood in production values and dramatic appeal. It is likely that *The Open Door* was one of the Handy films made for theatrical viewing.

THE AMERICAN DREAM CIRCA 1945

The opening scene of Jim coming home from a day at the factory is a picture of postwar American prosperity driven by a manufacturing economy. Jim lives in a picturesque house on a tree-lined suburban street. Solid middle class. From his driveway, Jim can hear strains of his daughter practicing at the piano. A metronome is clicking as she works through a Czerny etude. Her playing is full of mistakes. She's just a normal kid, as is her sibling, a freckled boy in a baseball cap who looks up with a wide grin: "Hello, Daddy." Jim's return from work is an event the whole family eagerly awaits. Finally, together again. The bliss of family life. But Jim is troubled. Not all is well at work. The elation of his recent promotion has worn off.

The director, Haford Kerbawy, flashes back to that happy day, when the boss, Mr. Vance, summoned Jim to his office. Lean, fit, exuding competence and authority, Vance wears a wide-lapelled suit and leans back in his chair, the picture of the competent executive. Vance delivers a disquisition on moving up and what it takes to be an executive. Jim, having been accepted into an exclusive club, is now entitled to understand the selection process. All the while Jim was operating a big, brutish stamping machine on the factory floor, *they* had kept an eye on him and found he'd been doing a "good job."

Vance tells Jim they want to promote him to foreman. They will train him, but they can't teach him the intangibles. Jim will have to prove he's executive material by showing he can lead people. If Jim proves he's the born leader they believe he is, then he'll keep climbing the ladder. The company, says Vance, always picks its foreman with "an eye on that ladder. Of course, sometimes we make mistakes and pick the wrong man."

Vance's talk sets down the rules of the game. This is the promise American business holds out to all who would scale its heights. First, a painful truth typically glossed over, especially in recent times: not everybody has what it takes, has "got it, down inside." Education, "all the training in the world," can't help a person who lacks "the natural ability to handle and understand people." This, like the ability to throw a baseball 90 miles an hour, is innate. Executives, leaders, are born, not made. Those who have "it" will succeed anywhere. Their ability is applicable to any enterprise; nothing holds them down. As Vance put it, if a man has "got the ability, he'll keep on climbing the ladder. He'll keep on getting promotions no matter where he works. It can be the factory, the Army, or anywhere else."

Vance's adjutant, an old man in suspenders, who serves as his superior's eyes and ears, suggests that perhaps one day, Jim will have *his* job. It's possible, Vance allows, now that Jim is on salary and commands more responsibilities and commensurate benefits. If he continues to prove himself, both will increase.

Thus concludes Jim's rite of passage. He is now an initiate into management and entitled to try for the grand prize: executive.

SUCCESS IN BUSINESS

One of the earliest orphan films about office life is an anonymous silent film titled *Success in Business* (1928).[9] Although the film's director, sponsor, and intended audience have been lost to time, its message is familiar. The film is one of countless narrative variations on upward mobility. *Success in Business* lays out the rules of success, which is attainable to any person willing apply those hoary virtues known to all: initiative and industry. Success is defined by implication as the accumulation of maximum power and wealth. *Success in Business* is also noteworthy for its language. The words and phrases preserved on the title cards capture the ideology of American business just prior to the Great Crash of 1929. It's interesting to note, for example, the weight and opprobrium assigned to the term *dead-end job*—the most terrible of plights because it precludes advancement. *Success in Business* anticipates *The Open Door*, and, like the latter, valorizes "executive" and "leadership," which shows how long these words and their attendant narratives have occupied cultural eminence. (The possibility that *Success in Business* might be an early Jam Handy film would be a remarkable coincidence!)

STUCK IN A DEAD-END JOB

Success in Business's protagonist is Bob Gregory, one of the faceless, nameless employees of a large organization, chained to a dead-end job. Bob and other low-ranking employees are seated at massive, wooden desks in a cavernous room. Several wear bow-ties. Telephones with conical earpieces sit on the desks. Also present is a secretary, the only woman in the room. There is a common coat stand. There is no privacy, no partitions. An officious man wearing a Theodore Roosevelt-style mustache enters with papers in hand, which he exchanges for more papers with a seated underling. This action passes for a typical day at the office.

That evening, Bob is home with his wife and two children. Still in office attire, he reads the paper while his wife knits. She asks how will they buy the kids new clothes this month.

Bob answers indirectly, as though musing on a problem: all businesses strive for productivity—and therein lies his chance of reward. He knows how to get twice as much out of his coworkers, but dead-end jobs scotch initiative. He decides to quit and hunt for a job with a "future."

But Bob's wife has a better idea: he should persuade his boss to let him create his own job.

Yes, of course. A grand idea that all dead-enders should broach—well perhaps only those with initiative and imagination.

Bob is next seen walking down a corridor that looks like a sleeper car and leads to a private office, the mark of status. The upper halves of the office's walls are glass, allowing the boss to watch his secretary; the upper-floor windows of this skyscraper afford a cityscape. A much older man offers Bob a seat and listens. Age signifies rank. As they shake hands and part, the gray executive says, "I don't think much of your idea, but I'll give you a chance to try it out."

The early going is rough. Bob *is* the new department, which sells a "new type of service to the public." Of what Bob is an innovator isn't revealed. Everything is abstract, interchangeable. This broadens the applicability of this training or motivational film's message to all office work.

Bob's climb is effected through the systematic application of the rules of success, which presuppose the mastery of certain skills, especially persuasion. When Bob's new big idea is rejected, he does a lot of hand shaking and talking hunched over desks. Finally, a man of obvious import (his desk houses two telephones) says, "I'll give you my answer tomorrow."

Bob never quits doing whatever it is he's doing, and it pays off. The business grows. More salesmen are hired, and Bob "institutes informal conferences." Bob is a leader on the rise. His ideas matter. No more private arm twisting. The conferences become formal. We see Bob animatedly addressing a semicircle of 11 suited men. The 12th (there must be *twelve*, of course) sits up front in judgment. It's the gray executive, the original nay-sayer who doubted but gave Bob a chance—to fail. Bob draws bigger and bigger audiences; standing room only, like packed political meetings, proof of inspirational "leadership."

Bob's incremental steps upward finally pay off. At home one evening, he shows his wife a letter. She is seated at a piano (they've moved from the cramped apartment in the first scene). The letter reads: "Mr. Robert Gregory: In recognition of your fine work we have decided to organize your activities into a separate department with yourself as head. In view of its importance you salary will be increased." Bob glows. At last, he's a "real executive."

The office has also changed. Befitting success is an expansive high-backed letter container and a new clerk sliding papers into its honeycombed slots. Bob, as department head, now oversees four employees of both genders. Like students in a stern classroom, they sit behind desks, which, to our modern sensibilities, conditioned by cost-cutting shoddy materials, seem oversized and luxuriously oaken. The men are bent over their desks, engrossed in writing, like hopefuls taking a civil service exam.

As the years recede, Bob, step by step, continues to advance. It's dinnertime at home with Bob, his wife, and two children. (The successful American family always seems to number two children, and always a boy and a girl.) Bob's wife draws something steaming from a silver serving set; upon the dining table are candles, flowers, and crystal goblets. A uniformed maid serves the family, which dresses for dinner.

Amid all this opulence, Bob makes a startling announcement: "I'm not going to work for Johnson & Bailey any longer." This draws a long look from his wife. He slides his chair close to hers, as if to brace her for tragedy.

"No," Bob Gregory continues, "I'm going to work for Johnson, Bailey & Gregory!" That rascal. He's made partner!

The business continues to grow in both size and complexity because of Bob's "leadership." Throughout the film, prosperity (growth) is symbolized by the number of desks, which are now legion. As for complexity (technological progress), a clerk stands before what appears to be a pipe organ, which is actually one of those tubular contraptions for sending paperwork to different floors.

Bob must be content. Making partner is about as good as it gets. Well, no—not for a man of Bob's ambition.

Eight people are seated at a rectangular table. Bob is standing, a clear sign of power, and he will not sit still until "he becomes president of the board whose policies affect the entire organization down to the humble position whence he started."

Success in Business ends with a close-up of what looks like a chimney: the most prominent shape among a slew of odd-sized rectangles that pass for an organizational chart—the most convoluted schematic imaginable. The chart isn't pyramidic, but more like a boxy building whose bricks contain titles. The bottom rung is Salesman, above which are Local Sales Manger, District Sales Manager, Assistant General Sales Manager, and Sales Manager lateral to Controller and Production Manager. On top of this dwelling is the "chimney," which houses the General Manager, the President, the Directors, and the Owners. These are the rungs in the modern business organization, a ladder that beckons those who dare to succeed. Bob Gregory did it, from Salesman to President of the Board. How?

Leadership—the ticket to the top. The film explains that, "Wherever people act together leaders will be found—whether among boys at play— or among a gang of men at work." Cut to a shot of grubby foundry workers laboring with molten iron; they look like prisoners. True leaders, no matter their origins, eventually attain executive titles because they share three traits: ambition, decision, and fairness. *Success in Business* illustrates these as three arched doorways cut into a cartoonish brick wall. Above the arches is the supreme skill in American business, "Leadership," sought and royally compensated by company owners.

But, like in a Hans Christian Andersen fairy tale, to get the gold, you must pass the test by negotiating each of the three doors, just like Bob Gregory. Bob hop-scotched across the organization chart until he landed on the last square. A push from his wife propelled him upward. But Bob possessed the intangibles that *Success in Business* was made to promote. These are the secrets of success, circa 1928. But they presume honest, intelligent management that rewards the deserving. No envy, favoritism, incompetence, or pettiness from above thwarted Bob's quest. Thus does *Success in Business* idealize American business.

One of the mysteries of such forgotten industrial films is who they intended to reach. Perhaps *Success in Business* was made to boost productivity by inspiring the bottom rungs—salesmen and clerks—to strive for more: as in all success fables, Bob started at the bottom.

OFFICE ETIQUETTE

The Open Door and *Success in Business* portray a male-dominated business culture. Executives, with very, very few exceptions, were all male and typically physically imposing and well spoken. The next two sponsored films show women in office life. Although the rules of success are gender neutral, women's career paths were vastly different than men's. It's certain that foreman Jim Baxter and salesman Bob Gregory possessed no more than a high school education, if that. Yet this was no impediment, for executives are born, not made. Yet two of the women featured in the next sponsored films are not only business college graduates, but they too possess industry, skill, and drive. However, their career trajectories seem to stop short of the executive suite, just a fact of life for most women in the 1950s.

Office Etiquette (1950)[10] appears to have been intended as a training film for secretarial schools. The only facts known about this 15-minute film are that it was jointly made by Encyclopaedia Britannica Films and Columbia University. Its message is that humility, diligence, and perseverance will enable the semiskilled to move upward. It also shows that record-keeping, correspondence, and personal and personable customer contact were once the essential facets of office life and were handled almost entirely by women. As an exemplar of what office life *should* be, *Office Etiquette* is Pollyannaish, although it does present its own version of *Goofus and Gallant*, a cartoon that teaches children social skills (it appears in *Highlights* magazine, found in all dental offices). *Office Etiquette* presents office life in much the same way the sitcom *The Adventures of Ozzie and Harriet* (1952–1967) presented family life: as a general state of happiness with a few rough patches that spur self-improvement.

Office Etiquette follows a recent secretarial school graduate, Joan Spencer, throughout the first few months on her first job and beyond. In all her actions, she is guided by the voice of Miss Purcell, the old pro who taught Joan's beginning typing class. But Joan learned that typing was a relatively unimportant skill in the grand scheme: the most important skill is getting along. Miss Purcell looks like the prototypical teacher in the days when, excepting universities, all teachers were female, their only other career path being office work. Miss Purcell is tall, matronly, wears small pearl earrings, and is kindly in a velvet-hammer manner. She is wont to stop her typing classes to make one of "her little speeches." In her fun-or-hard speech, for example, Miss Purcell tells her students that the Golden Rule also applies to offices. They must know their work and learn to enjoy it and their colleagues. Consideration of others, particularly one's employer, is cardinal. A new career can be fun or hard; this depends entirely upon a person's attitude.

Good advice indeed. One *can* be happy in an office, but there are many snares to avoid. Contentment stems from a *decision* to be happy with one's lot. The bit about enjoying people is sage advice, but this rarely happens automatically. One must work at cultivating this habit; more than tedium, it's other people that make office life so unbearable.

Joan Spencer admits she didn't understand some of the things Miss Purcell said until she landed her first job (on Miss Purcell's recommendation). The portly, balding man who hires Joan tells her they're a small company that values getting along with others. Can she do that?

Oh yes, says Joan, who is hired as a stenographer and file clerk. She reports for work wearing a checked, woolen suit, with an open jacket and a chic black cap. Very Parisian. It's her good suit, plain and neat and just right for an office, which is a formal place. No first names. It's Miss Spencer and Miss Hamilton—except for the secretarial pool women, who are the "girls."

Although Joan was worried about that first job, Miss Purcell's advice, which kept running through her head, sustains her. She lunches with the other "girls" and joins their bowling league. While Joan finds it easy to enjoy her colleagues, learning her job is harder. During her first weeks, she spends her evenings at home studying the company's forms and procedures and practicing her shorthand. A close-up shows Joan surrounded by stacks of notebooks. She's learning business terms. Other lessons, however, come harder.

One day, after handing a suited man a letter she has typed, Joan turns her attention to filing; and then it comes:

"Oh, Miss Spencer . . ."
"Yes, Mr. Kane?"

It's the letter she typed that morning. She's made a mistake: a passage makes no sense. Kane says he couldn't have dictated those words. He handles Joan gently.

She, however, turns defiant: No, she couldn't possibly be wrong. That's precisely what he said. She has it in her notebook and proffers the hard evidence.

Kind Mr. Kane sizes up the situation. He is too wise to berate Joan or flash his temper. He simply stretches out the word "Well," impregnating it to mean: "I get the picture; you're new and can't handle criticism. But I'm going to give you at least one more chance to see the error of your ways."

This is excellent management. Leading the employee to conclude that she was wrong rather than telling her induces growth while preserving self-esteem and stemming aggression.

Joan gets it. She had, of course, made a mistake. Henceforth, she learns to gracefully admit mistakes instead of arguing. She learns to ask questions instead of making wild guesses. And she learns not to brood over criticism. She also learns her dos and don'ts by watching others.

DOS AND DON'TS

Not all of Joan's colleagues are model employees. *Office Etiquette* surveys the types of people who violate office protocol.

A young, stocky woman, heavily lipsticked, sits in front of her typewriter. She reaches into a drawer and extracts a piece of chocolate that that she blatantly chews open-mouthed, dropping morsels on her paperwork. The chocolate drips down one hand while she attempts to clean her other by furiously licking her palm. Continuing her licking, she picks up a letter, smudging the document.

Miss Purcell would not approve. Consideration includes doing only office work during office hours.

Cut to a thin, older, man seated in front of an enormous ledger book, which he lifts to reveal a newspaper's sports section. After a furtive glance, he brings the book down. It's his routine: a little bit of office work, a little bit of reading.

Pan to a secretary typing away. A close-up reveals what she's writing: "don't you dare forget." She laughs to herself as she concludes her letter: "with gobs and gobs of . . ." She closes with a series of XXXs, puckers her lips, and directs a loud kiss at the machine.

Then there is the blonde gabbing on phone: "And who do you think we ran into . . . oh I was so mad I could have slapped her face. No! You wouldn't think she was that kind, would you."

Cut to a crew-cut, buttoned-down young man holding a pencil. He yawns as he hands someone a stack of papers. His head droops and he nods off. He is spent from late-night activities and has nothing left for work, thereby cheating the company.

Joan learns to work "right up till the end of the day" and also that a date after work is no cause to violate the rules of business attire. Cut to a woman in an evening dress looking at her watch. It's not yet five o'clock, but she has shut down for the day and occupies herself by staring into a compact mirror and patting her hair.

Some people have no consideration for their colleagues, such as the man who switches on a fan that creates a gale that blows away all the papers on another person's desk. Joan observes that thoughtlessness creates extra work and hard feelings.

Minding your own business is a cardinal rule of office life. A creature called Jimmy parks himself in front of Joan's desk waiting to retrieve a list of numbers for the boss, Mr. Arnold. Sheet in hand, Jimmy peeks at the numbers.

"You know you shouldn't do that, Jimmy," says Joan.
"Do whaaaat?" says Jimmy as he continues reading the columns of numbers.

Finally, the camera turns to Joan, hard at work. The rat-tat-tat of her typing is musical. She's obviously a 100-word-per-minute typist. Yes, it's possible to learn what not to do from poor performers, but Joan's most valuable lessons have come from stellar employees. They are neat and organized and manage their time so well they are able to help others, who reciprocate. So well has Joan learned these lessons that she becomes Mr. Arnold's secretary.

JOAN MOVES UP

Now secretary to the boss, Joan's new duties include public relations and personnel matters. She answers the telephone like the consummate professional she has become: "Mr. Arnold's office. No, he's in conference. May I help you? The Acme Printing Company ... no, that order was for $20,000, may we expect it next Tuesday?"

But executive secretary isn't the final rung. *Office Etiquette* ends with a shot of a new desk with the nameplate: "Joan Spencer, Personnel." Joan is now responsible for hiring.

She interviews a young applicant called Miss Collins. Joan commends her score on the employment test. But that's no surprise; Miss Collins was recommended by Miss Purcell. Does she still make her office etiquette speech? asks Joan.

Certainly, says Miss Collins, who knows it by heart: know and enjoy our work and those you work with ...

Yes, says Joan, those rules certainly helped her. She'll see Miss Collins first thing in the morning then?

Yes, very early, says the new hire.

THE BRIGHT YOUNG NEWCOMER

This short training film examines a perennial source of friction in offices: an ambitious new hire attempts to change the way things have always been done. *The Bright Young Newcomer* (1958)[11] is notable on several counts. It was made by the Calvin Company, a pioneer in the use of film as an advertising medium. In 1931, Forrest O. Calvin and his wife Betty founded an advertising company (in Kansas City) whose business films rivaled those made by the Jam Handy Organization. The Calvin Company would come to list DuPont, Westinghouse, and Goodyear among its clients. *The Bright Young Newcomer* was sponsored by the Aluminum Company of America (Alcoa) in cooperation with the National Office Management Association (Alcoa's Education and Training Department furnished the typical office problem confronting managers who supervise women). The film offers no solution; it was made to discuss at training seminars.

The McGraw-Hill Book Company, a textbook publisher that sought to expand its product line by venturing into educational films, distributed *The Bright Young Newcomer*. The film is notable for its picture of office life during the dawning of the Space Age.

THE MODERN OFFICE AND WOMEN

The opening shot pans file cabinets, four desks, four women, and a water cooler in an open room attached to the manager's private office. The manager, George Barnes, walks into the common space and heads for the water cooler. The narrator assumes the voice of opinionated wisdom as he comments on what transpires: "You know, sometimes I feel sorry for people who have to run an office setup. Especially if it employs a number of girls. So darn many things can develop out of nothing. I've always thought it was good common sense to ignore petty situations. But then again, you never know."

The "you never know" is a dig at George Barnes, foreshadowing his clumsy handling of conflict. Betty is the leader of the eight or nine "girls" who work for George. Every office has a Betty: short on personality, but "darned efficient." Betty, who has worked in the office nearly as long as George, set up many of their procedures and filing systems. But then, George hires a new "girl," Joan. In welcoming her, he treats her as a cut above the other employees and seems to give her a mandate to take charge. Unwisely, perhaps, he's too quick to laud Joan's work experience and her college training—*college* meaning two-year business or secretarial school. Perhaps she'll look around the office and come up with some new ideas.

However, when Joan proposes a more efficient filing system, Betty takes offense. She developed the old system, and now this newcomer wants to change it.

New ideas from any quarter always produce anxiety and resistance. Competent veterans are quick to take umbrage at new hires who haven't learned to wear their spurs, that is, to defer to their seniors until they've spent some time in harness.

Betty complains about Joan to Mr. Barnes: just because Joan's been to college, she acts superior and wants to change everything, particularly the things that Betty herself developed. For eight years they've used Betty's filing system, and now it's no good!

Barnes promises Betty that he will talk to Joan. Although efficient and conscientious, George Barnes is also busy and forgetful. He never does talk to Joan. Loathe to create disharmony in the office by confronting the issue, he does nothing, thinking it will pass. However, months later, Betty is hurt to discover that Joan and "the girls" have changed the filing system. Joan is conciliatory and offers to teach Betty. Betty explodes. She confronts Barnes: what did Joan say when he talked to her?

Barnes admits it slipped his mind.

Betty says she doesn't feel appreciated.

Not true, says Barnes, but he didn't expect her to be so resistant to change.

The scene fades and the film ends with a question, "Why *did* Betty resist the new ideas?"

Chapter 5

The Organization Man and His Kin: Preachers and Salesmen

THE ORGANIZATION MAN

In 1956, William H. Whyte, Jr., a writer for *Fortune* magazine, turned a series of articles featuring interviews with the CEOs of Ford and General Electric into *The Organization Man*, a lengthy polemic about the loss of individuality.[1] The book scrutinizes the mentality of subservience endemic to office life. In the half-century since its debut (equivalent to the interregnum between the Civil War and World War I) the book has been translated into 17 languages and sales have topped two million.

Today, the casual reader leafing through *The Organization Man* would think it highbrow, with its copious citations of thinkers such as Max Weber, Thorstein Veblen, and John Dewey. This characterization, however, has more to do with the decline of the reading public and the demise of American education, factors that explain why yesterday's popular culture is often today (mis)cast as highbrow. Nonetheless, *The Organization Man* is an exemplar of popular media (the book is still in print). In documenting the mindset of its era, it displayed the critical bite that defines the best reportage. It also enriched our language by popularizing the term *organization man*, still a put-down today—evidence that our anything-for-money culture is also schizophrenic.

Whyte wrote from a quasiscientific stance. He used popular culture to corroborate his ideas but looked down upon it as inferior to hefty academic studies. Whyte claimed that the ascent of American business also represented the decline of the Protestant Ethic—i.e., thrift and industry are evidence of (worthiness for) salvation—even though the captains of industry still invoked the old Puritan tenet about the sanctity of "hard work." In actual practice, however, big business had gutted the moral center from the immortal virtue of "hard work," which, as all the self-help books and inspirational biographies reveal, is the secret of "making it."

But the ideology of individual success was once fused with a moral component, namely, the welfare of others. Accumulation for its own sake was considered immoral. Flouting it was taboo: "old money" lived by the code "wealth whispers."[2] Getting ahead was justified as a means of elevating the common lot. In looking back on making *Wall Street*, Oliver Stone reiterated this foundational American belief, if not wishful fantasy: individual success, he said, ripples outward, helping to create a rising tide that elevates all boats; one person's success needn't mean another's failure.

In the aftermath of World War II, America may have been flush with prosperity, but something subtler and much more insidious had also taken root: a pervasive and unrestrained prostration to authority, to the "system." The once rugged and towering American spirit, born of revolution and nurtured in westward expansion, had twisted itself into a craven shape. For Whyte, a Princeton graduate and ex-Marine, the contrast in attitudes between the sturdy, moral-fibered citizens of the 1930s—his college years—and a post–World War II America teeming with "yes-men" was alarming.

Using the popular culture of his day—novels, magazine articles, and movies—as a gauge, Whyte documented that pressure to conform pervaded the country. The bellwether for the abdication of individuality, which Whyte considered a type of moral degradation, was the period's best-selling novel, *The Caine Mutiny*. Herman Wouk's World War II story won the 1951 Pulitzer Prize and topped the *New York Times* best seller list for 47 weeks during a 122-week run. (Humphrey Bogart starred in the movie version, *The Caine Mutiny* [1954], which was nominated for seven Oscars. *The Caine Mutiny Court Martial*, Wouk's adaptation for Broadway, opened in 1954, starring Henry Fonda, and also aired on live television in 1955.)

Whyte interprets the novel's surprise ending as disturbingly symptomatic of the malaise infecting the country: the rise of organization men, the middle managers and junior executives, who now swelled the ranks of corporate America. As *The Cain Mutiny* nears its climax, Wouk pits Lieutenant Maryk against his commanding officer, Captain Queeg, skipper of the USS *Cain*, a mine sweeper. When the ship gets caught in a typhoon, Queeg, a hectoring, incompetent coward, steers away from the wind. But Maryk knows that steering *into* the wind affords the only chance of survival. Unable to convince the blubbering Queeg to change his course, Maryk manages to temporarily relieve Queeg of command on medical grounds by citing a Navy regulation. Maryk saves the ship but is court martialed.

As Whyte remarks, Maryk's decision is a moral one: he "must do what he thinks is right or do what the system thinks is right."[3] The court exonerates Maryk and thereby destroys Queeg's career. Individualism wins. Or does it? There's a twist. At a celebratory cocktail party, Greenwald, the lawyer who so skillfully defended Maryk and his fellow junior officers, suddenly tosses his drink in an acquitted officer's face. They, the newly exonerated, not Queeg, are the real scoundrels, Greenwald proclaims. The trial over, his duty done, Greenwald is now free to confess that he felt ashamed to vilify Queeg on the stand. Greenwald rebukes the celebrants, the "victors," telling them that his mother could have been "melted down into a bar of soap"—the fate of European Jewry—were it not for men like Queeg. Regular officers like Queeg, he argues, uphold the system, they keep afloat the ships that protect America. Wouk's denouement is unequivocal. It's couched in the words that a junior officer confides to his diary: "I see that we were in the wrong. The idea is, once you get an incompetent ass of a skipper—and it's a chance of war—there's nothing to do but serve him as though he were the wisest and the best, cover his mistakes, keep the ship going, and bear up."[4]

It's wrong, then, for the individual to buck the system. Ever. "Did Americans gag" on this "extraordinary point of view?" asks Whyte. Quite the contrary. *The Cain Mutiny*'s critical reception revealed that the public overwhelmingly sided with Wouk. Whyte summarized the predominant attitude of the mid-1950s as, "The 'smart' people who question things, who upset people—they are the wrong ones."[5]

TWO-FACED (IN) SUBORDINATION: THE RISE OF THE YES-MAN

World War II was a war of liberation, but ironically, its aftermath brought a wave of inner repression. Smart people—at least those who needed to feed their families—discovered that questioning things didn't pay. Rather than upsetting their bosses, they donned masks—became organization men. Of course, toadyism isn't new. And popular culture has widely reviled the practice by aptly naming such types *yes-men*. Originally an idiom from nineteenth-century politics, the term *yes-man* has proven an enduring epithet. Even so, in actual practice, insincerity, however subtle or blatant, has been normalized. Lying—to put it bluntly—is considered smart, a necessary ploy not just to get ahead but to keep a job.

However, 1950s pop culture gave the impression that a new sort of submissiveness had suddenly swept the country, as though centuries of psychic evolution had been compressed into a decade. This may be seen by contrasting two fictional characters a mere 10 years apart: Tom Rath, the hero of Sloan Wilson's best-selling novel *The Man in the Gray Flannel Suit* (1955), and Jim Baxter, the hero of the Jam Handy Organization film *The Open Door: The Story of Foreman Jim Baxter His Family and His Job* (1945).

Both the novel and the film dramatize a fundamental law of office life: hierarchic organizations pressure even good people into some degree of two-faced behavior. Even so, the postwar character, Tom Rath, thinks thoughts that would have been as inconceivable to Jim Baxter as to Patrick Henry. Foreman Baxter is a throwback to that time in American history, which is to say for *most* of American history, when groveling at the feet of authority was considered shameful. Again, although a scant 10 years separates Jim Baxter and Tom Rath, the ethical gulf between them could be measured in centuries. For during that decade, if Whyte is correct, a blight spread throughout American culture: where individuality withered, the yes-man germinated.

GRAY FLANNEL

One of the most compelling passages in *The Man in the Gray Flannel Suit* is the sketch of a yes-man's anatomy that emerges in an argument between Tom Rath and his wife Betsy.

Rath, a brand-new hire, works as a speechwriter for the CEO of a major New York television network. His burning goal in life is more money. The way to get ahead, he explains to Betsy, is to "Tell the [boss] what he wants to hear."[6] But, he cautions, before committing yourself, first feel the boss out to find out what he thinks.

Tom laughs as he tells Betsy how it's done. It's like the trick fortune tellers use: make a bunch of hedged contradictory statements while scrutinizing the customer's face and use those that seem to please to steer what you say; that way, you can string the boss along by "telling him exactly what he wants to hear."

Betsy doesn't laugh: "Is that what they do?"

Yes, says Tom, who plans to read his boss by telling him that the speech he, the boss, wrote contains "wonderful" passages. If the boss lights up at the word *wonderful*, then Rath will suggest only minor revisions.

However, if the boss seems perplexed at the judgment "wonderful," Rath will say the speech doesn't work and needs major revisions.

Betsy blanches. But Tom shrugs it off as normal corporate behavior, necessary for advancement.[7]

Betsy screams her disgust at this two-faced ploy.

Her husband has genuinely found his boss's speech terrible. Rath thinks this because he still thinks for himself. His judgment has yet to be corroded by office life, by more years and pressures. As to the inevitable corruption of his mind, Rath is sanguine. He views it as nothing more than, in his words, completing his business education, as if he were talking about dropping a few pounds to make varsity.

"In a few years," he tells Betsy, "I'll be able to suspend judgment entirely until I learn what [the boss] thinks, and then I'll really and truly feel the way he does. That way I won't have to be dishonest any more."[8]

Let's pause here and reflect upon what Rath is saying. In a corporate environment, critical judgment, which Rath is still capable of, is a problem. And, incredibly, he views independent thinking as a liability because it makes him a poor liar.

Rath seems to be looking forward to the day of his metamorphosis, the day his corporate mask congeals into his real face. Then, Rath's mind will have been so completely colonized that he will, without effort, think like an organization man.

But even now, Rath's thinking has already become so twisted that he spouts the perverted idea that once he allows his mind to be co-opted, he will become a more honest person.

More honest? Compare this Tom Rath to the Tom Rath who interviewed for the job just months earlier. He was placed in a room with a typewriter and given one hour to write as much of his autobiography as he could possibly manage and told to finish it by completing this sentence fragment: "The most significant fact about me is . . ."[9]

Rath had then amused himself by thinking wouldn't it be something if I wrote the truth:

The most significant fact about me is that I detest the United Broadcasting Corporation, with all its soap operas, commercials, and yammering studio audiences, and the only reason I'm willing to spend my life in such a ridiculous enterprise is that I want to buy a more expensive house and a better brand of gin.[10]

Rath didn't go that far, but he did refuse to play this silly psychological game. And instead of frantically pounding out as much nonsense as possible with one nervous eye on the clock, Rath calmly walked out of the room with a full 15 minutes left on the clock and submitted just one paragraph that ended thus:

"I will be glad to answer any questions which seem relevant, but after considerable thought, I have decided that I do not wish to attempt an autobiography as part of an application for a job."[11]

That was Tom Rath before his emersion into corporate culture. That he is now so willing to sell out signifies a toppling of the American past—albeit largely mythic—and the rise of a new set of values anchored in postwar conformity: the new type of company man was more than willing to abandon autonomy and integrity for a shot at the next rung.

Honesty, which once gave weight to the American character, had become so much ballast holding back the hordes of one-dimensional creatures clambering up the pyramid.

Betsy represents the past, pre–World War II America. She comes from Puritan stock. She's never worked in an office and can't comprehend her husband's acquiescence in a corporate way of life so hostile to traditional American values.

Betsy's lashing eventually brings Rath back to himself. Ultimately, he refuses to con his boss. But that a straight-arrow war hero like Rath even considered selling out shows how insidiously and pervasively this corporate fungus had infected American morals.

That this disease would scorch the leaves of individualism seemed beyond possibility just a decade earlier. Representative of the previous era is Jim Baxter, the hero of the film Jam Handy made for General Motors, *The Open Door: The Story of Foreman Jim Baxter His Family and His Job.*[12]

FOREMAN JIM BAXTER

Jim says that like everybody else, he wants to get ahead in the world, to make something of himself for his wife and kids. With his recent promotion to foreman at a GM factory, Baxter has reached the first rung. "But I'm not going to stop there," he says. "I'm going to be plant superintendent some day. And maybe even higher than that."

At first, Baxter thought he had the best job in the world. But after a few months, the shine starting wearing off of his badge and worry and doubt began to torment him. Baxter had, foolishly he admitted, overlooked a few small incidents on the shop floor, just to show his subordinates that his new title hadn't gone to his head. "It cost me some of the respect of my men," he said.

Baxter also feels pressure from above. The assistant superintendent is too abrupt and impatient with him.

Baxter finds himself trapped in a type of purgatory. He is in between two strata, belonging to neither, and neither is welcoming. In his words, he's no longer one of the boys and not a real boss, just someone who catches hell from both above and below. Baxter concludes that he and all the other foremen are just management stooges.

His wife is rational. She urges him to speak with his boss, who was once a foreman himself; it defies reason that the company would want disgruntled foremen.

But Jim perceives confiding in his boss a sign of weakness, a lack of character. Mistrustful of authority, Jim believes his supervisor would pounce on him for not being up to the job.

After another incident, however, the pressure becomes too much, and Jim Baxter speaks to his boss. For men of his generation and ethos, there are only two reasons for visiting the boss's office: to toady or to quit.

Jim quits. Vociferously. Titles mean nothing. Personal dignity is everything. Jim is an American citizen and, no matter what his station, is inferior to no one. Fearlessly, defiantly, he speaks: The entire operation is a mess and everybody knows it, and the plant foremen are "getting a lousy deal. Maybe the other guys won't tell you, but I will."

For Jim Baxter, who represents the rugged individualism of America's past, the shop floor may be caked with grease and grime, but it's cleaner than the corporate offices coveted by the new breed, where nothing is as it seems, especially what people say.

Prostration before power is essentially an act of insubordination, not only against personal integrity but also against the supreme authority, truth.

But why this quisling stance? What drives it? No one can say for sure, but "sanctimonious materialism," to pick one of dozens of candidates, is as plausible and "valid" as any other platitude. It may, of course, say absolutely nothing remotely accurate about life on earth, but it does, nonetheless, have a basis in the historical and literary record. Likewise, it's also possible to pick any number of chronological starting points. It all depends upon when and where an author wants to begin his or her story. (A common tactic, especially in journalism and nonfiction stories, is to begin with some obscure causal link the writer dug out of the muck and shined up as a game changer.) General consensus seems to settle on "after the Civil War" as a good starting point for the rise of materialism. Mark Twain, for example, subtitled *The Gilded Age* (1873), his novel of greed and railroad corruption, *A Tale of Today*. He should know—at least he was there.

RUSSELL CONWELL'S *ACRES OF DIAMONDS*

Throughout the late nineteenth century and early into the next, public lectures occupied the cultural space that movies would fill. One of the most popular speakers of the day was a Baptist minister called Russell H. Conwell (1843–1925). Conwell, Mark Twain, and William Jennings Bryan were several of the Chautauqua ("cultural enrichment") lecture circuit's stars. Named for a lake in upstate New York, the site of the first cultural enrichment series, hundreds of Chautauqua programs were performed in tents across the country between the 1870s and 1920s. At the first Chautauqua, Sunday school teachers gave outdoor lectures about moral issues. Organizers broadened the programs by bringing in great orators, music, and theater. Theodore Roosevelt called Chautauqua "The most American thing in America."[13]

Conwell's best-known speech was *Acres of Diamonds*, which he claimed to have performed more than 6,000 times and to have used the proceeds to found Temple University (in 1884). The speech subverted common attitudes about money as the root of evil and rich businessmen as contemptuous. Conwell claimed that 98 percent of businessmen were honest. (How he arrived at this fabrication is curious; perhaps he thought 98 sounded more credible than 99.) Conwell argued that it was a person's *duty* to get rich,[14] a radical idea for audiences weaned on the parable of Jesus and the money changers. Audaciously, Conwell claimed that the American people had *misread* the Bible. Money was not the root of evil, he would thunder; the evil lies in the *love* of money.

Conwell was one of the first apostles of wealth, and maybe the greatest. The origins of the modern motivational industry, with its inspirational speakers and how-to-get-ahead books and tapes, are in Conwell. At one time, the training centers of major corporations such as AT&T housed libraries of motivational tapes freely available to their employees. Among the most widely circulated tapes were Earl Nightingale's, one of Conwell's twentieth-century acolytes. In his *Lead the Field* series, for example, Nightingale liberally appropriated *Acres*'s opening Persian tale, Conwell's anecdotes about getting rich by providing what people want, and Conwell's maxim that people are paid exactly what they are worth. Napoleon Hill and Dale Carnegie are also indebted to Conwell, as are today's merchants of "success," whether they know it or not. Their "secrets" are Conwell's laws: do one thing and only one thing at a time with all of your might; wealth lies within the grasp of those with character and imagination; and failure ultimately stems from personal deficiencies, especially negative thoughts—not outside factors.

These adages are the ideological core of office life. They constitute the ironclad rules of success. Conwell was one of the more successful agitators in American history. The arguments he advanced in *Acres of Diamonds* are pervasive today, but only piecemeal, truncated and de-contextualized. *Acres* is funny and wise and decidedly *Puritan*. This last moralizing or ethical strain—the essence of Conwell's message—is what has been lopped off. Missing are two essential qualifiers: wealth is attained not to horde but to serve the greater good; and reward is commensurate to the degree of social benefit rendered.

Of New England Yankee stock, Conwell attended Yale University and served in the Union army before trying lawyering, journalism, and finally oration. *Acres* is a classic of American oratory, compelling storytelling with a simple message: you needn't traipse about the globe searching for fortune when there are acres of diamonds in your own backyard. The "diamonds," of course, are fortune-making opportunities discoverable only to persons of imagination, industry, and fortitude.

When *Acres* was written is not known, but 1870 has surfaced as the year that Conwell heard the story that serves as the running metaphor throughout his speech. Conwell claimed he got the story from the Arab guide who led him and a party of English tourists down the banks of the Tigris and Euphrates on camels. (Setting the tale in cradle of civilization, the Garden of Eden's locale, is a nice touch.) Conwell said he quickly divined the ancient Persian tale was roundabout advice directed at *him*: a certain young American would do better back home than gallivanting around old Bagdad.

The tale concerns an enormously wealthy and happy land owner, one Ali Hafed, who lived near the Indus River. A Buddhist priest told Ali about the origin of the world and its minerals and gems. This discontented Ali. Greedy for even more, Ali sold his gardens and orchards and began an odyssey throughout the Middle East and Europe in search of diamonds, "congealed drops of sunlight." It didn't end well. Ali's quixotic search exhausted his money and health. In despair, he threw himself into a great tidal wave between the pillars of Hercules. Meanwhile, the new owner of Ali's land, watering a camel in a sandy brook, found a black stone that glistened rainbow hues—and then many more stones. He had discovered the world's most magnificent diamond mine, Golconda. "The Kohinoor, and the Orloff of the crown jewels of England and Russia, the largest on earth, came from that mine."[15] Conwell said the story made no sense—because its hero dies in the first chapter—until the concluding moral. The guide's denouement, said Conwell, gave him the bones of a lecture that carried "1,674 young men" through college (Temple University):

Had Ali Hafed remained at home and dug in his own cellar, or underneath his own wheat fields, or in his own garden, instead of wretchedness, starvation, and death by suicide in a strange land, he would have had "acres of diamonds." For every acre of that old farm, yes, every shovelful, afterward revealed gems which since have decorated the crowns of monarchs.[16]

Years later, Conwell would tell Philadelphia audiences that he, too, had made the same mistake about their city as they were now making. Right here in Philadelphia, within their reach, were " 'acres of diamonds,' opportunities to get largely wealthy."[17] Conwell said many of the "pious brethren" will think it "awful" to find a Christian minister running up and down the country "advising young people to get rich, to get money." Conwell delivers the clincher in a rhetorical question: why is he preaching about making money instead of the Gospel? He *is* preaching the Gospel— making money honestly *is* preaching the Gospel.[18] In making his next cardinal points, Conwell expresses prevalent nineteenth-century attitudes: some have been told all their lives that people with money are dishonest, dishonorable, mean, and contemptible; if you think that, "my friend," says Conwell, that "is the reason why you have none." The rich are entrusted with the nation's wealth, with the management of its great enterprises, precisely because they are honest.[19] Conversely, it's best to be niggardly toward the poor; the number that deserve sympathy is small. Poverty is evidence of God's punishment. It would thus be "wrong" to interfere with God's judgment by conferring sympathy on "a man who God has punished for his sins." It would be wrong to offer help "when God would still continue a just punishment." And, "there is not a poor person in the United States who was not made poor by his own shortcomings."[20]

Conwell castigated the notion that only the "awfully poor and awfully dirty" are pious, and what he called the universal prejudice of his age, that "godly men" should not attain wealth. However,

He who tries to attain unto it too quickly, or dishonestly, will fall into many snares, no doubt about that. The love of money. What is that? It is making an idol of money, and idolatry pure and simple everywhere is condemned by the Holy Scriptures and by man's common sense. The man that worships the dollar instead of thinking of the purposes for which it ought to be used, the man who idolizes simply money, the miser that hordes his money in the cellar, or hides it in his stocking, or refuses to invest it where it will do the world good, that man who hugs the dollar until the eagle squeals has in him the root of all evil.[21]

RAGS TO RICHES

Finally, Conwell promulgated the idea of working from the bottom up. He cites "the good sense of the elder Vanderbilt," by whom he means one of Commodore Cornelius Vanderbilt's (1794–1877) sons. The son asked his father if he had in fact earned all of his money. Yes, said the father, he built his fortune by beginning to work on a ferryboat for 25 cents a day. (In rising as a ferryman, Vanderbilt earned the honorarium "Commodore.") Following this example, the son shunned his father's money—(as if the "real" Commodore, who withheld money from at least one pleading son, would have given him any!)—and tried to get work on a ferryboat. The boy couldn't get work on a ferryboat, but did find a job for $3 a week. "Of course," said Conwell, "if a rich man's son will do that, he will get the discipline of a poor boy that is worth more than a university education to any man."[22]

Here Conwell is reflecting the core American beliefs that figure in all rags-to-riches legends and myths. Virtue leads to wealth. The worth of book-smarts was suspect; college men were soft—at least those from the fancy "finishing schools." (As late as 1985, for example, in the movie *Wall Street*, Gordon Gekko says he would never hire a Harvard MBA—they ain't "dog shit." Gekko's ideal hire is poor, smart, and ruthless.) There is no straighter path than honest manual toil. For many of these reasons, at least up until World War II, office work was considered effeminate.

However, in the 1920s, in creating new myths that valorized businessmen, the advertising legend Bruce Barton put forth at least one type of office work—sales—as heroic.

BRUCE BARTON

Ad man Bruce Barton (1887–1967) was raised to be high minded and self-reliant, as if his father William had followed Conwell's admonishment about building character by starting at the bottom—just as William himself had done. William started as a circuit-riding preacher in Tennessee in 1886 and eventually worked his way up to a ministry in Oak Park, Illinois. His father insisted he attend Berea College in Kentucky, where Bruce set type, proofread, and handled a press in the printing office for eight cents a day. Next, Bruce worked his way through Amherst College, selling pots and pans. He also worked 10-hour days in a Montana construction camp for $65 a month before leaving for Chicago, where he distinguished himself as a salesman, copywriter, editor, and essayist. In 1918, Barton and two other admen created Barton, Durstine, and Osborn, which became BBD&O with the addition of the George Batton Company in 1928. BBD&O's clients would include General Electric, General Motors, and U.S. Steel.[23]

JESUS THE (STRONG) BUSINESSMAN

Barton's melding of religion and business in inspirational tracts—particularly those he wrote for the *Woman's Home Companion* during the 1920s—raised Conwell's gospel of wealth to a different magnitude by highlighting the primacy of leadership. Barton understood the power of imagery. As he put it: "I am and have been concerned with the ways in which words, design and color may carry conviction to people, with the art-science of bringing others to your point of view."[24] He used these skills to re-create Jesus's image. From his boyhood onward, Barton had been put off by Jesus because every picture he'd seen portrayed the Man from Galilee as a down-in-the-mouth 90-pound weakling, a sissy: "a pale young man with no muscle and a sad expression." And then there was the "Lamb of God" appellation, which Barton associated with "Mary's little lamb." Barton decided to overhaul Jesus's public image.

Barton's myth-making further elevated leadership in American culture: it was business—not political—leaders, who exuded physical strength and a lust for life. "Only strong men inspire greatly and build greatly," said Barton. Because Jesus inspired millions and changed the world, and perhaps because he was a preacher's son, Barton recast Jesus as *the* exemplar of business leadership. His opening salvo: Jesus was a

physical weakling! Where did they get that idea? Jesus pushed a plane and swung an adz; He was a good carpenter. He slept outdoors and spent His days walking around His favorite lake. His muscles were so strong that when He drove the moneychangers out, nobody dared to oppose Him![25]

Barton was writing during the Jazz Age. Merriment was in, dourness out. Thus Barton's second salvo: Jesus was a

kill-joy! He was the most popular dinner guest in Jerusalem! The criticism which proper people made was that He spent too much time with publicans and sinners (very good fellows, on the whole, the man thought) and enjoyed society too much. They called Him a "wine bibber and a gluttonous man."[26]

Here is Barton's last salvo: Jesus was a "failure! He picked up twelve humble men and created an organization that won the world."[27] Food, clothing, housing, transportation—these essential needs and services— are business sectors. Thus, says Barton, "*all* business is his Father's business. All work is worship; all useful service prayer."[28] Following Barton's Jesus-was-the-first-CEO logic, offices *are* churches and skyscrapers cathedrals.

Such reasoning may be cast as ludicrous or poetic. But Barton's sincerity is indisputable. In his early days as head of BBDO, legend said Barton paid himself a salary of $5,000—annually. In later years, Barton said, "it would be a scandal if people knew how little I make as chairman of BBD&O. I think it's almost a disgrace for a man to die rich."[29]

Compare Barton to Lloyd Blankfein, the CEO of Goldman Sachs who paid himself a salary of $68 million in 2007—tops on Wall Street—and then owned $500 million in company stock. In 2009, Blankfein told *The Times* of London he was doing "God's work."[30]

Hey Lloyd, that's Bruce's line. If you're going to "borrow" from your betters, get the story straight. Doing "God's work" means feeding, clothing, and *housing* the masses, not slaying their jobs and laying waste to their pensions, investments, and savings for selfish gain. Don't you remember? You and your ilk were the types driven *out* of the temple.[31]

THE SALESMAN AS HERO

As the cultural historian Warren I. Susman pointed out, Barton tried to redefine older (i.e., nineteenth-century) values, namely self-development and human dignity, to fit an increasingly impersonal and complex world characterized by mass technology.[32] For Barton, the salesman became the hero of the new era: "in an age of increasing consumer orientation stressing sales and spending and joy rather than self-denial," Barton "glorified the salesman-businessman."[33]

Sixty years later, the jocular motivational speaker and sales trainer Zig Ziglar more or less echoed Barton: "I believe America is a great nation because we are a nation of salespeople. America was discovered by a salesman."[34] Columbus was a salesman? Yes, but unlike Barton's Jesus, Ziglar's Columbus had failings. Although he made the sale to Queen Isabella, he failed to "service the client" and lost the "account" to Amerigo Vespucci.

Thus we became the United States of America rather than the United States of Columbus.[35]

Ziglar is peeved at how salesmen are portrayed as fast-talking con artists in popular entertainment—or as "losers," as in Arthur Miller's *Death of a Salesman* (1949). Perhaps Ziglar has a point. Presumably, professions are value neutral; it's the *people* inserted into these who are either honorable or dishonorable. However, in the case of sales, popular culture mounts evidence to the contrary, suggesting that the pressures and frustrations endemic to the profession shape the personalities of salesmen. This may be seen in the four examples that follow. The first two are first-person exposés, the third a documentary film, and the last a Hollywood feature. Although the last example is fictive, it was influenced by the documentary that precedes it.

I will begin with William H. Whyte's account of working as a salesman in the 1930s because it counterbalances Bruce Barton's nebulous salesman-as-hero rhetoric—while it was still fresh—with a view from the muddy roads of Kentucky.

SALESMEN IN THE FIELD: THE ENEMY IS THE CUSTOMER

Some of the most compelling passages in *The Organization Man* (1957) are those in which William H. Whyte, Jr. recalls his days on the bottom rung of the corporate ladder. Whyte's reportage portrays Depression-era corporate culture as mean-spirited and duplicitous. Straight out of high school, Whyte became a salesman for the Vicks Chemical Company (known today as the makers of Vicks VapoRub.)

Paying your dues in the field as a salesman for nearly a year was touted as a "new" type of corporate training program. But Whyte would discover the new wrinkle in training was empty hype to lure and retain new hires by leading them to believe they were hired as "potential" managers. Vicks's promise of reward was great, but only to those who proved themselves under fire—as salesmen in rough terrain. Thus, Whyte and his class worked as hirelings without regular job assignments. These would come when management judged the novices had sufficiently introjected Vicks's corporate culture, had learned to do things the Vicks way. This slow-track inculcation could last anywhere from two to five years.

Vicks was big on semantic tricks. Graduating high school seniors weren't applying for a "job" with a chemical company. They were applying for admission into the Vicks School of Applied Merchandising, which the company advertised as a "postgraduate training institution set up by a farsighted management." Nor were applicants "hired." They were "selected" for a year-long study of "modern merchandising" that began in September. (The month must have reinforced the pseudo-collegiate veneer, a clever ruse in an era when a university education was a rare mark of distinction.) But Vicks's most outrageous ploy was its contention that "fairness" required that the new hires should pay "tuition," should *pay* for the privilege of working at Vicks. Although they would be asked to do some work—said to be related to their education—the company contended that its expenses "far outweighed" the worth of such meager "incidental services." Vicks's education program consisted of a smattering of classes in New York and 11 months of field training. Even though Vicks claimed it was losing money on all this "schooling," it magnanimously paid its trainees a $75-a-month salary, plus all travel expenses.[36]

A VIEW FROM THE EXECUTIVE SUITE

Whyte's postgraduate education was brief. He learned about the discovery of VapoRub, watched the goop being mixed, was battered with aptitude tests, and memorized Vicks's list prices and sales techniques, as well as those of its main competitor, Plough, Inc.[37] As their "classroom" education came to a close and just before the recruits were to ship out to the hinterlands for field work, they were given a tour of the corporation's executive suite. They met the company president (one H. S. Richardson) atop the Chrysler Building at the Cloud Club. The symbolism was clear to all as they looked down upon Manhattan's skyscrapers: "Golconda stretched out before us," writes Whyte, referencing the capital of an ancient kingdom in India. In other words, gold and diamonds lay before them for the taking—but only for a select few. "One day, we gathered, some of us would be coming back up again—and not as temporary guests either. Some would not. The race would be to the swiftest."[38] Vicks executives talked virtue, but the prizes would go to the most cunning, the most cutthroat.

Over coffee, President Richardson tossed the rookies a hypothetical problem designed to illustrate the Vicks way, the values showcased in Vicks's sales philosophy. (Richardson laid out precisely the type of conundrum known as the case study, which the Harvard Business School adopted as its pedagogical method early on owing to the absence of textbooks. Such business programs truly did make it up as they went along.)

Here was the case: You are the manufacturer of a product that is packaged in paper cartons. For years now, these cartons have been made by a small firm that is dependent solely upon your orders—its only product is *your* cartons. The relationship is symbiotic. One day, however, a new organism encroaches upon this harmonious environment: a new carton maker angling for your business claims it can undercut your loyal supplier. What do you do?

The trainees peppered Richardson with questions. Could they give the old supplier time to match the new bid? Richardson grew impatient. There was no need for elaboration. There was only one answer. It was black and white. The solution was nakedly simple and could be found in the trainee's temperament: "Either you were a businessman or you were not a businessman. The new man, obviously, should get the contract."

Richardson was big on this piece of advice: trainees must guard "against letting sentimentality obscure fundamentals." Richardson emphasized that "Business was survival of the fittest." Darwin's rules also applied within the corporation. The Vicks people played a strict numbers game. If every single one of the 38 trainees who drank coffee in the Cloud Club that day turned out to be wonderful, it wouldn't matter in the least. "The rules of the game," said Whyte, "dictated that only six or seven of us would be asked to stay with Vick [sic]."[39]

OUT IN THE STICKS

After Whyte completed the "merchandising" course in New York, he was bivouacked in Kentucky's hill country to complete his field work. Like each trainee, he was given "a panel delivery truck, a full supply of signs, a ladder, a stock of samples, and an order pad. After several days under the eye of a senior salesman, we were each assigned a string of counties and left to shift for ourselves."[40]

Rookies were not entrusted to target druggists. Rather, they made sales calls only to groceries and general stores. Whyte described a typical day of his training in merchandising: he awoke around 6 a.m.

in some bleak boarding house or run-down hotel and after a greasy breakfast set off to squeeze in some advertising practice before the first [sales] call. This consisted of bostitching [without permission!] a quota of large fiber signs on barns and clamping smaller metal ones to telephone poles and trees by hog rings. By eight, we would have arrived at a general store. . . . Our assignment was to persuade the dealer to take a year's supply all at once, or, preferably, more than a year's supply, so that he would have no money or shelf space left for other brands.[41]

An integral part of the Vicks sales technique involved inducing the client into a euphoric state. At the onset of the call, Whyte would command the merchant to recline his head. As he obeyed, Whyte would quickly shoot a dropper full of a decongestant called Vatronol down the victim's nostrils. The drug, a type of methamphetamine, produced an adrenaline rush. "His eyes smarting from the sting, the dealer would smile with simple pleasure." Facing no resistance, Whyte could then do what he came to do, plaster the hell out of the establishment with cardboard signs. All along his way to the next merchant, 10 miles down a mud road, Whyte would deface barns with Vicks signs. After a day of eight or nine such calls and no sales, Whyte would return to his lodgings for dinner around 6 p.m., then fill out report forms for several hours.

Each week, a letter would arrive from the home office, which was preoccupied with sales. To underscore the point, the letters would speak of trainees who were no longer in the program. Naturally, the office commiserated over the departed. But the message was clear. The fault lay within; and the same fate could befall *you*. Not meeting your quota? Perhaps you need to rise earlier. Whyte said he began to feel sorry for himself. The company dispatched its head training supervisor, who spent several days with Whyte until he diagnosed the problem. Whyte's state of mind; his attitude, his understanding of people, was all wrong: " 'Fella,' he told me, 'you will never sell anybody anything until you learn one simple thing. The man on the other side of the counter is the *enemy*.' " Finally, it clicked for Whyte. The Vicks training program was actually a "gladiator's school." Strife was the supreme value. "Combat was the ideal—combat with the dealer, combat with the 'chiseling competitors,' and combat with each other . . . our success depended entirely on beating our fellow students . . . " In the ensuing months, a gradual rapaciousness seeped into Whyte's consciousness. He spoke of losing his innocence and of finally being able to manipulate "a person into doing what we wanted him to do."[42]

After six months of tacking up tacky signs and squirting methamphetamine into yokels' nasal passages, the trainees were finally allowed to hit drugstores. A wily Vicks veteran gave the youngsters pep talks and taught them his sales tricks. The salesmen observed how the veteran handled proprietors, interactions he dissected in postmortem sessions: "As we gathered around him, like Fagan's brood, he would demonstrate how to watch for the victim's shoulders to relax before throwing the clincher . . . how to feign suppressed worry that maybe the deal was too big for 'the smaller druggist like yourself' . . . how to disarm the nervous druggist by fumbling and dropping a pencil. No mercy, he would tell us; give the devils no mercy." The acid test of the trainees' gall was a challenge the company set down: how many drugstores could they "desecrate" with "flange" signs. These weren't the usual throwaway cardboard signs. They were "hideous" metal that were screwed into "the druggists' cherished oak cabinets."[43]

Following is the technique Whyte learned, a *tour de force* of psychological manipulation. After a sale is made, tension ebbs and the client feels amiable. This is the moment the salesman would strike by asking the druggist for a ladder—an odd request, but granted. The salesman would continue bantering until the druggist turned to a customer. Then the salesman would say, "Just going to get this sign up for you," and bound up the ladder with an electric screw driver and a Vicks sign. As the druggist began to ken what was happening, the salesman would produce a second sign, depicting a blonde irrigating her nostrils, and, with a wink and a leer, proceed to deface the druggist's cabinet.[44]

Whyte's recollections of his foray into sales describe how Vicks promulgated its values or culture. Corporate culture is sustained through symbols (language and titles) and symbolic behavior (rites and rituals). Every corporation develops its own vocabulary to transmit its particular values. Vicks's president used language whose surface meaning only hinted at the violence underneath. "Beware of sentimentality" actually meant show no mercy—a supreme Vicks value, as Whyte would discover in the field. This was also couched in the question, are you a "real businessman," that is, are you cold-blooded? And finally, the customer is the "enemy."

Today, anyone who invests, has a mortgage, or deals with an airline or a credit card company feels the corporate enmity in their bones. This, it appears, is not entirely a function of recent deregulation, but perennial. Perhaps businesses were better at dissembling back then. Today they wield such power they needn't bother feigning courtesy.

Whyte's field training served as a boot camp that squeezed out "sentimentality." Training was a rite of passage during which the inductees proved their hard-heartedness by deliberately breaching their clients' trust. They symbolically vanquished the enemy by desecrating his shop, his sanctum, with garish signage. They planted the Vicks flag in enemy territory. It would be too easy to couch this act of aggression in vulgar terms.

Most telling, however, is how Whyte looked back upon his Vicks inculcation 25 years later. He allowed that in maturity, he should be ashamed of his youthful exploits, but isn't. Upon entering a drug store, Whyte thinks about how he mounted all those ugly signs: "the sound of the awl biting irretrievably into the druggist's lined oak." And when he and his Vicks brethren gather for informal reunions, they reminisce about "what really separated the men from the boys."[45]

Whyte's feelings are like those of a retired cavalry officer. He knows his company's treatment of the Pawnee was rough, even cruel, but nonetheless, those who rode with him share a bond forged under fire.

SELLING LIFE INSURANCE

In 1966, James Gollin, a Yale graduate with a Master's degree in English, became a life insurance salesman. He turned his experiences into an exposé, a book entitled, *Pay Now, Die Later* (1966).

Gollin called life insurance an "insane product." The only way to get 20 million Americans to buy life insurance was through salesmen. But insurance companies face a common problem: call them what you will, super-salesmen, hustlers, con artists—there are only so many people with a gift for persuasion. Thus, insurance companies are forced to hire desperate, mediocre people: "losers" recently fired from some other profession who could be coerced into doing anything. This led the insurance business to spawn the American Agency System, a corporate network that could turn the average man into a salesman. Thus the term insurance *agent*. Established in the nineteenth century, the Agency System faced two big problems: life insurance is too complicated for the average person to understand, explain and sell; and the average man can't endure the physical and emotional tolls of frustration and rejection.[46]

Therefore, the Agency System was designed squeeze the most out of "total failures." These are people unable to earn enough to pay rent and buy food. In big companies, the Agency System is entrenched in the sales department, which is headed by a senior officer, under whom are regional vice presidents, district managers, and branch managers. Branch managers resemble franchise owners. They run the ubiquitous insurance offices that abut Chinese restaurants, drugstores, and dentists' offices. According to census data, they are outnumbered only by gas stations, restaurants, laundries, and other small retailers. In days past, branch managers, who have assistant managers bucking for their own agencies some day, had total independence to run things as they pleased. They lost autonomy in the 1960s when their pay became tied to corporate mandates that sales *must* increase every year. To further this goal, the company and its branch managers have a tacit agreement. As long as they keep exceeding quotas, branches can write their own rules. They should try to avoid outright fraud, but if not, "above all, don't get caught."[47]

HIRING SALESMEN THROUGH DECEIT

Salesmen occupy the bottom rung of the Agency System. They are not true employees of the company but actually independent contractors. But many salesmen don't realize this because they're duped during the hiring process. The rarely spoken truth of the insurance business is that its agencies are designed to function as mills—lubricated by promises, deceit and coercion—through which, Gollin says, average men are turned into salesmen or "discarded."[48]

Newspaper ads in big cities, with their steady streams of applicants, are blatantly deceptive. Gollin illustrates this by reproducing two newspaper ads. The first is typical: "SALES CAREER—Salary $400–$700 + comm. Outstanding opty for highly motivated man who has owned his own business or served in mgmnt capacity either sales or administration." The second ad is one of the most sophisticated Gollin ever came across; it appeared in the Sunday business section of at least one New York newspaper: "WANTED: Extremely intelligent, highly articulate, independent minded executive age 35–45. The man we're looking for must be successful, aggressive, willing to take direction but still and all very much his own kind of guy. We're specialists in developing such men into professionals in the fields of employee compensation, estate analysis, and business planning. I you think you qualify, call or write . . ."[49]

The "qualifications" or trigger words in both ads are sham: *owned his own business, served in management capacity, administration, executive age, must be successful,* and *independent minded.* Neither ad states that the job is selling insurance, a fact that at least half of all ads suppress, says Gollin.

The point of such ads is to whitewash the job and give the impression that the company has high standards. In truth, they will hire anybody with a pulse. The pretense of selectivity is kept up during the job interview. Candidates take a bogus 45-minute sales-aptitude test on which it's almost impossible to give wrong answers. After the test is "graded," the applicant is told that he scored "extraordinarily, amazingly well." One assistant manager, whom Gollin judged "not particularly cynical," said the only thing the company is looking for is "whether the candidate can read." But the candidate thinks he's being screened because the company devotes such care and attention to hiring salesmen. After the interview with the branch manager, they let the candidate linger for several days, telling him they'll get back and let him know if he's passed muster.

The actual hiring or final interview occurs in the manager's office. This is

a velvet-smooth sales presentation conducted by an expert whose sincerity and conviction will be impressive. . . . The shrewd manager won't attempt to hide the fact that the life insurance business has its drawbacks. But, the manager will always add, the problems of selling life insurance only serve to bring out a man's best qualities: perseverance, courage, industriousness, intelligence.[50]

The manager lays it on thick by stressing his judgment of the prospect's "natural ability," how well they will work together, and how much the salesman will grow and improve his life. For managers who lack eloquence and imagination, the company provides canned spiels. The punch line is always something like: " 'just in case you're not a charitable institution'—he smiles—[we can] 'make you, frankly, richer than you ever dreamed you'd be. So how about it? will you give us a chance?' "[51]

WIFESMANSHIP

Gollin says in the "old days," companies lavished more time and care in hiring. The applicant was obligated to take a medical exam. The manager would meet his wife and invite the couple to dinner at an expensive restaurant. This was called "wifesmanship" and was considered an important executive skill, because according to "management folklore," it was the wife who determined if her husband's income was acceptable for the marriage and how quickly he should demand a raise. In *The Man in the Gray Flannel Suit*, it's Tom Rath's wife, Betsy, who compels him to leave his job at a charitable organization, where he's perfectly happy, because he makes only $7,000 annually. Rath takes a job he detests—corporate public relations—only because it pays $9,000. Betsy had said she wanted more and was tired of living in a dump—actually a charming Cape Cod in Connecticut. " 'We want a man who's frankly running a little bit scared,' one manager states. 'If the wife has expensive tastes and wants to live well, she'll push the man better than we can' "[52]

All this subterfuge is necessary because "the insurance industry must compete against businesses that not only pay salaries but offer generous fringe benefits as well." An arcane compensation system called a validation agreement is used to bludgeon the salesman by threatening to withhold his salary. The pressure is excruciating, says Gollin, who reckons in nearly every single one of the thousands of life insurance agencies, "salesmen are driven to commit fraud and near-fraud in order to keep on validating their so-called salaries." Harried salesmen typically falsify figures by quoting the customer a lower price than he will be billed. If the customer discovers this, the salesman simply apologizes for his "error."

Big companies view everything in terms of results. Salesmen are just a number. Whether the hiring policy is honest or dishonest, "so many men are recruited, so many hired, so much insurance is sold, and so many men are terminated. Only the sales statistics really matter. The success or failure of the individual salesmen means nothing whatever."[53]

Bruce Barton contended that all business was "his Father's business." Hence, the inherent nobility of business and the glorification of the businessman/salesman. If these things obtain, there can be no calling more noble than selling Bibles, the subject of the Maysles brothers documentary *Salesman.* This film is particularly significant because it captures two motivational speeches that show how embedded the ideas of and Russell Conwell and Bruce Barton have become in office culture.

SALESMAN: THE DOCUMENTARY

Salesman is a classic piece of direct cinema—hand-held camera work that empathizes with its subjects. The film neither condemns nor glorifies. Rather, it simply strives to document an aspect of contemporary life. David Maysles got the idea of returning home to Boston to take a look at the type of people he and his brother Albert grew up with. (David and Charlotte Zwerin edited the film; Albert shot it.) David did this through the eyes of four salesmen as they try to sell Bibles in working-class Catholic neighborhoods in Boston and Dade County, Florida.

Salesman documents a dying piece of Americana, door-to-door selling, whose roots go back to nineteenth-century Yankee peddlers. The Maysles brothers' intent was sociological: they wanted to document Boston Irish Catholic culture; trailing four Irish salesmen on their sales calls enabled them to enter homes and record how people lived and spoke. Business practices and mores, were secondary, even accidental, to the Maysles's purpose, yet they are salient throughout, an intertwining of ethnic and business subcultures. What salesmen do is most profoundly understood against the horizon of American business: peering into the lives of Bible salesmen is a way of unveiling business culture's values and mores.

Sales, of one type or another, give form and content to office life. Office work is auxiliary to sales. Salesmen are part of office culture, but they exist outside of it in a type of limbo. Salesmen may have desks and telephones in offices, but they are seldom seen there; their money is made in homes or other offices. Or salesmen may work in temporary "offices," telephone booths and motel rooms. Neither do they work set hours; their day may began at dawn and extend well into dark. Salesmen may work as much or as little as they please. If a salesman makes three sales before noon, he may opt to spend the rest of the day golfing.

A LOSER IN A DYING PROFESSION

The featured character in *Salesman* is Paul "the Badger" Brennan. Paul is the smart kid that never did what he was supposed to. Unlike his brother, who graduated from college with honors, Paul blew off school.

And now, middle-aged and married, he's stuck in a graveyard job peddling a product people don't want and can't afford. Paul is wont put on the brogue and wistfully imitate his father, who came straight from Ireland, became a policeman, and urged his son to do the same: Paulie, if you're smart, you'll join the force and get your pension. Fishtailing on snowy side streets in blue-collar Boston, Paul sings, "I wish I was a rich man" from *Fiddler on the Roof*. He later varies the lyric: "I wish I was a rich man, then I wouldn't have to go to shit land."

Paul is the only salesman who fails to make a sale. His colleagues blame his poor attitude. Among Paul's gripes are that the Italians (actually Hispanics in Florida) and the Irish (in Boston) are "dead," they lack religious enthusiasm. Half the time, says Paul, he can't even get past the front door. And when he does, it doesn't matter how hard he tries, he leaves empty handed, such as the call he spent two hours "breaking his ass" on. Paul says he doesn't want to sound negative, but he sees nothing but delinquent accounts in the Boston parish they're working. And in Florida, Paul gets lost driving around Opa Locka, essentially an incorporated housing development outside of Miami. More bad luck, he moans, he got stuck with a Muslim district, evidenced by Opa Locka's Moorish revival architecture and street names such as Sharazzad, Sinbad, Bagdad, Ali Baba, Ahmad, and Harem. "It's not the bum territory," someone reminds Paul good-naturedly, "it's the bum in the territory."

Depressed because he can't break out of his slump, Paul laments to one of his confreres, Charles "the Gipper" McDevitt, that theirs is a dying profession. You said this business was on the "fringes" eight years ago, Charles reminds him. And it's still on the fringes, says Paul. Remember in the old days when they had surreys? he says. (Surreys were four-wheeled, two-seated horse-drawn carriages covered with fringed canopies. Surreys were immortalized by Richard Rodgers and Oscar Hammerstein's hit from *Oklahoma!* [1943], "The Surrey with the Fringe on Top," which became a jazz standard, most famously interpreted by Miles Davis.) "Well, this business is the surrey," says Paul, "and the tassels aren't even left. They're nothing but shredded."

SELLING THE HOLY BIBLE IN UNHOLY WAYS

The main product the salesmen push is an illustrated Bible, which sells for $49.95—or more depending on the binding. They also sell *The Catholic Encyclopedia*—using brochures; the tome's too massive to lug into homes—and missals. At a big sales meeting in Chicago, the designer of these books, Dr. Melbourne I. Feltman, tries to fire up the Mid-American Bible Company's sales force, which numbers about 100.

They must stop thinking of themselves as Bible peddlers, Feltman tells the gathering. Their self-esteem will rise when they realize theirs is a privileged position. Some salesmen may have once held higher-paying jobs, but none have ever held a position of higher esteem "in the minds of the world," or a position that held greater self-satisfaction. [Cut to a shot that finds Paul in the audience looking glum.] For what they do is their "Father's" business. They are different from the many people who know and can quote from the Bible. For they know the "business," not in the crass sense of selling of Bibles for dollars and cents; rather, they know "the good that comes from the selling of Bibles, and the getting of Bibles, and the reading of Bibles." And in the year ahead and in the years to come, says Feltman, "God grant you an abundant harvest."

The salesmen get their leads—names and addresses on three-by-five cards—from the parish priest. Religion is the only thing that qualifies a prospect. When they knock on doors, the salesmen introduce themselves as "from the church." Paul even tells one couple he got their name and the "approval" of the monsignor to call on them. The bare sales pitch is, the Bible runs as little as $49.95, we offer three payment plans—cash, C.O.D., and "the Catholic honor plan"—which would work best for you?

In a motel room, the salesmen's boss, Kennie Turner, goes over the basic sales pitch and how to overcome objections. The stock opening is that they work "under the full authority of the church" and their products carry "the recommendation of his holiness, Pope Paul." Before buying "anything Catholic," the customer is told, it's prudent to check if the product bears the Church's imprimatur, as do all of the Bible Company's products.

Playing along and testing his boss, a salesman raises the primary objection: $40 is a lot for a Bible. "Not when you figure out you're going to have it for a lifetime," says Kennie.

Another objection is thrown at Kennie: the customer's wife is of a different faith and may be offended by Catholic literature in the house.

Kennie answers that he's not a theologian or missionary, just "a Bible salesman." He then asks the customer if he'd be pleased if his wife converted to Catholicism? Well, then such a beautiful Bible might spur her interest. If this tactic doesn't work, they can always pique the customer by asking who wears the pants in his family: what kind of *man* needs his wife's approval to buy something for his own use?

Kennie is quick to go for an assumptive close: he doesn't ask the customer if he *wants* to buy, but whether he prefers the $2.50-a-week or the $10-a-month plan.

The salesman hems and haws.

Kennie turns aggressive: "Do you want it? Then quit making excuses and sign right here."

The salesman says he just trying to figure out something.

"Quit figuring and start writing," Kennie orders.

See, that's how it's done. Nothing to it. Feltman's Bruce Barton-like motivational pitch that selling Bibles is not about dollars and cents but a continuation of Lord's work, a way of serving people by bringing goodness into their lives, is nothing but corporate double-talk. That salesmen are taught to exploit poor people using their presumed obedience to the church or their religious devotion is an indication of the gulf between sincerity and hypocrisy. What Feltman describes, especially the apparent disdain of money, is actually charitable work. But that's not the way the game works. It's all about money and nothing but money. Kennie made this clear during *his* motivational speech, which opened the sales conference at which Feltman spoke, held in a ballroom at the famous Edgewater Beach Hotel. The salesmen were seated in rows. All were male, in dark suits, name tags, white shirts, and thin dark ties, except for the bow-tied Jamie "the Rabbit" Baker. The last row is occupied by a handful of beehived women, perhaps management wives who've made the train trip.

Kennie stresses that money is being made in the Bible business. If salesmen aren't making money, it's "their fault" because the business is "fabulous" and the money is "out there." Kennie is tired of salesmen who "goof off" on Fridays and Saturdays. If they worked instead of playing gin rummy and poker, they would double their earnings, the company would double their volume, and all parties would be better off. If the salesmen were to look around the ballroom, they would see a few missing faces. They've "eliminated" a few men, the sour apples who spoiled the barrel. Kennie wants all to know that the next man that "gets off base" with him will be tagged out.

Kennie's main thread comes from Russell Conwell's ideology of success. His speech exemplifies how these rules of success, long since appropriated by American business, are inculcated or force-fed to lower-ranking employees: if a person fails to prosper, the fault is entirely his. Look around, there are diamonds laying all about waiting for some industrious soul to pick them up. Pinning personal failings on external conditions is buck passing and alibi making.

After Kennie's speech, the salesmen are encouraged to stand up and testify, as in a revival meeting. Their testimonies are meant to affirm the staunchness of their beliefs in the rules of success.

The Gipper stands up and says, "I'm going to triple my production for the year. Believe me." Applause.

A WASPy-looking salesman stands and says he takes Kennie's point that people are making half the money they're capable of. He, for one, intends to make the upcoming year special because his wife talked him "into buying a big house and she wants to have a few more kids and all this kind of rot, so I'm going to make $35,000 this coming year."

"I believe that," Kennie says.

A thin salesman stands up. It's all so fantastic, he's been with the company only three months—"three long months," someone interjects— "damn," he wishes it had been "three or four years. I mean it. I expect to make $50,000—not $35,000—or better! And I think I can do it."

As a point of reference, earning $25,000 a year in the 1960s was considered having it "made." When Robert Townsend became *president* of Avis in 1962, he took a salary of $37,500.

There is nothing subtle about Kennie's threats: sell or else. He pals around with the Badger, the Gipper, the Rabbit, and Raymond "the Bull" Martos, plays poker with them, and visits their motel rooms evenings to ask about the day's sales. But they're never fully at ease in his presence. At breakfast on their first day in Florida, Kennie, who speaks in a soft Southern accent, delivers a little speech to the four salesmen: he's not trying to give anybody a hard time, but they must know there is potential in this market and he doesn't want any excuses. Today, "we want to hit 'em early, wrap this up as soon as possible. Get out there and get 'em."

"I will be successful," says one of the men.

"Well, you're eating like you're successful," says Kennie.

PRESSURED

Salesman shows that the pressure to sell forces even decent, likeable men to use deceptive tactics. Office life is a state of mind. Even though the "offices" these salesmen work in are people's homes, outside supervision's range, their faces still wear the stresses and strains of hierarchical office life, particularly Paul, who is easygoing. All of his bitching and moaning is soft-spoken self-deprecation. He is not given to lashing out in anger. Yet on a sales call, Paul belittles a woman.

Paul began by telling the woman he sells Bibles because he's devout and believes every Catholic family should have one. She should understand because they're both Irish.

"I'm Polish," she says.

Well the Poles are good people too, says Paul.

She doesn't want to buy, but Paul keeps pressing. Sale or not, he still has enjoyed talking to her. This isn't "Irish blarney," he says, it's "straight from the heart."

No dice.

Paul fires one, frustrated parting shot: "Forty-nine-ninety-five!" A carton of cigarettes costs $3 a week—can't she afford a dollar a week? "I don't understand. Honest to God, I've been selling Bibles for ten years."

A quieter desperation shows itself in Paul's closes, which resemble ridiculous pick-up lines. Why not give her husband a surprise, he tells a housewife. "Does he have a birthday coming up? It'd be a lovely gift. The Bible's still the best seller in the world."

One couple says they simply can't afford the steep price.

Well, borrow the money from your neighbors, Paul suggests. But their neighbors are in even worse shape—their house is on the verge of repossession.

On another call, Paul engages in outright fraud to hammer a poor and naïve couple the Gipper (McDevitt) had earlier deceived. When it became obvious they couldn't afford a Bible, the Gipper tricked them into signing a purchase order: "Would you mind writing your name and your address right here?" Had he asked them for the required partial payment, they would have caught on.

So Paul calls on the house pretending to be the district manager and asks for the down payment on their purchase. Taken aback, the woman says she never wanted to buy anything—cancel the order.

Impossible, says Paul. Kind Mr. McDevitt has already mailed out the order.

Well, call me tonight (when her husband will be in), she says.

Impossible. Paul won't be there, he'll have moved on to a new territory. If she won't pay, says Paul, he will be forced to "give Mr. McDevitt a penalty."

This pains the woman. How much will that nice man be forced to pay?

The amount of the down payment, $7.50.

The woman scrounges around and hands Paul all of her pin money.

Thus, the schizophrenic messages the salesmen received in Chicago resolve themselves in the field: No, ma'am, we are not Bible peddlers, we bring goodness into homes, versus get the cash by any means necessary. Not that any salesman confused the outside consultant's surface meaning with his true meaning, which he ended with: "God grant you an abundant harvest." Of what, good deeds? souls?

The Maysles brothers' *Salesman* influenced the movie *Glengarry Glen Ross* (1992), which parallels the documentary in several ways. *Glengarry* tracks four salesmen, each a different type. The movie also features a motivational speech by an outsider, whose message is the same as Kennie's in all but tone and language. American business has always been profit hungry, and its fundamental ideology has remained unchanged since the early days. But *Glengarry*, in one of the most brutal portrayals of office life in popular culture, shreds the pretense of public service and civility covering these ideological raiments.

GLENGARRY GLEN ROSS: THE MOVIE

In adapting his 1984 Pulitzer Prize-winning play for film, David Mamet changed the locale from Chicago to the Sheepshead Bay section of Brooklyn. Mamet's salesmen try to sell swampland in Florida, parcels in developments called Glengarry Highlands and Glen Ross Farms. The incongruity of faux Scottish Highlands with pink flamingos, as depicted in sales brochures, reveals what type of men—Mitch and Murray—own the company and drive their salesmen to commit fraud. Like in a Samuel Beckett or Harold Pinter play, Mitch and Murray are never seen. They represent a distant land called "downtown."

The salesmen work out of a shabby storefront office in a low-rent neighborhood, within earshot of an elevated railway's ceaseless clacking. Their agency is called Premiere Properties. The inside is a cramped and dingy open room with crummy blinds, standard gray file cabinets, a beat-up mail credenza, and a bookcase filled with three-ringed colored binders. Above the old coffee maker is a sales map stuck with pins. The salesmen's desks are almost on top of each other. Their telephone receivers have shoulder harnesses. Only the manager has a private office—with a big observation window. On the walls are a few placards with sales adages: "A Man Only Hits What He Aims For" and "Salesmen Are Born Not Made."

The salesmen constantly duck in and out of the Chinese restaurant next door for drinks and conversation. It serves as another office. The eldest salesman, Shelly "the Machine" Levene (played by Jack Lemmon), is in a terrible slump. He is such a regular at the Chinese place that he tells the coat check woman: "If my daughter calls, if anybody calls, tell 'em I'm over at the office." Compared to other office jobs, salesmen, of course, are free to come and go as they please. But their profession is waning. (It will soon enough be supplanted by telemarketing and robo-calls.) Ricky Roma (played by Al Pacino), is the top seller and merciless—which are not unrelated. Not all salesmen hate their jobs. They love the independence. And for the big earners, outwitting the "enemy" induces a type of euphoria. Ricky senses a change in American culture: "It is not a world of men," he says. "It's a world of clock watchers, bureaucrats, office holders . . . No adventure to it. Dying breed. Yes it is. We're the members of a dying breed. That's . . . that's why we got to stick together."

The big sales meeting conducted by Blake, the man from downtown, starts at 7:30 p.m.

THE MOTIVATIONAL SPEECH

The salesmen aren't happy about being yanked into a "sales conference" at 7:30 p.m. Dave Moss (played by Ed Harris), who is lazy and wont to blame others, bitches the loudest: no one's ever made a "god-damn dime" [sitting in a meeting]. All that happens is "some jerk shoots his mouth off." He's figured out their game. The salesmen are suckers. They get a lowly 10 percent commission, so some jerk in an office can take 90 percent for saying go out and close and win a Cadillac. Angrily, he queries the office manager, John Williamson (played by Kevin Spacey), "A sales conference?"

The strategy comes from downtown, says John, who is soft spoken, mean spirited, and despised by all. Dave says he thinks he'll pass. John advises him to be there.

David Mamet augmented his play by adding a new part to the movie script, Blake (played by Alec Baldwin), the motivator from New York City who deigns to address these losers as a "special favor" to Mitch and Murray. Baldwin said he found the character so despicable he didn't want to play the role; and that "now," 10 years later, he couldn't do it because he's aged "spiritually."[54] Blake's speech pierces the ideological veil of corporate America; that business raises the standard of living by satisfying consumer demands, and that corporate profits equate to more jobs and a stronger nation. Blake's foul-mouthed diatribe reveals the true spirit lurking behind the veil: increase profits at any cost, and by all means, bleed the customer to death, and any employee that can't or won't do this must be axed. If a business titan dispensed with the bland corporate-speak and fake smile and spoke his heart to his sales force, he would sound like Blake.

Precisely at 7:30 p.m. Blake struts out of the manager's office. His head is down, his steps deliberate. He will speak near a green chalkboard with September's sales tallies. Ricky Roma has blown off the meeting but faces no consequences. He's the sales leader with $90,000, and there are differ-ent rules for stars. Blake paces as he speaks. He wears an expensive dark blue suit. He begins by saying he doesn't want to hear excuses about nobody wanting to buy the land they're selling. Suddenly, in mid-sentence, Blake stops: "Put that coffee down." He pauses after each word, which conveys power. The coffee remark is directed at Shelly, who is standing in the back pouring himself a cup.

Shelly doesn't understand what he's hearing. Is this a joke, he asks.

Blake pounces. "Coffee is for closers only." Shelly is dead last on the monthly quota board. This is no joke. "Your name's Levene? . . . You call yourself a salesman, you son of a bitch?" Blake pronounces "salesman" with reverence. It's an honorific reserved for only the nervy and coura-geous.

Moss rises in protest, "I don't got to listen to this shit."

No, he certainly doesn't, says Blake, because he and all the others are fired—beginning tonight, they have one week to regain their jobs. To give them extra incentive, they've sweetened the monthly sales contest by add-ing more prizes to the Cadillac Eldorado. A set of steak knives for second prize, and "third prize is you're fired." They've been given leads, for which Mitch and Murray paid good money. If they can't close these, they "can't close shit." They "are shit!" So Moss is free to beat it, because he will surely fail.

Shelly: "The leads are weak." This is true.
 Blake: "The f****** leads are weak? You're weak. I've been in this business fif-teen years."

Moss demands Blake's name.

His name, says Blake, is f*** you because he drove an $80,000 BMW to the meeting while Moss drove a Hyundai.

Blake turns back to Shelly, telling him he can't compete in this man's game, he lacks what it takes to close. And anybody who can't close sales should go home "and tell your wife your troubles. Because only one thing counts in this life: get them to sign on the line which is dotted! You hear me, you f****** faggots!"

Blake flips the green quota board over to reveal acronyms: A (attention), I (interest), D (decision), A (action)—AIDA. On the left half of the board is, ABC (Always Be Closing). That stringing such silly, meaningless words together would have any bearing on anything is ludicrous. But such is the world of consulting and training. Blake repeats each slogan, then directs the first acronym at the three salesmen: does he have their Attention? their Interest? Have they made their decisions "for Christ?" Good. Now it's time for action. Get out there and mine these leads, "A guy don't walk on the lot lest he wants to buy. They're sitting out there waiting to give you their money. Are you going to take it? Are you man enough to take it?"

Moss doesn't buy it. He smiles and shakes his head, "Crap." If Blake is so rich, such a hero, why's he here wasting his time on a bunch of bums?

Blake removes his massive gold Rolex and places it on Moss's desk. Does Moss see the watch? It cost more than Moss's car. Blake made $970,000 last year—how much did Moss make?

That is who Blake *is*. His identity is his bank account and his status objects. Because Moss can't match these, he's "nothing." Is Moss a nice guy? a good father? Blake doesn't "give a shit." Moss should go home and play with his kids. But if he wants to work here, he must close sales.

Blake descends on George Aaronow (played by Alan Arkin), the newcomer, a former schoolteacher forced into sales. Extremely inept, George lacks the ruthless aggression necessary to succeed at this game. Blake uses George to explain his bastard-as-motivator strategy. If these men can't take Blake's abuse, how can they take what awaits them in the field? Blake says he could take the leads they've been given, go out and make himself $15,000 in two hours. Right now. Tonight. Can they? Blake pounds a wooden divider. "Get mad you son of a bitches. Get mad!" Do they know what it takes to sell real estate? These, Blake says, turning his back and spinning around dangling a pair of brass balls on a string.

The money is out there, says Blake. It's theirs. All they have to do is pick it up. If they don't close tonight, they'll be shining his shoes and sitting around in a bar, a bunch of "losers" saying they used to be salesmen, what a tough racket. Blake holds up a handful of index cards. The Glengarry leads: pure gold. But they don't get them. They're for closers only.

Blake's fictional speech is an X-rated version of the message the Maysles brothers filmed Kennie Turner delivering at the Edgewater Hotel in 1967. Blake, an aloof corporate creep, and Turner, who is one of the guys, are both transmogrifications of Russell Conwell: wealth is lying all around you, reach down and get it; if you can't see it, you're internally deficient.

This message has colored hierarchal office life for more than a century. If a person fails to climb, the problem is within. The strain, guilt, and deception this produces is easier to see in salesmen, the outliers of office life, whose pay and fate are precariously balanced on accelerated production demands. If they don't sell today, tomorrow they're gone.

The old pro Shelly Levine embodies everything the public finds repugnant about salesmen. *Glengarry* may be viewed as pop culture reinforcing biased attitudes or pop culture telling the truth. Or both.

SLEAZY TACTICS

Levine is a practiced liar. And he's desperate. In telephone cold-calling, a salesman has about 20 or 30 seconds to make an interest-creating remark that will lead to a face-to-face sales pitch. The following call Levine places to a Dr. Lowstein contains at least eight lies. The only truth Levine utters is his name. He gets the doctor's wife. It's important he speak with the doctor himself. A "situation" has just come up on the Rio Ranch estates. The president of Levine's company is in town for one day only. He has given Levine a special "hold" on certain "choice parcels" for only the next 48 hours. When the woman brushes him off, Levine turns aggressive: "Listen, I've got 48 hours to make you a lot of money. What do you mean the doctor's not there. It's fairly urgent. No, I can't be reached. I'll get back to him."

Levine is also capable of outright fraud. He calls a woman claiming to be with Consolidated Properties of Arizona and tells her she's been chosen for a real estate prize by the company's computer. Even though she's not engaged in Consolidated's "land development plan," federal law stipulates she *must* be awarded the prize, but both she and her husband must sign for its receipt. He just may be in her area tonight, possibly tomorrow. Yes, of course he'll hold.

George the new hire is a virgin liar. After all, he was a schoolteacher. He has no choice. He must lie. Truth doesn't work in peddling worthless land. So he imitates the veterans. Claiming to be the vice president of Rio Rancho Properties in Furman, Arizona, George telephones a man, telling him he's calling from the airport with "rather unusual and rather good information" on a property. Consulting his map, he sees the man and his wife live nearby . . .

Like a tiger cub learning to hunt, George paws harmlessly at a baby buffalo, which soon flees. He will soon learn to survive—or perish. This is how "organizational culture" is spread and how some offices become toxic.

GLENGARRY AS A TRAINING VIDEO

When *Glengarry* the movie was released, it flopped. Small wonder. A *tour de force* for aficionados of the actor's art, but not much mass appeal. I'd seen Mamet's play when it opened on Broadway—some memorable lines and acting, but its effect was mild compared with the movie. Setting aside the movie's many merits, such as the riveting cinematography, which saturated the characters in blue light, and the casting—the interplay among truly superb actors in *every* role—the main difference between the two versions was the addition of Blake: the motivational speech, which reveals the seamy underbelly of the business world. Money trumps all. Family, sacred ground in most cultures, isn't even a close second. In fact, it's unmanly to spend too much time with the wife and kids. Doing so excludes a person from the big leagues.

Since *Glengarry* moved from the big screen—it ran about one week in most cities—to DVD, it seems to have found a new audience. James Foley, the director, mentioned that his sister belongs to the world of corporate retreats, in cities such as Honolulu and Las Vegas. She reports that *Glengarry* is in big demand at retreats—as a training tool. The movie, said Foley, is used "to invigorate the sales force." As Foley put it, sales companies are telling their employees, "We know what we're asking you to do is perverse . . . but isn't it great."[55]

Yes, it is great that corporations are finally unveiling their profound cynicism and admitting their contempt for the cover story they've been peddling to their employees and the public all these years.

Chapter 6

The Office in Drama and Comedy during the 1950s and 1960s

EXECUTIVE SUITE

In spite of its airiness, the American Dream is an idea understood the world over as "making it." One of the ultimate symbols of making it, and the goal of every corporate climber, is attaining a perch in the "executive suite." As a free-floating signifier, the executive suite points to a nebulous place and vacuous promises of happiness, just like the American Dream itself, somewhere beyond the reach of everyday cares. One of the classic formulations of this notion opens the movie *Executive Suite* (1954).[1] Based on Cameron Hawley's novel, the picture features many of the era's greatest actors: William Holden, June Allyson, Barbara Stanwyck, Fredric March, Walter Pidgeon, Shelley Winters, Paul Douglas, Louis Calhern, Dean Jagger, Nina Foch (nominated for Best Supporting Actress), and Tim Considine. The director, Robert Wise, opens the movie with an upward pan of skyscrapers as the narrator intones: "It is always up there close to the clouds on the topmost floors of the sky-reaching towers of big business. And because it is high in the sky, you may think that those who work there are somehow above and beyond the tensions and temptations of the lower floors." And then comes the hook: "This is to say that it isn't so."

Executive Suite shows upper management as troubled and unhappy as everybody else, if not more so. Reaching the upper echelons does not afford automatic bliss. But this is old news. Much of *Executive Suite*'s enduring value lies in how it documents the tensions and attitudes that would come to shape American business in the coming decades. It was one of the few serious movies about business until Oliver Stone made *Wall Street* 30 years later. One example of the film's prescience is how it anticipates the rationale for "outsourcing," a euphemism tied to a yet murkier euphemism, "globalization." In the place of booming factories in Ohio, Michigan, and Pennsylvania, their machinery having been dismantled and shipped to Latin America, are rubble-strewn deserted lots. Why?

You won't find a more concise and truthful explanation than that voiced in disgust by Don Walling (played by William Holden), the engineer hero of *Executive Suite*: "Improve the profits, but never the product. That's Shaw's [the power-hungry controller] philosophy. To him the whole company is just a curve on a chart." This is the logic of outsourcing laid bare long before that strategy wrecked the American Dream for millions. Strip away all the past and present propaganda about transforming the United States into a "service economy"—right . . . "Do you want fries with that?"—and you have the corporate mindset whose logical conclusion is globalization: cheapen the product—incessantly!—and increase profits. That is the credo of modern business taught at the best universities: cut costs at all costs. Nothing else matters, neither the nation nor its citizens. For example, in 2011, Intel Corporation, that Silicon Valley darling of new American enterprise—the nonhierarchical "anti-Eastern establishment" corporation—deemed its Chinese operation too expensive, so it began relocating to Vietnam. One can foresee a day when Vietnam becomes too expensive and the company moves its manufacturing to Uganda. Perhaps 50 years hence, the cheapest labor on earth will be found in a ruined, abject land once called the United States of America.

Executive Suite's exposition of the public-be-damned ethos of American business is seminal in mass entertainment. Whether this malignancy is a uniquely American postwar growth or a universal aberration inherent in the nature of corporations that ripen—or more properly, rot— under the right conditions is an open question. The movie's plot is universal. The emperor dies. Who among his top lieutenants will succeed him? The emperor is Avery Bullard. His empire is Tredway Corporation, the country's number-three manufacturer of fine furniture. As the movie progresses, key characters articulate the competing ideologies of modern business in a running debate that culminates in a boardroom showdown that resembles a courtroom drama. Also worth recounting are the ambient details that contextualize American business and culture at the mid-century mark.

In those days, the speed of "light" was the telegraph. It's striking to recall how much was done by hand in a world of copper wires, trains, buzzers and intercoms; two telephones on one desk signaled a big shot. President Bullard himself, rather than a subordinate, pencils in the Western Union form to telegraph his secretary that he will arrive on the 5:49 p.m. train from New York that day, a Friday; she is to call an executive committee meeting for 6:00 p.m.

By word of mouth, Bullard's directive travels throughout Tredway's headquarters in Millburgh, Pennsylvania. Those summoned stop in their tracks. They call home. Plans are hastily rearranged. The head of sales cancels his flight to Chicago. But within minutes of sending the telegram, Bullard keels over on a busy Wall Street sidewalk while trying to hail a cab: a heart attack at age 57. Perhaps it's not so sweet in the executive suite. Bullard's body lies directly beneath the upper-floor offices of his investment banker, with whom he has just concluded a meeting. George Caswell (played by Louis Calhern), a member of Tredway's board of directors, was in the banker's office. He hears a siren, looks down, and sees Bullard's lifeless body lifted into an ambulance.

Instantly, Caswell gets his broker on the phone and orders him to start selling Tredway short in the broker's name, not his—as many shares as he can before the Stock Exchange's closing bell. Gleefully, Caswell turns to the investment banker, one Julius Steigel, and crows: when Wall Street learns of Bullard's death in the morning, Tredway's stock will plummet and he'll be able to buy it back for 10 points less than he sold it. It's just the type of gamble he likes: a sure thing.

The elderly German-accented Steigel shakes his head. There are some ways to make money that don't seem right, he says. He is the voice of the older generation's ethical wing.

But old or new, ethical or not, they all play or played the same Wall Street game. The objective is to control a company by buying or selling its stock. How quaint from a modern vantage to see that Tredway's value is rooted in tangibles such as its plant and machinery. Back then, they actually manufactured things and spent money on research and development. Developing new manufacturing processes is design engineer Don Walling's passion. He faces generational resistance. The aging plant manager remarks that when he was starting out, he didn't need the college-educated "boy wonders and slide-rule experts" to show him how to do things.

The news of Bullard's death triggers the angling for succession. There are seven board members; four votes elects a new president. Loren Shaw, the controller (played by Fredric March) wants to be president in the worst way. The treasurer, Fred Alderson (played by Walter Pidgeon), wants to put Don Walling up for president. But Don doesn't want it. He tells his wife Mary (June Allyson), "I'm not going to die young at the top of the tower worrying about bond issues and stockholder's meetings. . . . I'm a designer, not a politician." Don and Mary had spoken often about office politics. She once told him he was "dying a slow death" at Tredway. They disagree about personalities. Don thinks Shaw is a bad guy who is always trying to cut funding for his design experiments, while Bullard was the good guy who supported his projects. Mary disagrees: maybe at one time, but Bullard changed, and Shaw, not Don, was the guy he listened to.

Naturally, the board members form factions. Fred Alderson, the treasurer, confers with Don about voting in Walt Dudley (played by Paul Douglas), a big lug who is vice president of sales. No, says Don, "He's just dead weight, something we'd have to ease out of place every time we wanted to get anything done."

Since talking to his wife, Don has had a change of heart. He proposes himself. Fred now says no.

Don turns bitter: "I'm not ready yet. Is that it? Five more years to be properly seasoned while the company goes down the drain. . . . I've never had my picture in *Fortune*. I get my hands dirty [on the shop floor] once in a while. I don't know the rules. I'm not old and tired, or weak and afraid."

Fred reminds Don that he had asked him to be president the night before. Don's outburst causes Fred to doubt his initial assessment of Don. Executives don't blow up, which shows disrespect. Bullard was always respectful. Maybe Fred didn't realize how hot headed this young hot shot really is. Plus, Don doesn't defer to his elders, which grates. But even without Fred's allegiance, the presidency is still attainable.

However, Don's wife cools to his change of mind. As Don as hurriedly knots his tie, readying himself for the meeting to elect a new president, Mary unloads: she's stood by for five years watching him succumb to harassment, frustration, and rejection. "Look at your face in the mirror, look at your hands," she says. What's he doing this for? She wants back the man she married. She can't let him do this to himself.

Mary touches a universal truth. Battling for—and holding—power is damaging and all consuming. But Don defends his motives as altruistic. He can't "stand by and let the company fall into the hands of a weakling like Dudley or an adding machine like Shaw." Tredway affects too many lives. The entire town depends on its viability.

Don leaves for the boardroom showdown. He is the sheriff, the defender of ethical business practices. If business abjures its tacit pledge to work for the nation's well-being, there can be no American Dream.

The fight is wider than internal politics: "The whole town is at stake." Millburgh's vibrancy depends on Tredway's jobs, on full employment. This is shown in a scene of a Little League baseball game. The bleachers are packed. The whole, happy town is there, enjoying the leisure that attends prosperity, an idyllic picture of sunny suburban life.

The gunslinger is Loren Shaw, the controller, the people-be-damned numbers guy. The only thing that matters to Shaw is the highest possible return on investment. This is a fight for the soul of Tredway, a stand-in for American business. Shaw begins by arguing that corporations must be run in a way that yields the highest and safest return to investors. The interests of shareholders can be the only "sound basis for corporation management today." Corporations must be managed as though they were financial institutions, which is why today they draw more of their leaders from the controller ranks. The problems "that come to the president's office today are predominantly financial."

"I get it," says Fred. "Manufacturing and selling don't count anymore."

They count, says Shaw, but only as means to an end, not ends in themselves. Take Tredway's case. They've been experimenting with manufacturing techniques and have done a "wonderful job" of reducing costs on their finishing operation. However, in truth, these things, even when successful, add little to net earnings—less than a quarter of what Tredway gained from the new tax accounting procedure Shaw got the government to approve.

Fred interrupts, "Yeah, we see, all right. While Jesse and Don are turning out products, you figure jugglers and chart men are busy flyspecking it with decimal points. Well, some of us have had enough of it."

Shaw fights back. He knows what they think of him. "Efficiency has become a dirty word. Budget control has a bad odor." But his job "is to plug every profit leak," every single source of waste and inefficiency. And if Shaw has to "step on toes and hurt feelings," so be it. But he has the company's best interests at heart and no one can say otherwise. He challenges his fellow board members to take a look at *his* record of the last three years.

So much for teamwork and the contributions of others. It's all about Shaw's one-man show.

"*Your* record?" says Don.

Shaw: "Couldn't have been done without me." He allows that Avery Bullard was the right choice for president when Tredway was floundering. Bullard put the ship right and charted the course to prosperity. But now, Tredway needs to move in a different direction, which requires a different type of management, "one that will dedicate itself to paying the maximum dividends to the stockholders."

Then Don asks *the* question. Why would anyone *want* to be president? Indeed, philosophers the world over have concluded that only mad or bad men covet power. What incentive, asks Don, would a person have knowing he'd have to devote heart and soul to the company? Trapped in an office day and night with mounting pressures—what kind of life is that?

Well, outside of salary, says Shaw, "There's such a thing as success, isn't there. The sense of accomplishment."

Exactly, says Don. Continuing his cross examination, he asks Shaw if he were the man at the top, would he be content to measure his life's work by how much he raised the dividend? Would he consider his life a success because he "managed to get the dividend to three dollars, four, five, or six or seven? Would that be enough? Is that what you want engraved on your tombstone when you die? The dividend record of the Tredway Corporation?"

Shaw: "Are you suggesting earnings aren't important?"

They are, says Don. But an even bigger obligation to shareholders is to keep the company alive for a long time, not just a year or two. Sometimes it's necessary to pump profits back into the company for growth instead of paying "them all out in dividends to impress the stockholders with your management record. There's your waste, there's your inefficiency. Stop growing and you die. Turn your back on experimentation and planning for tomorrow because they don't contribute to dividends today and you wouldn't have a tomorrow because there won't be any company."

Bullard was wrong, says Don, in the same way a lot of people are wrong today: he lacked faith in the future, so he only went for the quick and easy sure thing. Bullard became so consumed with building a great manufacturing company that he lost sight of why he was doing it. Bullard began with faith, which oriented him, but lost it and began groping for something he couldn't find.

Bullard was driven by pride, says Don, and that was his failing as a human being and as a corporate head. Bullard may have done what no other man on earth could do, but only to glorify himself. Hence, he neither needed nor wanted anyone else. Bullard was the man all alone at the top of the tower.

But what's wrong with a man having pride if he's earned it? asks big, dumb Jesse.

Nothing, says Don, "But why should that set him apart from the people he's working with? . . . You can't make men work for money alone, you starve their souls when you try it. And you can starve a company to death the same way."

Don's argument carries the day. But corporate America will eventually side with Shaw, jettisoning jobs, suppressing wages, and turning proud communities into ghost towns for the enrichment of a few. Even as early as 1954, Hawley hints at things to come: Shaw manages to increase profits not through sales but by the stroke of a pen. He petitions the government to change an accounting rule for figuring taxes, a whisper of the fusillade of deregulation to come.

DESK SET

Automation would soon enough be used to starve souls *and* companies. A foreboding of this runs throughout *Desk Set* (1957),[2] a romantic comedy set in the Manhattan headquarters of a fictional television network modeled after CBS. Walter Lang directed the picture, which starred Kate Hepburn as Bunny Watson, a reference librarian at the Federal Broadcasting Network, and Spencer Tracy as Richard Sumner, an efficiency expert who installs a giant computer that will render fact gathering by humans obsolete. Of historical note, to set the action in a skyscraper, Lang begins *Desk Set* with an upward pan of the old RCA Building (now the GE Building), which suggests the grandeur and power of the American corporation.

Because *Desk Set* encapsulates the beliefs and values of its era in a highly entertaining and vivid manner, it serves as a compelling baseline of American culture at the mid-century mark. *Desk Set* is significant historically because it probes the ideological core of American culture from the vantage of two of its constituent myths: love and getting ahead— myths that hold out the promise—or the lie—of happiness. In addition, *Desk Set* is a wry comment on corporate culture and automation.

The story takes place during the Christmas season, which renders the firing of employees due to automation all the more poignant. *Desk Set* shows a general bifurcation in office work that goes back to the turn of the century: women worked at semiskilled positions until they married; men climbed the ladder of success. Bunny and her three research assistants are single. They receive a Christmas card from a former colleague who is pictured with her new husband and baby. It's either work or, preferably, marriage, but not both. All the women at Federal Broadcasting consider Mike Cutler—played by Gig Young—the prize catch. Mike is nominally in charge of the research department. However, as a librarian remarks, "[Bunny] runs it, but he's her boss."

Bunny and Mike are an item. Bunny hopes for marriage, but Mike has kept her waiting for seven years. Mike contends everything is fine just the way it is, so why go changing things? Mike is a "climber." He has no qualms about taking credit for the reports Bunny cheerfully and brilliantly writes for him, much like the smart girl longing for affection who does the star quarterback's homework. Mike's sense of reality is entirely self-centered and rooted in the belief that women are frivolous creatures incapable of the serious work that men do. So deeply set is this frame of reference that Mike is blind to all evidence to the contrary.

OFFICE ROMANCE

As always, whenever Mike leaves his office to visit the research department on the twenty-ninth floor, the executive secretaries, like well-placed Indian scouts, heat up the telephone wires alerting the lower-rung employees that the boss is on his way down. Bunny frantically searches for her lipstick. She can't find it. Mike arrives and kisses her, or tries to.

"Mike, for the five hundredth time," Bunny protests, "there's a glass wall behind you." Her office is a glass cube ensconced within a larger space that contains library shelves, file cabinets, and the desks of her research assistants, who can all see what's going on. But Mike doesn't believe decorum is necessary. He is, after all, the boss.

"Everybody knows you haven't got a brain in your head," he says. "The only way you keep your job is by being nice to me."

This line is delivered after the director has spent 20 minutes establishing Bunny's remarkable intelligence: not only is she emotionally and intellectually superior to her boss, but she has also outwitted a Ph.D. from MIT, one Richard Sumner, the inventor of a computer.

Bunny keeps up Mike's pretense: "Well a girl has to work."

Work? Oh yes, work, says Mike, revealing his disdain for work. Then he gets to the real reason for his visit. Would Bunny mind taking a look at the financial report he drew up? "They're screaming for it upstairs," but he doesn't want to turn it in until Bunny's looked at it. "Look at" means fix it and make it sing. Mike isn't sure about the projected spending.

Bunny says she'd be glad to take a look. He throws her a bone: he's missed her, hasn't seen her in years.

"A week ago Monday," Bunny corrects.

Mike says the "boys upstairs" have been pressuring him because the annual board meeting is coming up.

Bunny dismisses this as "their annual war dance."

Mike says he doesn't know why the bigwigs make him so nervous; he shouldn't still be so unsettled after so many years at the company.

At this admission, Bunny turns serious. They actually do that to you, she says. In primitive times, men demonstrated their valor in battle. In civilized times, their blood sport is business. A woman may overlook many defects in a man, but not lack of spine. Bunny, however, seems to immediately dismiss the thought. It's a door she doesn't want to enter. Her familiar face returns. Get out of here, she tells Mike, or she'll never get his report done.

Yes, go over it good and send it up this afternoon—or better yet, bring it up yourself, he says and kisses her. As he leaves, he addresses the three assistants: "Bye, girls. Always a pleasure seeing your freshly scrubbed, smiling faces. Remember our motto: Be on time, do your work, be down in the bar at 5:30."

Mike's exit may be facetious, but it captures a basic truth about office life. Many in executive positions don't do much of anything, and office work holds no inherent interest for them. They're all bluff and perfectly expendable. But when business is bad, it's the poorly paid subordinates—those who actually do the work—who are let go.

CLIMBING THE LADDER

Peg, a wisecracking research assistant played by Joan Blondell, sees how Mike is using Bunny and chides her friend, calling her "Bunny Watson, spare tire." Peg proves prescient. It's Friday at the office. Mike and Bunny have a big date. They're going away for a special weekend. Perhaps Mike will even pop the question. Out of breath, Bunny enters the library. She's in a hurry to run out to her 4 p.m. hair appointment. She spots Mike in her office with a lavish white bouquet. How thoughtful. She hugs him. But the flowers are an apology. He begins a familiar refrain, which Bunny harmonizes:

"When you work for a network, you have to expect this sort of thing."

The sorrow in Mike's voice, however, soon lifts. The network's president, a man called Azae, has chosen him, Mike, over half a dozen other young bucks to fly to Chicago for the annual war dance.

"I think you're moving up, boy," says Bunny.

Mike beams: "Thanks to you. That financial report had a lot to do with this. . . . I got quite a few compliments on it."

"Remind me to louse it up next year," she says, and pins one of his flowers in his lapel. "Here, for a rising young executive."

An idea hits Mike about how they can salvage their date: Bunny can drive out to the airport to see him off and watch all the happy couples boarding *their* flights. How considerate. Bunny declines.

CONSULTANTS AND COMPUTERS

In *Desk Set*, the office is depicted as a displaced or sublimated hunting ground. Women hunt for men. Men hunt for trophies of war called promotions, which Bunny sees and laughs off as a status game played by the domesticated savages who prowl corporate corridors. But this is a secondary theme. Central to the plot is the idea of "scientific management," an attempt to maximize production that involves breaking tasks down into discrete movements. This idea, created and marketed by a man called Frederick Taylor, spawned legions of note-taking hucksters armed with stopwatches and tape measures. Enter Richard Sumner, who pronounces himself a "methods engineer." Sumner buffaloes Azae, the network's president, with gibberish. "Visual read-offs are all centralized, miniaturized, and set on schematic panels now," he says.

Azae says he doesn't understand a single word of it, but if Sumner says so, that's good enough for him. Here the fictional Azae mirrors thousands of real-life business leaders who have been and continue to be taken in by consultants spouting pseudoscientific jargon. The next new thing has arrived, be it a slogan or a machine, and they're buying. When Bunny first encounters Sumner, she sizes him up as an "efficiency expert" and asks what his like would be doing "in our little iron lung."

Sumner replies: "Well, you'd be surprised how a little scientific application can improve the work/man-hour relationship . . . time is money."

Yes, Bunny has heard that.

Desk Set is set in the infancy of the computer age. Bunny has seen a demonstration of the new "electronic brain" at IMB's offices.[3] She and her colleagues are alarmed. They know that Federal Broadcasting's entire payroll department was pink-slipped, replaced by one of Sumner's machines. Sumner has now turned his attention to the research department, where he has installed an enormous mainframe computer—the EMERAC, an allusion to UNIVAC and ENIAC, two of the first computers. Sumner lovingly calls his electronic brain Miss Emmy. The women in research nervously gather in front of the room-sized computer that they fear will superannuate their jobs. The company brass, naturally, are also present for Sumner's demonstration and sales pitch.

"The purpose of the machine is to free the worker," he exclaims.

"You can say that again," Bunny mutters under her breath. Her intonation turns "free" into a *double entendre*, as in free the worker from her wages.

Sumner continues. Yes, free the worker "from the routine and repetitive tasks and liberate his time for more important work."

But Sumner is sincere. The network isn't going to fire any one in research. There's been a terrible misunderstanding. In fact, owing to an upcoming merger, they're actually going to add personnel. However, the women in research aren't happy. They take pride in their work, and their self-worth is at stake. For Sumner to submit his machine is superior to the human brain—to their brains—is galling.

But all ends well. In a scene that recalls John Henry's contest against the steam drill, the computer fails to best the humans. Instead of information about the island of Corfu, it spits out bits of the poem, "Curfew Must Not Ring Tonight" (by Rose Hartwick Thorpe, one of the nineteenth century's most popular poems).

Then comes the romantic climax: Mike, it seems, will finally propose. He turns up at Bunny's office with gorgeous red flowers. Mike has been promoted to head the network's West Coast operations. We know the scenario all too well. Bunny will quit her job, move out to L.A., live a rich material existence, and never have to work again. But, Sumner interrupts their *tete-a-tete*. He punch-cards Miss Emmy two questions: should Bunny Watson marry Mike Cutler? "No," reads the printout; and, should Bunny Watson marry Richard Sumner?

Bunny beats the machine to the punch with an empathic "No." Sumner is stunned. Bunny explains. She'd always be second fiddle to his first love, Miss Emmy. Not true, Sumner protests. He doesn't care a thing about the electronic brain, only Bunny. This he proves by allowing Bunny to pull the dreaded red lever that short-circuits Miss Emmy. The computer goes haywire. They laugh. The picture ends.

POP AND HIGH CULTURE

The line between pop culture and high art is blurry, if not artificial and snobbish. An artifact's historical value isn't necessarily correlated to its genre or original intent. For example, Sumner's sales spiel about using machines to liberate the worker is right out of Walter Gropius's Bauhaus manifesto. That it's mouthed by a loveable corporate shill in a Hollywood movie does not negate the message. In fact, the passage of time has added a deeper layer of meaning. Viewed from today's perspective, this scene is a trenchant analysis of the power of corporations to co-op all opposing ideologies—which pretty much sums up the fate of critical thought throughout the twentieth century. And finally, the movie's fairy-tale ending points to an inherent dilemma in the pursuit of happiness, American style: more often than not, love and getting ahead are antithetical paths to self-fulfillment. Mike got his big promotion, but he didn't get the girl. Climbing the ladder and a happy home life don't mix.

SCIENTIFIC MANAGEMENT

Knowing the genealogy of the ideas that shaped business in the 1950s and the 1960s and beyond is crucial in understanding modern office life.

Desk Set confronts the doctrine of efficiency, which spawned the consulting industry. The mantra of efficiency began appearing in early twentieth-century accounts of office life. In her World War I–era novels, Edna Ferber said that the mania for efficiency started in Germany and migrated to the United States. Perhaps there's truth in that. However, in the United States more than anywhere else, an engineer called Frederick W. Taylor propagated the cult of efficiency, which now permeates all facets of American culture. In 1911, Taylor published a study—actually a manifesto—titled *The Principles of Scientific Management*,[4] which warrants a brief look.

Taylor cites President Theodore Roosevelt saying next to the conservation of natural resources, increasing efficiency is the nation's most pressing need. Taylor says inefficiency is entrenched in American business owing to antiquated ideas about hiring and manager–employee relations. In hiring, said Taylor, managers are guided by a wrong assumption: they search for "the ready-made, competent man" to fill positions from "the presidents of our great companies down to our household servants." Of course, there are few such ready-made or experienced people. Only when managers realize, writes Taylor, that it is their duty to "systematically" co-operate "to train and to make this competent man, instead of in hunting for a man whom some one else has trained, that we shall be on the road to national efficiency."[5]

The key word is *systematically*. Taylor argued that there was only one best way to conduct any task: the most efficient way, which could be determined scientifically. In essence, scientific management meant measuring performance with stopwatches and such and begat white-smocked efficiency experts who patrolled offices and factories with clipboards and tape measures. This led to time-motion studies, rearranging desks and machines, even dropping room temperatures. (It was thought that the women who assembled telephones for Western Electric might work faster with chattering teeth. They didn't.) Recall that when Bunny first meets Richard Sumner, she instantly tags him as an "efficiency expert," so pervasive had that ilk become throughout business and industry by mid-century.

Scientific management castigated individual initiative and style—"rule-of-thumb methods"—as wasted effort inimical to the "system." Taylor put it thus: "In the past the man has been first; in the future the system must be first." The idea was to work at the fastest pace possible with maximum efficiency. Taylor promoted a utopian vision. Scientific management would yield such vast gains in production that labor and management would no longer squabble over how to share of the profits. There would be more than enough to satiate both quarters. But fear, based on erroneous beliefs, causes workers to deliberately loaf or "soldier," as it was called in Taylor's day. Why is it, Taylor asks, that,

Whenever an American workman plays baseball, or an English workman plays cricket it is safe to say that he strains every nerve to secure victory for his side. He does his very best to make the largest possible number of runs. The universal sentiment is so strong that any man who fails to give out all there is in him in sport is branded as a "quitter," and treated with contempt by those who are around him.[6]

Yet when this same man returns to work the following day,

instead of using every effort to turn out the largest possible amount of work, in a majority of the cases this man deliberately plans to do as little as he safely can . . . in many instances to do not more than one-third to one-half of a proper day's work.[7]

Workers soldier because they fear an increase in productivity would eliminate jobs; soldiering, or working as slowly as possible, protects employee self-interests. Working at a slow, easy pace also stems from "natural instinct." Once workers and managers drop their enmity and realize their interests intersect, "systematic soldiering" will cease, maximum efficiency will obtain, and prosperity will reign across the nation.

In the 1960s, television portrayed a fully automated future in which work amounted to pushing buttons. However, this didn't result in a surfeit of happiness.

THE JETSONS

The Jetsons debuted on Sunday, September 23, 1962 (and ran through March 3, 1963). The animated sitcom set 100 years into the future was the first program ABC-TV broadcast in color. But it aired opposite NBC-TV's *Walt Disney's Wonderful World of Color*, got drubbed in the ratings, and was cancelled after 24 episodes. *The Jetsons*, however, was revived for syndication. Between 1985 and 1987, an additional 65 episodes were made (with nearly all of the original voice actors). These ran, intermingled with the original 24 episodes, during the Saturday morning jamboree of children's programs. Those who would dismiss cartoons as a lower art form slander the genre. A remarkable amount of talent and care converged to make *The Jetsons'* now classic first season: the voice actors recorded their parts in sessions that lasted for six hours, so particular was Joseph Barbera about what he wanted. In contrast, the 1980s'

Jetsons were recorded in just one hour. The actors included the best in the business. Mel Blanc played the curmudgeonly boss, Cosmo Spacely. (Blanc, of course, was famous for doing the voices of Bugs Bunny, Daffy Duck, Porky Pig, Tweety Bird, and Woody Woodpecker.) In the first episode, the pro's pro Jean Vander Pyl voiced seven characters, including Miss Galaxy, Spacely's baby-voiced secretary, and Rosie the Robot. Looking back 40 years after the first season, Janet Waldo, who voiced teenaged Judy Jetson, said Vander Pyl gave this advice about doing cartoons: "be as bad as you can . . . be a little worse, let it all out and you'll be perfect." The other main voices in the original episodes were George O'Hanlon (George Jetson), Penny Singleton (Jane Jetson), Daws Butler (Elroy Jetson), and Don Messick (Astro, the family dog). After the voices were recorded, the animators began their work, playing off of mannerisms in the voices and drawing those into the characters. Pop culture's level of sophistication in 1962 is worth noting. A French maid robot Jane Jetson considers hiring is named Blanche Carte; such little jokes presuppose an intelligent mass audience.

Written for both adults and children, *The Jetsons* transposed the ideal middle-class nuclear family into a technologically driven utopia, if utopia may be defined as freedom from manual labor. George, an affable office drone, is the breadwinner, his wife Jane, is a pert homemaker. They have a boy-crazy teenager, Judy; a precocious six-year-old, Elroy; a dog, Astro; and a maid, Rosie the Robot. The future is conceived as cities in the sky, with elevated buildings on thin circular pillars. Cars are bubble-topped flying saucers that navigate upper and lower sky lanes, but there are still traffic jams. It's the same old rat race, and George, unable to afford a larger saucer, complains of "compact saucer cramp." The year 2062 is 1962 with a technological facelift. When Judy tells her mom, "You're crazy," Jane says, "Don't be smart. Is that any way to talk to your mother?" Of course it is, says Judy, that's how teenagers used to say, "I love you," something she learned in her ancient history class. Ancient history is "now," 1962, replete with assimilated beatnik slang. And people still use cash, dollar bills! But they are surrounded by futuristic appliances. But so imaginatively did the program look into the future, claimed Waldo, that *The Jetsons* "invented" or anticipated moving walkways, called "slidewalks," and the microwave oven, the Food-a-Rack-a-Cycle.

OFFICE LIFE

The Jetsons depicts office life as immutable, and for good reason. Essentially, office life is and has always been a way of structuring interpersonal relationships around the ostensible goal of productivity. Offices give rise to perennial tensions and naturally these seep into and affect home life. For example, *The Jetsons'* first episode, "Rosie the Robot,"[8] treats two familiar rituals of office life, asking for a raise and having the boss over for dinner, which are not unconnected. Such "informal" dinners were once one of the hurdles of promotion. Like a military dress parade, family and home were put out for inspection. George's salary becomes an issue when their Food-a-Rack-a-Cycle goes haywire. Jane "cooks" George's breakfast by pushing its buttons, but the machine serves up raw bacon, and, instead of coffee, tea with oatmeal floes. "When we were first married," George chides Jane, "you could punch out a breakfast like mother used to make, now you're all thumbs."

But it's this "antique monster's" fault, says Jane, who wants a new Food-a-Rack. (She also hates washing, ironing, and vacuuming, which amounts to pushing three buttons, so Jane plans to get a robot maid on a free one-day trial.)

But they can't afford a new Food-a-Rack, says George.

Then why not ask Mr. Spacely for a raise, says Jane.

Because Spacely is a "penny-pinching old crab," says George.

George works at Spacely Space Sprockets, Inc. Parking isn't a problem; his flying saucer folds up into a briefcase. A slidewalk conveys him into his office, whose main feature is a circular chair, which anticipates the Bubble Chair Eero Aarnio designed in 1968! The walls are decorated with squares and rectangles that look like clean hieroglyphics, a streamlined Adolph Gottlieb painting from the 1940s. (Thus is the past transposed in imagining the future.) George spends his day leaning back in a picture of repose: his feet crossed, his head braced by interlocking hands. His job consists of pushing a button. When he returns home and Jane asks if he had a hard day at the office, George answers, Just brutal. He had to push a button on and off five times. Spacely's a slave driver.

At the office, George begins to think Jane is right, he should ask Spacely for a raise: he deserves a raise, he's a darn good "digital index operator," or button pusher; it takes brains to know which one of two buttons to push. In fact, Spacely couldn't get along without him, he thinks, working up his courage. "I'll just march right in, and I'll ask him for a raise right now."

Spacely's pretty, young blond secretary is called Miss Galaxy. By convention, pretty secretaries aren't bright, and Miss Galaxy is no exception. (Jean Vander Pyl uses a thick Brooklyn accent to convey Miss Galaxy's lack of smarts.) No, George can't see Mr. Spacely at the moment because he's on the picture phone (which looks like those unveiled at the 1939 World's Fair). Actually, Spacely is being badgered by his wife, Stella. She won't be cooking tonight because she's going to a protest at the United Planets Building. Stella is excited. She gets to carry a "Martians Go Home" sign.

When Miss Galaxy tells Spacely someone called Jetson is here, Spacely doesn't recognize the name, so preoccupied is he with personal problems. His secretary reminds him what Jetson does and Spacely thinks he has summoned him because "butterfingers Jetson" must have screwed up again.

Intimidated before the boss, George stammers something about "thinking."

Spacely cuts him off: Don't think. Leave the thinking to the machines.

Jetson blurts out that asking for a raise was his wife's idea. But all Spacely hears is "wife," which sets off a chain of envious associations. Spacely wishes he were like Jetson again, young and struggling, and most of all, Spacely longs for home cooking: hash, meatloaf, soup bones, beans. He's sick of restaurants. He dreams he's young and struggling and, most important, he eats home cooking.

Spacely invites himself over for dinner. It's understood that if the meal is good and George's family is to his liking, Spacely will grant the raise.

"Now back to work Jetson," says Spacely, tossing him out by kicking Jetson's chair and repeating his mantra: "Busy, busy, busy, busy."

George, of course, gets his raise. His family passes muster, and Spacely loves Rosie the Robot's cooking. Spacely isn't a bad sort, and he clearly sees George's shortcomings. But in granting a raise, it's as if Spacely were also hiring the entire family, including Rosie, and they make up for George's deficiencies. As Spacely says, "We'll have to try the whole dinner bit again if it's all right with Rosie."

In a worker's utopia, beyond Frederick Taylor's imaginings, nothing much has changed. There is always something to complain about, and social life is still about keeping up with the Joneses. The real future has yet to arrive, but *The Jetsons* is cautionary about equating happiness with freedom from drudgery. Fully automated machines and smart robots with human personalities can be designed to do all the drudge work. But if the present is any indication, these devices will inevitably malfunction, and there will always be a newer, improved model to strive for.

REAL AND FAUX AD MEN

Throughout popular culture, business signifies conformity—narrowness of mind and purpose. In the early 1960s, for example, the prototypical plastic man wore a suit, the antithesis of such transient adventurers as cowboys, hobos, and beatniks. Ad men in particular were put down for creating the false needs that drove a wasteful consumer culture.

However, pop culture also contains representations of ad men that flip such clichés about business and advertising. Three such examples are the television program *Mad Men* and books by two creative giants, David Ogilvy and George Lois, whose personae *Mad Men* loosely draws upon. These examples show how fact and fiction nurture each other within popular culture, just as both shape our attitudes. Because of its pervasive influence in mythologizing the Madison Avenue of the 1960s, I will start with the present, *Mad Men*.

MAD MEN

Set during the years of the Kennedy administration, the recent hit cable television series *Mad Men* evokes an era remembered, through the glaze of nostalgic wistfulness, as idyllic. It's America's so-called "Camelot" period— a designation, however, not lacking in irony. *Mad Men*, which debuted in 2007, depicts the advertising business as a life-on-the-edge, high-wire act, an especially enticing métier in those years when behavioral psychologists and market research were starting to change the profession but hadn't yet completely superseded individual intuition and keen observation of emerging trends.

Office life at Sterling Cooper, a small Madison Avenue agency, shares a kinship with the stressful, make-it-up-as-you-go creative work in the television, movie, and recording industries of the day. The firm's executives, copywriters, and graphic artists set their own hours, blow off client presentations, belt Scotch during the day (executive offices contain liquor cabinets), wisecrack, and throw themselves at the secretaries.

Creative work may contain intrinsic rewards, but the same acquisitive drives and machinations that propel other businesses animate Sterling Cooper—perhaps more acutely. Even the firm's secretaries are power hungry; their status is derived in part from their bosses' stature, or from current or past romantic interludes with the hierarchy. Some of these women take pleasure in tormenting new secretaries by picking at the crust of exposed insecurities. An innocuous, mundane remark or the reply to a seemingly friendly question might be seized upon as though it were a serious breach of decorum or protocol that could only imply moral turpitude or stupidity.

Mad Men's main character, Donald Draper, the firm's brooding creative director—the boss of all the copy writers and graphic artists—represents a new type: the antithesis of the gray flannelled Tom Rath, even though, outwardly, their lives bear an uncanny similarity. Both are paid to manipulate public attitudes and perceptions—or, more charitably, to "inform" the citizenry; both commute from the suburbs; both possess beautiful but unhappy wives. Rath, however, must mind what he says. The role forced upon him precludes genuine expression. Fear is Rath's constant workmate. His role of company man infiltrates his private life.

In contrast, Draper's job, abetted by his company's culture, demands free and imaginative expression. His success hinges on eschewing fads and delivering the unexpected. Indeed, the accounts people, or the business side of the house, anticipate contentious and even condescending encounters with such creative types. And Draper, a tall dark figure with a razor intellect, has built his considerable reputation on his creative flights. He's also in flight from his past. He exudes a mysterious, introspective air. If Draper wears a mask or slips into a role, it's by choice. These are protective devices used to throw off scent those who would get too close.

To such an extreme does *Mad Men* glorify ad men—albeit with good reason based on historical accounts—that one of the gears driving the reviled engine of shallow materialism is portrayed as a bastion of cool. In twenty-first-century television land, being a retro ad man is hip. Just how hip is established in an episode called "Hobo Code,"[9] from *Mad Men*'s debut season, 2007.

THE SQUARE VS. THE BEATNIKS

Donald Draper is Madison Avenue's premier creative director. Unlike his real counterparts, David Ogilvy and George Lois, Draper is a loner with the brooding air of a 1950s French intellectual. And unlike Ogilvy and Lois, for whom 80-hour weeks were the norm, Draper, a family man, has time for unlimited affairs, such as the one with a spacey lady called Midge.

In her Greenwich Village apartment, Midge and Don and several beatniks smoke marijuana and listen to *Sketches of Spain* by Miles Davis. Soon enough, however, the beatniks shatter the mood by attacking the ad man. He creates the big lie. He manufactures need. His kind are nothing but ants in a colony. What follows is an existential clash of self-identities.

The beatniks have presumed superiority. They drain more out of life than the squares because they're unencumbered. Like Midge says, she doesn't make plans. But what they look down upon as Don's regimented office life takes a type of courage and strength beyond their comprehension. For all his philandering, Don possesses some measure of an artist's discipline. His clothes, his style, are immaterial. His profession is fraught with the risk and despair inherent in all sales work. Don's job demands a level of consciousness magnitudes above pretentious indolence masquerading as freedom. Work is the thing. Without work, there is no self-actualization, nor, to use the philosophical jargon of the era, can there be anything approaching "authentic being."

But the beatniks don't work. All they do is talk and point fingers at people like Don for society's injustices. They exude contempt. Dig the ad man's useless and pointless existence, selling detergent flakes and toothpaste. That won't bring back those murdered black kids in Biloxi, Mississippi.

No, and neither will leaning against Grand Central Station with a bottle of Tokaji wine pretending to be a vagrant, says Don. Nor does it make you make you free. Don pities these wastrels.

Why don't you make something of yourself, he asks.

Don seems to be prodding them to re-think the faulty premises of their indolent existence. He echoes Camus and Sartre: I hate to break it to you but there is no big lie. The universe is indifferent.

Like primates spooked by fire, the beatniks can only whimper.

Just that day, Don had received a $2,500 bonus check. Come on, he says to Midge, let's go to Idlewild (which would become JFK) and catch a flight to Paris for the weekend.

No, I can't, she says.

Can't? This is the woman who doesn't make plans? Who lives in the moment?

With that, the plastic man coolly signs his check over to her. Here, go buy yourself a car, he says, and walks out, leaving the posers in their invisible cage.

It's the man in the suit and tie, then, not the one wearing a fez and an earring, who truly lives on the edge, who is recklessly and magnanimously spontaneous. That he works in an office makes him even more "out there." It's also immaterial. The avant garde composer Charles Ives was an insurance man.

DAVID OGILVY

Before David Ogilvy (1911–1999) rose to the top of the advertising field, he distinguished himself as a pastry chef in an exquisite Parisian restaurant. He then tried door-to-door selling, and farming in Pennsylvania. Although the colorful Scotsman was expelled from Oxford for laziness, he apparently retained some schooling; his *Confessions of an Advertising Man* (1963)[10] is rich in literary allusions and untranslated Latin and French witticisms (more evidence that yesterday's pop culture seems decidedly highbrow by today's standards).

Ogilvy spent his 1962 summer vacation writing *Confessions*, which, he later admitted—perhaps in an ironic twist of "modesty"—was a shameless piece of self-promotion intended to lure new clients. Ogilvy claims he thought the book wouldn't sell—maybe 4,000 copies tops—and gave his son the book's copyrights for his twenty-first birthday. However, *Confessions* was an instant smash when it appeared in 1963, selling 600,000 copies. It has since been translated into 17 languages. Its status in the pop culture pantheon was reaffirmed when the book was mentioned by the characters on *Mad Men*—jealously, of course.

One of Ogilvy's most famous ads was one of his earliest. The first week the ad ran in the *New Yorker* in 1951, a sleepy shirt manufacturer from Maine sold out its entire inventory. On a whim, on the way to a photo shoot, Ogilvy stopped at a novelty story and bought a $1.50-eye patch, which he placed on the model. Thus Ogilvy created the debonair aristocrat who became the iconic symbol of Hathaway shirts and could well serve as his alter-ego.

Ogilvy looked like the prototypical man in the gray flannel suit, the title of Sloan Wilson's 1955 novel. Because the hero of Sloan's book was a publicity man, ad men got pinned as gray-flannelled yes-men who would do or say anything to land an account. Ogilvy, however, was never subservient. To anyone. In the following anecdote from his *Confessions*, Ogilvy finds himself in a demeaning position as he tries to land the account of the trade association that represents the nation's rayon manufacturers. To win the account, he must beat out the reps of other ad agencies in a sort of beauty contest.

Ogilvy is summoned into what he called "a pompous committee room." The big rayon chief tells him he has precisely 15 minutes to make his pitch. Then he will ring a bell to signal in the next agency's rep.

Unbowed, Ogilvy begins posing questions, as if *he* were auditioning the client. Were he to accept this account, how many people would have to approve his work?

A committee of 12, each from a different rayon company.

"Too many masters, too little money," thought Ogilvy. "Ring the bell," he said and walked out, laying sycophancy to waste.

GEORGE LOIS

George Lois (b. 1931) was a graphic artist with a flair for the outrageous. In 1960, he formed Papert, Koenig, Lois, the first ad agency to go public. There he created some of the most memorable and cleverest ads of that decade or any other. For Braniff Airlines, for example, he created a two-page spread of Andy Warhol and world heavyweight champion Sonny Liston as seatmates. In a black leather jacket, with an emphatic finger in the air, Warhol makes an animated point as Sonny listens intently. Lois had Liston, an ex-con and a former mob enforcer, dressed in a white shirt, suit and tie; he looks positively intellectual. The tag line reads: "Andy Warhol and Sonny Liston fly on Braniff. (When you got it—flaunt it.)" At the time, Sonny Liston was considered the most feared black man in America, a symbol of the brute strength and rage that could be unleashed upon white people. In 1963, Lois created a cover for *Esquire* magazine featuring a head shot of Sonny Liston wearing a Santa Claus hat. It caused instant outrage.

Lois's work showed that advertising carried some of the most radical ideas in a radical decade—that racial prejudice could be attacked using humor and novelty.

JIFFY LUBE

George Lois designed the Jiffy Lube logo, an excellent example of design that blurs the line between commercial art and Pop Art, reminding us that Pop Art is either a tribute to or a shameless appropriation of the best commercial art. But the logo would never have been approved had Lois not used his rapier wit to slay a boardroom philistine.

When Jiffy Lube hired Lois, they were a fledging quick-oil-change company in complete disarray. Potential customers drove right by their garages, whose signage failed to beckon. Lois saw they needed "branding." So he designed what he termed an "active" logo. Unlike passive logos, which just sit there, active logos grab the eye. Jiffy Lube's inner sanctum in upper New York State loved the new logo. However, Lois had yet to sell the corporate people in Baltimore. In a large conference room, he faced division heads and lawyers in what he called a "group grope." Reeling in his audience, Lois unsheathed the new logo, which looked like a traffic sign pointing to a Jiffy Lube service entrance, a brilliant design that marries form and content.

The room applauded. But then a short pudgy lawyer asked for the floor. There's a problem: the design is *phallic*.

"I don't know what *your* peepee" looks like, said Lois, "but mine don't look like that."[11]

Portrayals of ad men in popular culture remind us that individuality isn't exclusive to society's fringes. Conventional thinking posits a hostility between business and art. But commercialism doesn't preclude merit. Inherently, business and advertising are neither good nor bad. They are fluid concepts that describe and promote a necessity: human exchange. Commerce and advertising can drive social change, and radical ideas can emanate from offices on Madison Avenue—the heart of the Establishment.

BEWITCHED

Even a farfetched sitcom about an ad man can carry critical bite. Take, for example, an episode from *Bewitched*'s first season, 1964, called "The Witches Are Out."[12] It seems an odd vehicle for social commentary, but the episode contains layered dialogue that agitates for equal rights beneath the surface humor and silliness.

Darin Stephens is the brightest talent at McMann & Tate, one of the world's largest ad agencies, located on Madison Avenue. Darin is married to a witch, Samantha, whose mother and her coven disapprove of her marriage to a mortal. A maker of Halloween candies hires Darin to create an ad campaign with a highly identifiable trademark. Like many ignorant clients, this one, a Mr. Brinkman, thinks he knows more about advertising than the pros. He has an idea for a trademark and he wants Darin to design it. He wants a clichéd witch, a hag with a crooked nose, warts, and broken teeth, wearing a tall black hat and riding a broomstick.

While Brinkman and Darin are meeting in his office, Samantha is hosting a coven at their suburban home. The witches are meeting about their cause, the hideous stereotypes of witches harbored by straight society. Every time I see one of those "ugly old crone" images of a witch, I fly right home and cry myself to sleep, says Aunt Clara. Mary says, I don't see why we just don't come out. Let's tell everyone we're witches.

"Better take out lots of fire insurance first," says Bertha.

"Oh, Bertha," says Sam, "they stopped burning us years ago."

At home, Darin works up some sketches for the client. But Samantha has raised his consciousness, and his drawings are defiant. He refuses to perpetuate any further discrimination against this minority group by propagating the stereotypical images the client ordered. Darin has drawn beautiful witches, sexy and mini-skirted.

The client is incensed. "That's not what I wanted," Brinkman thunders. He goes over Darin's head to his boss Larry Tate.

"You know what the client wants," says Tate. Give it to him.

Darin takes a stand. "Put someone else on the account," he says. He will not engage in "witch discrimination." Tate persists. Darin walks out on his boss. He will quit his job before being a party to injustice.

That evening, the witches use their powers to mess with Brinkman's mind. They turn up in his bedroom bearing protest signs: "Witches Are People Too" and "Brinkman Unfair to Witches."

Back in the conference room the next day, all is well. "I'm glad you saw my point of view, Mr. Brinkman," says Darin, unveiling a poster of a gorgeous witch in high heels sunning herself near a palm tree. The tag line reads: "Only the Choicest Witches Eat Witches' Brew Candy."

Brinkman loves the campaign and all is well.

In playing the discrimination theme for laughs, *Bewitched* managed to raise the issue without ire. (The witches, of course, serve as a stand-in for any mistreated minority.) Business and advertising are portrayed as agents of social change. Their images and slogans enter the lexicon of popular culture—or more properly, re-enter; pop culture is the reservoir of symbols that advertisers plunder. To resonate with the masses, ad men must speak their language, which is pop. Notice Darin's appropriation of youth culture in word and dress. His tag line uses "choice," which meant superb, as in, "It's choice!" He also taps the latest thing from London, mini-skirts, popularized by the ultra-thin model Twiggy.

But ad men are salesmen who work in hierarchies, loose though they may be, and under tremendous pressure. Their work may be brilliant and socially sensitive, but they must please their bosses, who care only about pleasing clients, who care only about increasing sales. Any "good" an ad may do is incidental to these facts of office life.

Darin and Samantha are happy because the ad portrays witches in a positive light. But Brinkman and boss man Tate are blind to all but the bottom line. Social considerations had no influence whatsoever in the decision to run the ad. At a celebratory dinner with Darin and Samantha, Tate admits that he shared Brinkman's skepticism about beautiful witches. But then research reports came in that put both boss and client at ease, and Darin got the green light: "Mothers and children don't buy Halloween candy," said Tate, "fathers do. And that gorgeous witch on the billboard has kicked Brinkman's sales up twenty-seven percent!"

Chapter 7

Greed Is Good: The 1980s to Present-Day America

The 1980s was one of the more noisome decades in American history, a period marked by the dry rot of excess: rude, obscene levels of "me-first" gluttony. Laws and norms of conduct that had held business in check since the New Deal were overturned with shameless vengeance. Lying and cheating and disloyalty to the buying public and to the nation are now the norm. *Glengarry Glen Ross*'s[1] (a box office bomb) resuscitation as a motivational video at corporate retreats is indicative of the nose-dive into cynicism and contempt. Not that these things are new—they're ancient. But publicly parading these, especially as a display of ego, is new. Open allegiance to the new money culture coopted previously hostile territory, colleges and universities. Students in the 1960s and 1970s protested social inequality, spurned materialism, and regarded sitting behind a desk spiritual death.

The author Michael Lewis, who graduated from Princeton in 1982 (with a BA in art history), reports that during his senior year, for the first time in the university's history, economics became the most popular major: it was seen as the road to the most coveted career—financial analyst for an investment bank; in 1986, Yale graduated 1,300 students, 40 percent of whom applied to work at First Boston; and in 1987, Harvard added 40 sections of an economics course to serve 1,000 students; enrollment had tripled in 10 years.[2]

In his novel *Bonfire of the Vanities* (1987), Tom Wolfe, a Yale graduate (PhD, 1957), notes the change. The "sons of the great universities," the "legatees of Jefferson, Emerson, Thoreau, William James, Frederick Jackson Turner . . . now flocked" to Wall Street and bond trading.[3] To hell with the great American novel, travel, adventure, Hemingway, and all that rot about authenticity and forging your own path. Bright youth were in the throes of money culture.

Wall Street was awash in money. The buzz on every campus, said Wolfe, was you had to be stupid or lazy not to be making $250,000 a year within five years; if you weren't making more than $500,000 by age 30, you were probably mediocre; and only the incompetent or timid failed to earn $1 million a year by age 40. Mere boys on Wall Street were buying $3 million apartments on Park Avenue and 30-room summer places—with servants' wings—in Southampton; for their children's birthday parties, they covered their expansive lawns with trucked-in carnival rides operated by teams of workers.[4]

Ten years after *Bonfire*'s publication, a derivatives trader, Keith Styrcula, weighed in on Wall Street's new money culture in a short story called "At the Top of His Game," which I will later take up in greater detail. The hero of the story is a trader who takes stock of his "friends" at a cocktail party. The "Wall Street jerks"—bankers, brokers, traders, lawyers—in the room represent millions of dollars in Ivy League diplomas, licenses to steal, paid for by their parents. They skim a "disproportionate chunk of the country's GNP," which they and their trophy wives consume conspicuously on houses, vacations, cars, boats, and swimming pools. Their children are infected with this status virus and are "tragically conversant with the iconic symbolism of Tiffany and BMW." Wall Street jerks "confuse wealth with class," passing the former on to their children, but not the latter.[5]

After he published *Liar's Poker* in 1989, Lewis ran into an unexpected reaction during his visits to college campuses. *Liar's Poker*, said Lewis, was merely an attempt to leave a message in a bottle: "Unless some insider got all of this down on paper, I figured, no future human would believe that it had happened. . . ."[6]

Liar's Poker documents the insanity within Salomon Brothers, the first brokerage house to make obscene profits by trading mortgage bonds. It covers the years 1984 through 1987. By several turns of fate, Lewis, who holds master's degree in economics from the London School of Economics (1985), became a bond salesman at Salomon Brothers.

Lewis had hoped that *Liar's Poker* would induce young people to pursue their passions rather than selling out, that students would see the foolishness in turning phony just to work in finance. He wanted the bright kid at Ohio State to "spurn the offer from Goldman Sachs" and become the oceanographer he really wanted to be. But students read *Liar's Poker* as a how-to book and flooded Lewis with letters asking for more "secrets" about Wall Street. Even though the financial system had been discredited time and time again, "the big Wall Street banks at the center of it just kept on growing, along with the sums of money that they doled out to twenty-six-year-olds to perform tasks of no obvious social utility. The rebellion by American youth against the money culture never happened."[7]

Liar's Poker documents a twisted form of office life and the rise of an immoral ideology on Wall Street. The book is named after a form of gambling popular among traders at Salomon Brothers. Liar's poker involves 2 to 10 players holding dollar bills close to their chests and attempting to bluff or fool others about the serial numbers on their bills. Like in poker, bids or bets are placed and raised, and typically no more than several hundred dollars a hand is wagered. Most famously, Salomon Brothers' chairman, John Gutfreund, once publicly challenged the best player in the firm to, "One hand, one million dollars, no tears." The challenge was declined with the retort that they should play for "real" money—$10 million.

LIAR'S POKER

Fixing the beginning of the "greed is good decade" is done at the storyteller's discretion. Who can say? For Tom Wolfe, the causal chain dates to the Vietnam War, which President Lyndon B. Johnson financed by printing billions of dollars. This flood of new money insidiously spurred global inflation, which surfaced in the early 1970s when the Arabs raised oil prices and turned markets of all sorts into gambling emporiums: "gold, silver, copper, currencies, bank certificates, corporate notes—even bonds." Thus, bond trading came to gain prestige. Previously, bonds "had been the bedridden giant of Wall Street. . . .The less promising members of the firm were steered into bonds, where they could do no harm."[8] Lewis infers a less convoluted beginning date: September 30, 1981, when Congress passed a tax break that encouraged commercial banks to sell or trade the home mortgage loans they held—at a *loss*! Back then, the Glass-Steagall Act's (1933) provision that separated investment banking from commercial banking still held. (The provision was repealed by the Gramm-Leach-Bliley Act of 1999, which President Bill Clinton signed into law.) Glass-Steagall was designed to stop the type of speculation that spurred the Great Depression. Investment banks issued stocks and bonds, while commercial banks, or thrifts, accepted deposits and made home loans. Home mortgages in the United States represented

$1 trillion of debt. This tax break led to hundreds of billions of dollars of churning on Wall Street and proved an unexpected windfall for Salomon Brothers, which possessed the only fully staffed mortgage department on Wall Street.[9] Yet another plausible starting date for the greed decade is October 6, 1979, when the chairman of the Federal Reserve, Paul Volcker, announced that the money supply would be fixed rather than free-floating (or dictated by business cycles). Interest rates rose and the thrifts began disgorging money, losses that bond traders would feast upon. In the ensuing years, commercial banks would insanely sell their mortgages for as little as 65 cents on the dollar to traders who would resell them for up to 85 cents on the dollar. It was as though confused clown fish had swum into a school of sharks.

Naturally, the bond brokers at Salomon Brothers held the presidents of thrifts, whom they fleeced mercilessly, in contempt. The presidents were rubes, maroons, heedlessly unaware of the playing field and the financial acumen of their opponents. The brokers were brilliant salesmen and light- ening quick at grasping and exploiting any weaknesses in the markets; they saw the entire board, knew how to play all the angles, and were continually inventing new shots. In Salomon Brothers argot, thrift presidents—whom traders imagined wore polyester suits, drew paltry five-figure incomes, and worked "banker's hours"—belonged to the "3-6-3 club": the typical savings and loan president borrowed money at 3 percent, lent it at 6 percent, and was on the golf course by 3 o'clock.

Lewis relates a conversation between a broker and a 3-6-3 man. The remarkable thing is that the broker, tongue in cheek, improvised his forced close. The thrift president wanted to sell a $100 million bundle of 30-year loans and buy a different bundle of loans worth $100 million. The Salomon trader told him he'd buy the first bundle for 75 cents on the dollar and sell him the second bundle for 85 cents on the dollar, a $10 million loss for the thrift man, who complained about the deal. The broker allowed that, yes, it wasn't a good deal "from an economic point of view," but, he said, "look at it this way, if you *don't* do it, you're out of a job." The thrift man bought it. The brokers who overheard the sales pitch split their sides.[10]

At the bottom of the pecking order on the bond floor at Salomon Brothers were salesmen, followed by traders and senior management, all of whom had been traders. Salesmen were attached to particular traders, who set the salesmen's annual bonuses. The traders lorded over their anx- ious and scared salesmen, who deftly handled institutional investors such as pension funds and insurance companies. Traders would often persuade their salesmen to push or sell this or that bond to their clients.[11] Traders smoked cigars, played endless practical jokes on each other, and devoured prodigious amounts of food nonstop, starting with onion cheeseburgers at 8 a.m. In between the gluttony and jokes, traders bought and sold mortgage bonds and eventually moved on to the "raw material" for these, home loans, which they would learn to creatively package in various tranches. These early innovators created the template for the bizarre and fraudulent forms of selling repackaged mortgages that triggered the looting of public monies in 2008, the so-called "bailouts," a scheme designed by the investment banks and approved by their stooges in government.

Senior management, traders, and salesmen all occupied the 41st floor, Salomon's nerve center. Management, including CEO Gutfreund, "stalked" the floor—some 100 feet in length—which was "lined with connected desks." As Lewis described it,

Traders sitting elbow to elbow formed a human chain. Between the rows of desks there was not enough space for two people to pass each other without first turning sideways. . . . Most of the men were on two phones at once. Most of the men stared at small green screens full of numbers. They'd shout into one phone, then into the other, then at someone across the row of trading desks, then back into the phones, then point to the screen and scream, "F***!"[12]

In researching *Bonfire of the Vanities*, which featured a bond salesman protagonist, Tom Wolfe, ever the superb reporter, parked himself on Salomon's 41st floor. Wolfe sat near a legendary trader known as the Human Piranha, who once profited enormously on the French government's ineptness. (The French had issued a bond dubbed the Giscard after President Valery Giscard d'Estaing; the Giscard is featured in *Bonfire*.)

BONFIRE OF THE VANITIES

Following is how Wolfe fictionalized Salomon's now infamous 41st floor, as he follows the bond salesman Sherman McCoy to work. McCoy works at an investment bank called Pierce & Pierce, which occupies five floors near the top of a 60-story glass tower that rises up "from out of the gloomy groin of Wall Street." Eighty bond traders and salesmen occupy the entire 50th floor, a vast "oppressive space" emanating a "ferocious glare" and an "ungodly roar, like the roar of a mob."[13] Glancing about, one saw the "writhing silhouettes" made by the flailing arms and twisting torsos of young men, "few of them older than 40. They had their suit jackets off. They were moving about in an agitated manner and sweating early in the morning and shouting, which created the roar. It was the sound of well-educated young white men baying for money on the bond market."[14]

So preoccupied were these traders that they scarcely noticed or spoke a word to an elderly black man called Felix who "moved from desk to desk" throughout the day shining their shoes for $3, including his tip. Felix might represent "everyman," the lower strata, people whose lives are negligible—menials upon whom crumbs are scattered.

Sherman McCoy held no official rank, but as the top producer, he enjoyed "moral eminence." Sherman loved the "shouts, the imprecations, the gesticulations," and the "fear and greed" that "enveloped" him. Bond traders and salesmen were the ultimate office dwellers. They never left their desks, upon which rested telephones and a computer terminal. They didn't start their days "with small talk and coffee and perusals of *The Wall Street Journal* and the financial pages of the *Times*." They got on the phone and started making money. If they left the office, they gave an assistant the number they could be reached at in the event that a new issue of bonds came in and had to be moved quickly. Going out for lunch had "better have something directly to do with selling bonds for Pierce & Pierce. Otherwise—sit here by the telephone and order in from the deli like the rest of the squadron."[15]

Wolfe likened the end of the trading day to the end of a battle:

After five o'clock the Masters of the Universe took care of all the things people in other businesses spent the entire day doing. They figured out the "net net," which is to say, the actual profit and loss for the day's work. They reviewed the markets, reviewed strategies, discussed personnel problems, researched new issues, and did all the reading of the financial press that was forbidden during the daily battle. They told war stories and beat their breasts and yodeled, if they deserved it. The one thing you never did was simply go home to the wife'n'kiddies.[16]

The term "Masters of the Universe," now ubiquitous in news reports and editorials about Wall Street, originated in *Bonfire* as an ironic description of Sherman McCoy. "The Masters of the Universe were a set of lurid, rapacious plastic dolls that his otherwise perfect daughter liked to play with." Sherman is a philandering twit whose wife is on to him. We first meet Sherman, on his hands and knees, in his Park Avenue apartment building "ransacking his brain for white lies" with which to deceive his wife: "The world was upside down. What was he, a Master of the Universe, doing down here on the floor . . ."[17]

OUT FOR BLOOD: TRUST NO ONE

In *Liar's Poker*, Michael Lewis notes that Salomon Brothers' 41st floor housed the firm's most ambitious people, "and because there were no rules governing the pursuit of profit and glory, the men who worked there, including the more bloodthirsty, had a hunted look about them." The men worked under the jungle understanding that unreined "self-interest was healthy." Therefore, suspicion reigned. Had some cutthroat positioned himself to ambush you and steal your job?[18] Lewis quotes a once-prominent deposed person saying he was OK with what happened. In fact, the manner of his firing, underhanded as it was, reaffirmed his faith in capitalism, whose foundational axiom, he claimed, was only the fittest deserve to survive.

The eat-or-be-eaten mentality was reaffirmed two decades after *Liar's Poker* by a veteran derivatives specialist, Keith Styrcula, in "At the Top of His Game," a short story he wrote under the pen name Stephen Rhodes. Styrcula's Wall Street resumè includes senior positions at J.P. Morgan, Credit Suisse First Boston, and Union Bank of Switzerland (UBS).

Pundits have proffered various candy-cane explanations of what "caused" the great postmillennium Wall Street swindle. One narrative seems to have achieved such a degree of consensus that it's routinely put forth as definitive: those naughty boys who comprise the financial industry simply got a little too reckless gambling with house money (i.e., other people's). Journalists who invoke the cliché that Wall Street is a giant casino and "investments" are "bets" are wont to allude, perhaps unwittingly, to Tom Wolfe: the gamblers are "the Masters of the Universe"—a stupidly fawning, flattering moniker that chokes off contempt and indignation for the fraudulent acts that were committed. While this story line sounds metaphoric, it's most often intended literally. Such is the understanding of Wall Street's machinations among the commentators who share this world view—a perspective that amounts to nothing more than a mild rebuke for the usurious system that now drives the American economy.

In contrast, the metaphors in Styrcula's short story "At the Top of His Game"[19] evoke mobsters, a crime family, unbridled ambition propelling the invariable cycle of young Turks conspiring to muscle in on and capture rival territories. For example, the story's hero, Rich Barston, realizes that several colleagues have conspired "to put a bullet" in his head; and "kill or be killed" is Wall Street "in its purest form."[20] Murder is, of course, hyperbole for discharging a person.

Seventy-eight people report to the 36-year-old Barston. "Twenty-something stress addicts" populate the firm's trading floor. The "thrill and agony of trading derivative securities" is also in Barston's blood: "There's no Betty Ford clinic for this addiction," he says, "nor would I voluntarily twelve-step myself away from this high." Barston is a top revenue producer. The "assassination attempt" he survives shakes out thus: his nemesis is called Howard Ranieri, a "passive-aggressive, hair-challenged, beer-gutted, no-talent clown." Ranieri's tactics are common in office culture. He bad-mouths Barston to a higher-up, who was his Harvard roommate. Ranieri's roommate had created a "do-nothing job" for him, drop-kicking him into Barston's "sand-box as a co-head." The rationale had been that Ranieri had a lot to learn and could do so while helping Barston. But Ranieri doesn't want to share power. So he steals Barston's ideas, team, business, and revenues. Ranieri "systematically" slanders Barston to "senior management as 'redundant' and 'not a team player,' " while he and his former roommate wait for Barston's "mentor to be incommunicado somewhere" so they can pull their "lame-ass coup d'etat"

The resemblance to mob families is glaring. Both Barston and Ranieri are "made men" under the protection of competing capos. The "bosses" (senior management) resolve their dispute by putting "a bullet to the head" of Ranieri's capo. Barston has "crushed" his enemy, but he's uneasy. Ranieri's voice haunts him, *"You can postpone the inevitable only so long."* How many bullets can Barston dodge? How many of the smiling faces on the trading floor are now plotting to take the fiefdom that *he* built? Perhaps it's a "law of nature," Barston thinks: "Once you're at the top of your game, everyone becomes your enemy—rivals, friends, lawyers, lovers, superiors, subordinates. They plot and scheme and come after everything that matters to you, everything you love and care about." Barston's assistant, Terri, puts a steaming latte on his desk, her freckled face beaming. It's an intimate moment; together they triumphed over evil against great odds. "Yet at this moment, absolutely no one is beyond suspicion. *Et tu, Terri?*"[21]

In *Bonfire*, Wolfe's traders assure each other that their talent, not "dumb luck," begets their wealth. Certainly Wall Street contains brilliant minds and master salesmen, people with exceptional instincts for reading and exploiting others' foibles. But without dumb luck—tax breaks, deregulation—Wall Street would never have carted off obscene amounts of loot. In *Liar's Poker*, Lewis uses himself as an example: a 20-something, clueless geek. He started at Salomon at a *mere* $47,000—four times what a top professor at the London School of Economics made. When he quit two years later, in 1988, knowing full well had he stayed he would have become a millionaire, he was earning $225,000. This shook his faith in the traditional American values he was raised with: that the amount of money a person made was justly and directly proportional to his or her benefit to society. Lewis knew he didn't deserve *his* salary, a relative pittance though it was. He had, after all, sat at the center of "possibly the most absurd money game ever," which conferred benefits "all out of proportion" to the value rendered to society. All around him he saw hundreds of "equally undeserving people" raking it in. What Lewis saw, of course, was the appetizer to the main course Wall Street would feast on in the ensuing decades.[22]

Like Lewis, Stephen Rhodes in "At the Top of His Game," also remarks the role of dumb luck in the finance industry:

Rich Honeywell is yet another Greenwich hedge fund asshole, one of those Wall Street guys with marginal talent and a nine-figure chunk of someone else's family money behind him. A once-in-a-lifetime fluke—a federal deregulation of pension plans—has made him obscenely wealthy in his own right, and kept an endless convoy of Brinks trucks dumping mountains of money on [his office] doorstep . . .[23]

As a point of comparison between the new and the old Wall Street trader culture, I turn to a short story about a broker at the turn of the century.

A KIND BROKER, CIRCA 1901: BUYING ON MARGIN

The journalist Edwin Lefevre was noted for writing about Wall Street and the world of business. He also wrote fiction. In 1900, he published a collection of short stories called *Wall Street Stories*, which included "The Woman and Her Bonds."[24] The tale is both instructive and entertaining. Its plot hinges on short selling, a bizarre "trade" whereby a speculator sells shares he doesn't own and, as many have pointed out, profits only when others meet misfortune. Napoleon is said to have called short sellers "enemies of the state." Legend has it that the first shares shorted—in 1609—belonged to the Dutch East India Company. The practice was promptly banned in the Netherlands but reinstated within several years. The following century, the English outlawed the practice as well. Short selling was blamed for the crash of 1929. The concept of short selling spawned the creation of all manner of grotesque derivatives whose unregulated trading precipitated the Wall Street collapse of 2008.

In unfolding his plot, Lefevre lucidly explains and illustrates short selling. As O. Henry showed in "The Romance of a Busy Broker," the turn-of-the-century broker worked at the breakneck pace set by the New York Stock Exchange. So too Lefevre's fictional broker, Fullerton F. Colwell, who worked at the rapid tempo dictated by the incessant flow of information delivered by telephone, message boys, and the stuttering ticker tape machine: "Every quotation was of importance; a half-inch of tape might contain an epic of disaster. It was not wise to fail to read every printed character." Colwell was known as the busiest and "hardest-worked" man in the Wilson & Graves brokerage house. This is impressive because anyone who understands how offices work knows that "it is always the downtrodden clerks who do all the work and their employers who take all the profit and credit." Considering the pressures of his office, the patient and copious advice Colwell lavishes upon a "poor" widow makes his humanity appear all the more extraordinary. However, "The Woman and Her Bonds" serves as a cautionary tale against letting sentiment intrude upon business, an "updated" version of the old adage that cautions against mixing friendship and business.

Colwell had a friend, Harry Hunt, who had been careless about money matters. Harry wasn't one of the "big people," in the Wall Street parlance of the era. Nevertheless, when Harry died, Colwell spent considerable time untangling the mess he had left and then waived all the executor's fees that were his due. Colwell prudently invested the $38,000 Harry's estate amounted to, investing the sum in a trust fund that paid the Hunt widow 2.5 percent annual interest, or $79 per month. (Given the lawless mess that Wall Street is today, it is easy to forget that for much of the twentieth century, there actually were "sure" investments, such as AT&T, which, prior to its government-mandated breakup in 1984, was known as a "widows and orphans" stock because of its unspectacular but steady returns.)

Precisely at that hour of the day when "distractions were most undesirable," Mrs. Hunt calls upon Colwell, who was perplexed to see her. He'd set her up well. The $20 a week she earned in interest was more than three times the amount a semiskilled entry-level clerical job paid. Guessing she was still grieving, he told her to be brave, that time heals all. As he does with all his clients, "big people" or small, Colwell treats Mrs. Hunt with impeccable politeness. But while he stands, attentive and sympathetic, the woman hems and haws. The furious ticking of the tape machine tries his patience and spurs his imagination. What could all that tapping possibly mean? "Perhaps the bears were storming the Alabama Coal & Iron intrenchments of 'scaled buying orders . . .'"

But he can't possibly attend to dollars and cents while a distressed human being sits before him. She mustn't brood, he says. But bereavement isn't troubling her. It's money. She can't or won't live on $80 a month. Could Colwell find a higher-yielding investment? Yes, high-grade bonds, which will guarantee the safety of her principal and yield at least $110 a month—just to begin with. Mrs. Hunt is fearful. She's heard "so much about the money everybody loses in Wall Street." If she "tired" of the bonds, could she get her money back? Yes, she can always sell them, albeit at a little less or a little more than she paid for them.

She sends him a check for $35,000. Colwell maps out his strategy in a letter: When the Manhattan Electric bonds advance in price, as they surely must, he will sell some and keep the balance as an investment. Although the operation is speculative, he assures the widow her money is safe. By dribs and drabs, he will continue to increase her original capital. Within six months, Colwell hopes to double the widow's monthly interest income. Colwell performs these services gratis. (Modern investment advisors would be licking their chops over the fees such incessant buying and selling—or "churning"—would generate, not to mention their glee at getting their hands on a widow's life savings.)

Within days, the widow is back at Colwell's office. She's "so stupid" she doesn't understand the bonds she bought. Patiently, Colwell explains that he used a margin account—or borrowed money on her behalf—to purchase $96,000 worth of bonds. But Mrs. Hunt is upset she "owes" the firm of Wilson & Graves $61,000. "I've never met Mr. Wilson nor Mr. Graves. I don't even know how they look." However, she wouldn't mind owing the money to Fullerton Colwell, himself, as he's a friend and she knows he'd never take advantage of her. He manages her to calm her down, but makes the mistake of showing her how to track the bonds' daily movements in the newspaper's financial pages. (Buy-and-hold deity Warren Buffett used to advise small, amateur investors, not to follow the daily fluctuations, which lead to anxiety and panic.)

A few days later, the widow returns, perturbed. Her "financial matters"—jargon she's picked up from reading market reports—aren't well. Manhattan Electric Light is now trading for $95. Colwell smiles. It's nothing. Cease worrying, he tells her. No matter how low the price drops, she is not to panic. The investment is sound. He, of course, knows the market. Mrs. Hunt promises to be patient.

Mrs. Hunt, however, is now getting advice from a cousin's husband who knows nothing about investing, only how to worry the widow sleepless. He waters the seeds of insomnia by remarking any drop in price with "ominous hints and head-shakings." Mrs. Hunt confronts Colwell. It's in all the papers, she says, the *Tribune*, the *Times* and, the *Herald*. The bonds are now trading at $93. Colwell's smile fails to reassure her. She believes she's lost $3,000. She hasn't lost anything, he says, because he's not going to sell $93, but at $110 or so. Again, Colwell preaches patience: his strategy will take months to execute. The woman's mind races. What if the bonds fell to $90, or what if they dropped to $85? A friend had told her a one-point drop meant a $1,000 loss. Colwell tries using analogies of the real estate market—anything she might understand—to placate her, but fails. She regrets the whole deal and wishes she had her money back. Well why didn't she say so before, asks Colwell, suddenly buoyant at the thought of his divestiture from this pest.

Colwell summons a clerk to make out a $35,000 check to Mrs. Hunt and transfer the Manhattan Electric Light bonds to his personal account. He didn't tell her that to effect this transfer, he, in effect, paid $96,000 for bonds he could have purchased on the open market for $93,000. "He was the politest man in Wall Street; and, after all, he had known Hunt for many years."

One week later, the bonds climb to $96 and Mrs. Hunt returns to Colwell's office. Does he still have those bonds? Why, yes, of course. He will do for himself what he had planned to do for her. It's a sure thing, not that he tells her this. She, it seems, now wants the bonds back. At your service, madam. Telephone calls are placed. The bonds are now trading at 96.5, practically her original purchase price. But they were $93 when she sold them to Colwell, and that's the price she wants to pay. But he transferred them to his account at $96, which was duly recorded on the firm's books. She seems not to comprehend, let alone show gratitude for his $3,000 favor. Couldn't he let her have them for $93? No, they're now selling for $96.50 and he will purchase them for her at that price—or whatever the market price is—if she wants back in. But she wants them at $93. Why did he ever let her sell them? But they're selling for nearly her initial purchase price, he says. She doesn't budge. It's all his fault. He knew full well that she didn't know anything about business matters. Again, he is unfailingly polite as he tries to guide her: let him buy them at $96.50, it's a good deal. No—$93 or nothing. It shall be nothing, then, Colwell says, but do come back if you should change your mind.

Naturally, as Colwell knew they would, the bonds climbed steadily. Mrs. Hunt, flushed with more amateur advice from her relatives, calls again: "I came here to find out exactly what you propose to do about my bonds." *Her* bonds? What could this odd woman possibly mean? Had she taken his advice, she'd now be sitting on a $7,000 profit. She says she has decided to take his advice, and will reluctantly pay $96.50 even though she knows full well the price should be $93. That's impossible, says Colwell.

Why, she wants to know. Did he or did he not keep the bonds he purchased from *her*? And to whom do they belong, by rights? Well, to him, Colwell, of course. You mean he won't give them back to her, even for

$96.50? Her unfounded indignation has driven the most polite man on Wall Street to exasperation, to frankness. Quietly, he tells her:

For Harry's sake I was willing to pocket the first loss, in order that you might not worry. But I didn't see why I should make you a present of $3000. . . . If you had lost any money through my fault, it would have been different. But you had your original capital unimpaired. You had nothing to lose, if you bought back the same bonds at practically the same price. Now you come and ask me to sell you the bonds at 96½ that are selling in the market for 104, as a reward, I suppose, for your refusal to take my advice.

Mrs. Hunt isn't going to tolerate this. Colwell has "insulted" her. She will consult a lawyer "and see if I am going to be treated this way by a friend of my husband's. You've made a mistake, Mr. Colwell."

Yes, he certainly has. To ensure he avoids further mistakes, he asks Mrs. Hunt to oblige him by "never again calling at this office. By all means consult a lawyer."

Colwell hated losing his temper. Absentmindedly, he checks the ticker. During their unpleasant interlude, Manhattan Electric had gone up to $106\frac{1}{8}$.

Compare the fictional gentleman broker Colwell to a real-life counterpart some 100 years later, a Deutsche Bank salesman called Greg Lippmann, who went around giving presentations trying to convince people to short subprime mortgage bonds. (Like all the great hucksters, Wall Street salesmen baited their suckers semantically: "subprime" sounds innocuous compared to truer designations such as "worthless contracts" or "fraudulent obligations.") A money manager who heard Lippmann's pitch wanted to buy but hesitated. Because Lippmann controlled that market, he was the only person the money manager could sell to if he wanted out. Here is Lippmann assuaging his potential customer's fear: "You have no way out of this swimming pool but through me, and when you ask for the towel I'm going to rip your eyeballs out."[25]

OLIVER STONE'S *WALL STREET*

When *Wall Street*[26] opened in 1987, Oliver Stone took offense when critics called his tale of unhinged greed a "morality play." The Medieval term was presumably too rigid to register his characters' complexities. Perhaps he had a point. Take the corporate raider Gordon Gekko (played by Michael Douglas). His odiousness doesn't invalidate his insights about leveraged buyouts and a society that permits such destruction. Certainly *Wall Street* contains nuances; the drama has more levels than just good versus evil. But if audiences interpret the story as a morality play, that's how it's registered in the collective memory. As with speech, with which the masses have the power (of convention) to turn "incorrect" grammar into accepted usage, so too with the meanings of movies and books. (When has the public ever cared about the *auteur's* intentions, which can be esoteric? Stone, for example, intended the harshness of the florescent lighting on the trading floor to mean that the stockbrokers' milieu "burns out your brain." Without the benefit of Stone's commentary, this would have remained insensible—at least to me.)

Fundamentally, however, the story *is* a morality play—the activities of any salesman, trader, or raider contain a moral dimension. Time has also turned parts of the movie into a fairy tale; such is the gulf between *Wall Street's* ending and what passes for law enforcement today. In the movie, Gekko loses; he is sent to prison; his tool, Bud Fox, a salesman and Master of the Universe wannabe, is apprehended on the trading floor and led away in shame by a law enforcement team composed of officers from the U.S. Postal Office, the SEC, and the U.S. Attorney's Office. Insider trading and corporate espionage didn't pay then. Today, the thought that toothless regulatory agencies would punish anyone on Wall Street—as feeble and porous as what's left of the law might be—is ludicrous. That the schmucks who crashed the economy and continue their stranglehold abetted by the "people's" representatives in Washington would receive their comeuppance is a fairy tale.

Wall Street is a tale that shows how social forces shape people or extrude new social types. The movie captures the clash between traditional business values and an emerging form of corporate piracy—not that the impetus or drive for acquisition suddenly intensified in the 1980s, as though human nature had changed. What did change, however, was the sense of public shame formerly attached to ruthlessness and flaunting wealth. As the novelist Stephen Rhodes observed, old money was humble; past generations lived by the unspoken adage that "wealth whispers." Gekko brays and crows. He taunts and humiliates his adversaries—namely, anybody he does business with. Gekko represents the normalization of immoral behavior. Indeed, his signature phrase, "greed is good," now drives official U.S. policy.

GEKKO'S ACOLYTE

Bud Fox (played by Charlie Sheen) is a 20-something securities salesman for a brokerage house called Jackson-Steinem. Bud is obsessed with moving up. He tells his colleague Marv that his dream is to be like Gordon

Gekko. Bud idolizes Gekko for making $47 million on a single deal and $23 million on another before he was 40. Bud says Gekko makes 20 times what Yankee outfielder Dave Winfield makes in a year. (Several years prior, Winfield had signed a 10-year, $23 million contract, the richest in baseball.)

"And he had an ethical bypass at birth," says Marv.

A DAY IN A SALESMAN'S LIFE

Their office is a huge open room in a skyscraper they share with scores of other young men in white shirts and ties who sit at desks with computer monitors. Each morning, they leave their apartments and join the hordes of office workers who render subways and elevators claustrophobic. They arrive at their desks, remove their suit jackets and begin bantering. It's recess before school. Then an enormous digital clock flashes 9:30, a bell rings, and someone shouts, "OK, they're off and running," and the frenzy begins.

Buy and sell orders are barked into telephones: "That's right, 10,000." "Dump it." "You own it."

And as the trading day wanes, such snippets are overhead: "Put research on this. I need the information now, before the market closes in 10 minutes. At four o'clock I'm a dinosaur."

The salesmen are pressured both from without and within the firm. When a customer reneges on a buy order after the shares drop, Bud's manager tells him that if he can't make the sale stick, Bud will eat the $7,500 loss. "Somebody's got to pay. Ain't gonna be me," says the manager, walking away from Bud's desk with a fancy walking stick over his shoulder like a hunter's weapon.

This speaks to the oral nature of trading securities. Agreements are made by a simple "yes" or "no" via telephone. An unwritten code of honor governs these transactions. Speed is everything. There's no time for written contracts. For all the abuse salesmen take, customers can be as dishonest as the slimiest salesmen.

That evening, Bud laments his misfortune over beers with his dad, Carl, a maintenance supervisor for Bluestar Airlines.

Carl admonishes Bud. He could have been a doctor or a lawyer or even a customer relations supervisor at Bluestar. Anything would have been better than a "salesman."

Bud bristles at the word, as though a "carter" had been called a garbage man.

Bud insists he's an *account executive* who will soon move up into investment banking.

Carl isn't having it: "You get on the phone and ask strangers for money, right? You're a salesman."

But Bud rejects his dad's values. It's not what you do or how. It's how much you make: "I could make more money in one year as a broker than in five years at this airline."

THE GAGA YEARS

Gekko is an apostle of short-term profiteering. He plays an eye-gouging, zero-sum game. His ostentatious flaunting of wealth—his boorish taunting—is his victory dance. In *Wall Street*, the ghost of business past is Lou Mannheim (played by Hal Holbrook). Lou is an old-timer filling out his days as a middle-rung supervisor at Jackson-Steinem. He articulates the textbook version of the stock market's role in society by preaching about the sanctity of the stock market's purpose in a democracy. Lou tells Bud that he's a part of "something." The securities he sells will create jobs in science and research. This is Wall Street's moral obligation to the nation, an unwritten contract that underscores purposive activity for the greater good.

When Lou passes on a tip about a drug company to another fledgling, he meets disdain: the payoff is far too distant—at least five years away.

Lou's mantra is "fundamentals," the basic benchmarks of a company's actual and potential value. "Stick to the fundamentals," he tells Bud. "That's how IBM and Hilton were built. Good things sometimes take time." Lou says that every bull market produces quick-buck artists, but only the steady—those who stick to fundamentals—also make it through bear markets. But that old path is too slow and doesn't yield the level of wealth Bud covets.

"You've got to get to the big time first," says Bud. "Then you can be a pillar and do good things."

No, you can't get a little pregnant, says Lou: when you chase money as an end, it makes you do things you don't want to do.

THE WIT AND WISDOM OF GORDON GEKKO

Gekko is a City College grad who "bought his way in" to high society. It cost him $1 million to get on the Bronx Zoo's Board. WASPs, says Gekko, "love animals, they can't stand people."

Why can't fund managers beat the S&P 500? Because they're sheep and sheep get slaughtered.

As to loyalty, get a dog if you want a friend, says Gekko.

In something of a job interview, Gekko sizes up Bud's potential as a tool.

Is Bud willing to break the law? Is he willing to engage in insider trading and corporate espionage?

Bud is consumed with success, but not at any cost. Not if it means breaking the law.

Gekko dismisses Bud. He's useless.

But what about hard work? Bud asks in desperation, trying to salvage the interview.

Strictly for suckers, says Gekko, like his father, who "worked like an elephant pushing electrical supplies till he dropped dead at 49 with a heart attack and tax bills." You're either on the inside or the outside, Gekko says. An outsider is a "$400,000-a-year working Wall Street stiff flying first class and being comfortable." Insiders own their own jets, they're "players" who make $50 million or even $100 million a year.

Gekko's values are a twisted version of the American Dream, which he turns into a sales pitch. Bud had what "it took" to get into his office. Does he have what it takes to stay, namely the stomach to injure hundreds of thousands of working Americans by raiding their pension funds and wiping out their jobs? That's how it done. The new path to wealth: legal machinations.

GREED IS GOOD

Oliver Stone said he got the "greed is good" line from Ivan Boesky's 1986 commencement address at Berkeley. (Boesky was a notorious speculator convicted of insider trading.) Boesky had said something like "greed is healthy," which Stone remembered as "greed is right." In *Wall Street*, Gekko utters the line in a speech worth recounting because it shreds the veil that shrouds business and politics. If an American president with a philosophical mind were to publish a truthful memoir, it would corroborate Gekko's observations.

Gekko's speech is delivered at the annual shareholders meeting of a corporation he covets, Teldar Paper. A Teldar executive, one Mr. Cromwell, presumably on the board of directors, opens the meeting by telling the shareholders that their company is under attack by Gekko: "Teldar Paper is now leveraged to the hilt, like some piss-poor South American country." Cromwell says Gekko intends to shamelessly strip Teldar of all its assets, severely depressing the value of its stock. Shareholders must see through Gekko and reject his offer to buy the company. By the end of his diatribe, Cromwell is shouting like an old-time carnival barker who revels in the virtuosity of his enunciation.

Gekko takes the microphone and delivers a state-of-the-union address that justifies his actions. With its trade and fiscal deficits at nightmare proportions, he says, the United States has become a second-rate power. When the country was "a top industrial power there was accountability to the stockholder. The Carnegies, the Mellons, the men that built this great industrial empire, made sure of it because it was their money at stake. Today, management has no stake in the company!" Gekko points to two rows of about 10 men each sitting behind long, white-clothed tables, one elevated behind the other, Teldar's management. These men, says Gekko, own less than three percent of the company. As to Mr. Cromwell, who earns a million-dollar salary, he's invested in less than one percent of Teldar. The stockholders who own the company are "all being royally screwed over by these, these . . . bureaucrats with their steak luncheons, their hunting and fishing trips, their corporate jets and golden parachutes."

Cromwell shouts: "This is an outrage! You're out of line, Gekko!"

Gekko stands firm: Teldar Paper has 33 vice presidents, each making more than $200,000 a year. Scattered whistles. Gekko has spent two months analyzing what they all do and he still can't figure it out. Scattered chuckles. But Gekko knows Teldar lost $110 million last year. "And I'll bet that half of that was spent in all the paperwork going back and forth between all these vice presidents. The new law of evolution in corporate America seems to be survival of the un-fittest." In Gekko's book, you do it right or you're gone. Witness his last seven deals, which made 2.5 million stockholders a $12 billion pretax profit. He is not "a destroyer of companies," said Gekko, but their "liberator."

Then, calmly and deliberately, Gekko says,

The point is, ladies and gentlemen, that greed—for lack of a better word—is good. Greed is right. Greed works. Greed clarifies, cuts through and captures the essence of the evolutionary spirit. Greed, in all of its forms, greed for life, for money, for love, knowledge, has marked the upward surge of mankind. And greed—you mark my words—will not only save Teldar Paper, but that other malfunctioning corporation called the U.S.A. Thank you very much.

To a standing ovation, Gekko strides through the crowd smiling triumphantly. Gekko's wrath is righteous. Fumigating Teldar is patriotic. And, he promises, it will make the shareholders a bundle. Gekko's indictment of the general state of corporate management rings true. But he is, after all, a rank liar. His plausible claims and semantic tricks cover vicious intentions. In actual fact, everybody will lose—the shareholders, the employees, the nation. Everybody except Gekko.

HOW MUCH IS ENOUGH?

Portraying himself as Bluestar Airlines' savior, Gekko plans a takeover. He will break the airline into pieces and sell these off; and he will "make" $25 million by dissolving the company's pension fund—paying out the minimum in guaranteed annuities and pocketing the rest. Where the airline's hangers are, Gekko envisions condos.

When Bud catches on, he asks Gekko why wreck Bluestar and kill all those jobs?

"Because it's wreckable," says Gekko. "It's all about bucks, kid. The rest is conversation."

In spite of having acquired so much, Gekko is still restless. He seems engaged in business as a blood sport, a regression to an atavistic vanquishing of every one standing. "Gecko," of course, is a type of lizard. No longer constrained by society's mores, Gekko turns reptilian, unleashing the savagery that civilization represses.

In the presence of Gekko's opulence, Bud wants to know how much is enough.

"It's not a question of enough," says Gekko. "It's a zero game. Somebody wins, somebody loses."

This says nothing. Bud keeps pressing him. Who is this man? Why does he do these things?

Gekko responds with a picture of reality. He tells Bud how things really are. (In shaping his own thinking, Oliver Stone mentioned the influence of Buckminster Fuller's writings on "lawyer capitalism," which infested the United States after World War II.)

Says Gekko:

The richest one percent of this country owns half our country's wealth. Five trillion dollars. One third of that comes from hard work, two-thirds comes from an inheritance—interest on interest accumulating to widows and idiot sons—and what I do, stock and real estate speculation. . . . You got ninety per cent of the American public out there with little or no net worth. I create nothing. I own. We make the rules, pal. The news, war, peace, famine, upheaval, the price of a paper clip. We pick that rabbit out of the hat while everybody sits there wondering how the hell we did it. Now you're not naïve enough to think we're living in a democracy, are you, Buddy? It's the free market. And you're part of it.

The free market. Pirates are free to plunder. Democracy is a mirage. Keep your eyes on the flag and your nose to the grindstone, kid, while those who rule the country pick it apart, corporation by corporation— like they did Pan American World Airways.

PAN AM: AN AMERICAN TRAGEDY

By the time Oliver Stone had finished *Wall Street*, Pan American World Airways had been picked clean—from the inside. Although Pan Am officially ceased operations in 1991, by 1986, nothing was left of history's most glamorous airline but its name and carcass, an all too typical story of greed and incompetence at the top. But Pan Am wasn't just another company that fell in the 1980s. Its demise left a gaping hole in popular culture, both aesthetically and symbolically. Pan Am's death illustrates the corporate dereliction of social responsibility—that is, the stewardship of national treasures—and reminds us how much of American self-identity is tied to the vibrancy of its business sector. Brands and logos are an important facet of national image, both at home and abroad: Mickey Mouse, the Marlboro Man, McDonald's, Coca-Cola, Levi's. At one time, no logo was more storied or symbolic of American prestige and power than Pan Am's blue globe with white parabolic stripes. A great piece of commercial design, pop art before Pop Art, right up there with Raymond Loewy's Lucky Strike bull's eye package from 1942.

PAN AM AND NATIONAL IDENTITY

In 1955, Pan Am hired two New York architects, Edward Larrabee Barnes and Charles Forberg, to update the company's image. They designed Pan Am's now classic logo, which soon saturated mass culture and became a signifier for quality, adventure, and American culture. Since the late 1920s, Pan Am had been known as the U.S. government's "official" airline, and in subsequent news reports and images, Pan Am became entwined with American statecraft and diplomacy. The blue Pan Am logo on a white tailfin, surrounded by blue skies, accents the cover of Dave Brubeck's album *Jazz Impressions of Eurasia* (1958), where the logo signifies exotic travel and adventure. The Pan Am logo was a salient backdrop at the Beatles' 1964 JFK press conference. Stanley Kubrick's *2001: A Space Odyssey* (1968) features a Pan Am "Space Clipper." The company nicknamed their airships "Clippers" after the tall-masted nineteenth-century sailing ships. (*Star Trek*'s creator, Gene Roddenberry, piloted a Clipper in the 1940s.) Rolex reinforced Pan Am's cachet in an 1974 ad campaign themed "How a Pan Am 747 Pilot Tells Time." Rolex claimed it had designed its GMT Master Watch for Pan Am, which had supplied all its pilots with the watches since the 1950s.[27]

There was also the Pan Am Building on Park Avenue, a monument to the Bauhaus with its lean geometry. Walter Gropius, who founded the Bauhaus in 1919, assisted the architect of record, Emery Roth & Sons. The Pan Am Building opened in 1963 as the world's largest commercial office space. It took the entire fourth floor to house PANAMAC, the computer IBM built in 1964 to crunch reservations and hotels—one of Pan Am's many innovations.

Juan Trippe (1899–1981), a Yale graduate, started Pan American Airlines in 1927 after a stint as a Wall Street broker. Trippe won the government contract to fly mail between Key West and Havana. (He was not Cuban, but of European extraction.) Trippe had learned to fly as a WWI volunteer (he never saw action). In 1929, he and Charles Lindbergh began charting routes to Brazil and Latin America, and later, Pan Am developed its lucrative routes to Asia. Trippe ran Pan Am until 1968, when he resigned as its president. (Trippe burst back into pop culture in 2004 when Alec Baldwin played him in Martin Scorsese's *The Aviator*.)

By 1981, is was clear to many insiders that the company was listing. Two events frame Pan Am's last chapter: in 1981, management sold the Pan Am Building—a symbol of strength—to MetLife; and, in February 1986, Pan Am "transferred" its treasured Pacific routes, along with 2,500 flight attendants, to United.

THE QUIPPER: A GRAVEDIGGER'S STORY

These dates—1981 through 1986—also frame the birth and death of an underground flight attendant's (FA) newsletter, the *Pan Am Quipper*.[28] Its anonymous editors used biting humor to document and criticize gross mismanagement. In June 1981, the first mimeographed newsletters secretly began appearing in company mailboxes (in violation of corporate policy), under doors at layover hotels, and in Clipper "demo kits" (which contain oxygen masks and other safety props). The *Quipper* was also available through subscription—$10 for one year, cash only, mailed to a San Francisco address.

The *Quipper* tells the story of Pan Am's demise from the bottom of the pyramid: a "gravedigger's" perspective, which yields an uncommon truth. The term comes from Jimmy Breslin's *New York Herald Tribune* column about John F. Kennedy's funeral. Breslin had been loathe to report the funeral in hackneyed fashion by interviewing dignitaries or describing the bereaved. Instead, Breslin wrote a column about the man who dug the president's grave at Arlington National Cemetery, Clifton Pollard, who earned $3.01 an hour. (When his supervisor apologized for "pulling him out on a Sunday," Pollard said, "Oh, don't say that. It's an honor for me to be here.")

Karl Marx expressed an idea similar to the gravedigger approach, saying the "truth" of any society could be grasped most profoundly by viewing it through the eyes of its lowest stratum.

THE TOP VIEWED FROM THE BOTTOM

The *Quipper* is an unsanctioned account of business history, a submerged voice that bears testimony to an era of reckless destruction. History needn't be written and slanted by the "victors": employee newsletters represent a valuable means of corroborating or contradicting official versions. Significantly, the *Quipper* chronicles the beginning of the era of deregulation, of mergers and acquisitions, hostile takeovers, buyouts, and "downsizing." The airline industry, for example, had been treated as a utility until it was deregulated in 1978 to give free play to market forces. Previously, the Civil Aeronautics Board (CAB) had regulated domestic routes and set fares.

In its five-year, 20-edition run, the *Quipper* was one of the first organs to tell a now familiar story: a blue-chip company identified with American prestige and innovation is commandeered by people indifferent to its tradition and hostile to its employees. The vultures profit by piecemeal destruction.

As edition No. 3 (October 1981) notes: "Airplanes, hotel Subsidiaries, skyscrapers: once they are sold they can't be sold again." Confronting this "fact of nature," the CEO, from "high atop the (former) Pan Am Building," creates a new "product," the Clipper Climax Club, whose $3,000 fee entitles members to sexual favors from the stewardesses—or stewards. Predicting the doom of yet another once-great company, the newsletter extended Joni Mitchell's metaphor (in a song) likening the Pan Am building to a tomb: the building, said the *Quipper*, is "a tombstone in a graveyard of monuments to dead institutions."

The name *Pan Am Quipper* is an inside joke playing on Pan Am's inflight magazine and its corporate newsletter, both called *The Clipper*. In the first issue (June 1981), the *Quipper* announces its intention to laugh at the absurdity of the flight attendant's situation, caught between noncaring management and a clueless union. But it's difficult to laugh when flight attendant pay was just slashed 10 percent and words once avoided like a hex—"if the airline survives"—are now spoken aloud.

Issue No. 3 (October 1981) contains a narrative about dead-end jobs whose deep structure predates Pan Am and is endemic to office culture. The flight attendant's career path leads to a dead end. To survive, FAs must stick it out,

work as little as possible, acquire seniority, and get back at the company by collecting a salary that increases in parallel with self and corporate contempt. Whether or not one does a good job makes no difference. The only "promotions" available are to Purser; where you tell people who already know how to do their job how to do their job, while apologizing to passengers about the way they are doing their job.[29]

The passengers must be placated because management doesn't understand the importance of flight attendants and doesn't adequately fund the position. Given the sanctity of "service" in American business, this is a sign of rot at the top. The *Quipper* voices the universal lament that doing a good job doesn't matter. The FA job is seen as a dead end because the most viable step up, to Purser, isn't a serious option—the job amounts to telling FAs how to do their jobs. Of course, a flight attendant could move "into the Office." But that would be even worse than Purser. In the Office,

you become a paper-pushing Company Stooge who flits about from Telex to Xerox machine, taking everything "oh so seriously" until the next round of management layoffs arrives. Then, if the Union hasn't revoked too much of the seniority you were forced to purchase with dues back when you were a flight attendant, you get shoved back on the line where you bump someone junior to you onto the layoff list.[30]

The *Quipper* wishes that true "excellence"—untainted by seniority—were rewarded. But "maze bright" flight attendants learn to ignore the majority of passengers (tourist class) to butter up first-class passengers. The goal is to wheedle commendations: "my employer would be very happy to hear that you liked the flight; just mention my name."

In recognition of self-service at the expense of customer service—the play-acting that defines careerism in all organizations—the *Quipper* announced it would begin a campaign to recognize the most deserving among such "first class" employees: a new feature called the "Annoyee of the Month Award."

POOR MANAGEMENT

In the fall of 1981, chairman C. William Acker sent all "fellow" employees a letter thanking them for volunteering to accept a cut and freeze in
wages. The *Quipper* (No. 4, November-December 1981) warned Acker
and his management team against reading the employees' acceptance of
the pay cut as "a vote of confidence in your Company and in your Management." Rather, the prevailing sentiment is that, "Pan Am management
in general is hopeless. It's time for a massive overhaul." The *Quipper*'s
assessment of Pan Am anticipates Gordon Gekko's criticism of self-
serving, useless executives who suck companies dry: the FAs are working
for a company that the Harvard School of Business holds up to its students as a "classic example of mismanagement." Vice presidents sit in
offices "in the (former) Pan Am Building, sipping coffee and brandy,
and swinging big deals for their relatives: convention business to hotel
owing cousins in Florida; the ultra-fast sale of the Inter-Continental Hotel
Corporation with accompanying lucrative kickbacks." And under
William Seawell, Pan Am's previous chairman (1971 to 1981), the vice
presidents and their friends, relatives, and cronies "had priority over full
revenue passengers for seats in first class."

The *Quipper* (No. 18, May 1983) asserted that "The Colonel" (Seawell)
ran "the company like a feudal lord. He and his cronies . . . donned Rolex
watches and drifted about Pan Am's world (in First Class) arranging
sleazy business deals for friends and relatives." FAs, of course, know who
flies ticketless. (I heard of a pilot at another airline who refused to take
off until a freeloading friend of some executive was led off the plane—
protesting all the way.) The *Quipper* continues: "Anyone anywhere near
the top at Pan Am knows that the way to advance in this corporation is
not by doing quality work; one advances by collecting sufficient dirt on
one's superiors to be considered dangerous, hence, 'worthy' of promotion. No wonder they call them 'vice' Presidents! No wonder this is the
world's fastest receding airline!"

Finally, issue No. 3 presented the inaugural Annoyee of the Month
Award—William T. Seawell, albeit "posthumously" as he'd left Pan Am.
His achievements, however, were so voluminous that Seawell earned a
higher distinction: Annoyee of the Decade. Stated the Quipper: "We'd
simply like to thank Billy T. for a decade of monumental misdirection.
We'd like to thank him for setting an example of total incompetence that
everyone along the chain-of-command could emulate."

The *Quipper* shows that employees closest to the ground—those in the
air, actually—cared more about Pan Am's legacy than upper management

did. They were most affected by—and experienced first hand—the directives that impoverished service while enriching those at the top.

In the fall of 2011, ABC debuted a prime-time Sunday night drama called *Pan Am*, which instantly became the hottest program on television. Set in the 1960s—*everybody's* favorite decade, especially those who weren't there—the program glamorizes the airline. Deservedly so. Too bad and so sad, that government, aided and abetted by academics and their studies, helped wreck Pan Am and the entire airline industry through deregulation (which turned flying into bus travel, only with more service glitches). But who needs the real thing when you can watch make-believe TV?

OUTSOURCED

Integral to leveraged buyouts, greenmail, and hostile takeovers were junk bonds—low grade and high yielding—a quick way to raise capital. These were pioneered by Michael Milken while he headed Drexel Burnham Lambert's high-yield bond division in the 1970s. Milken justified junk bonds' use in leveraged buyouts with the same argument George Soros would use when accused of wrecking national economies by shorting their currencies. Soros, founder of the Quantum hedge fund, infamously "made" $1 billion overnight in 1992—"Black Wednesday"—by shorting the British pound, betting $10 billion against it. (The Bank of England lost more than £3 billion.) But Soros argued he wasn't an economic terrorist; rather, he performed an essential service: finding and exploiting flaws in economic systems and policies so they might be fixed. In a similar vein, Milken had argued junk bonds exposed deficiencies in the credit-rating system. That is, many American companies were erroneously over- or undervalued.

In *Liar's Poker*, Michael Lewis said that Milken often spoke to students at business schools. He would argue that bankrupting companies was difficult, countervailing forces were far greater—that is, those who wished to kill and loot companies were vastly outnumbered. To demonstrate how difficult it would be to wreck a company, Milken presented students with a hypothetical situation. (Actually, this "hypothetical" was exactly what the very real Lockheed Martin had done in the late 1970s.) First, locate the company's

major factory in an earthquake zone. Then let's infuriate our unions by paying the executives large sums of money while cutting wages. Third, let's select a company on the brink of bankruptcy to supply us with an essential irreplaceable component in our production line. And fourth, just in case our government is tempted to bail us out when we get into trouble, let's bribe a few indiscreet foreign officials.[31]

Rather than merely cutting wages, outsourcing as it is now practiced eclipses Milken's outlandish example—by far: a company fires *all* of its employees, shuts down *all* of its plants, and moves *all* of its operations to an impoverished country.

WELCOME TO INDIA

At first glance, John Jeffcoat's romantic comedy *Outsourced* (2006) looks like cotton candy, easily digested and easily forgotten, a 90-plus-minute distraction. However, this characterization is unjust. The picture presents a clear-eyed, even-handed look at outsourcing, laying bare the logic driving the practice. Furthermore, *Outsourced* captures the look and feel of modern office life: Frederick Taylor's practice of measuring efficiency with a stopwatch is the defining characteristic of call centers. The misnamed "service" economy is not just curtly impersonal, it is deliberately anonymous.

First, the movie offers a look at office life in Seattle. The hero, Todd, is a supervisor in a Seattle-based call center that sells patriotic-themed knick-knacks, such as painted plaster American eagles. Todd supervises a vast floor of order takers from an open cube workstation. Summoned by his boss, Dave, Todd turns flippant, "Is this going to take a while? I just ordered from Thai Garden and they're pretty fast." Todd's been with Western Novelty Products for four-and-one-half years. He knows he's good and thinks his boss is hazing him before his upcoming performance review.

"So you like spicy food, that's interesting," says Dave, a 50-something harmless-looking man in rimless glasses. His looks belie his message: "Any American job that's done online or over the phone is going overseas [to Mumbai]." Dave calls this mass dismissal of the company's workforce "restructuring."

This won't play with customers, says Todd. The factory worker in Wisconsin—(are there any left?)—won't cotton to buying patriotic kitsch from an overseas outfit. This scenario comes to pass, but the Indian order takers have been primed. A recently unemployed American rants when he hears the order taker's accent. These are the people taking American jobs. He insists on buying American. Calm down, a female supervisor tells him. They carry an American-made product line. He can have the item he wants, made in the good old U.S.A.—for a mere $212 more than the $40 Chinese version. The customer's indignation and patriotism drain away. Meekly, he buys Chinese.

But accent training will mitigate such episodes, says Dave. They will teach the Mumbai workers to pronounce "Internet" "Innernet" and to hold their noses when they say "Chicago."

Todd is told walk out on the office floor and tell everybody they've been fired. He blanches.

"You're free to quit," says Dave, "but you haven't vested your stock options yet, plus your pension and your medical. Quit now and you'll be out there in a bad job market with no unemployment benefits." Dave piles on: ask all those people out on the floor how it feels—"they'll know in about twenty minutes."

Todd must ship out to Mumbai to train his own replacement, who will earn all of $11,000—eight heads for the price of one, says Dave, pleased with himself.

THE BUNKER

The call center in India is an unfinished concrete box in a cow pasture. A sign bearing the word "Fulfillment" is the bunker's only adornment. Inside the office, fulfillment is defined as bringing down the "MPI," or minutes per incident. At the 12 minutes per order they're averaging, Todd claims they're losing money on each call. His goal is to get the MPI down to six minutes. "Work faster," a supervisor blares through a bullhorn. Too crude. Todd uses finesse. He bonds with his people. He likes them and they like him. They reach the magic number. They feel wonderful. They all go out to celebrate.

Boss Dave flies in to India just in time for the celebration. But he's not there to commend. He orders Todd to wipe all the data off all the hard drives. The Indian employees are told not to come to work the next day. They're all fired. The overqualified grunts are happy. Technical wizards all, they are now free to work for Microsoft. Only the nontechie supervisors are left in the lurch.

The operation is moving to China. Boss Dave says they'll be online upon the morrow. "China's the new India," he says. "Twenty heads for the price of one." They have been acquired by the largest direct-marketing firm in the United States. Their old company, Western, will be a small part of the new operation. The new company is going to outsource 4,000 call center jobs. Doubtless their algorithms have factored everything down to the Renminbi's transaction costs.

Today numbers rule, but not exactly as Frederick Taylor envisioned: efficiency has been realized beyond imagination, but management never did play nice. Turned out turn-of-the-century laborers were correct. They "soldiered" or worked at the slowest pace possible because they *knew* in their bones if production rose, employment would fall; and why wouldn't it given the nature of those at the top, whom they rightly viewed as their natural enemies? (Why else the need for unions and child-labor and minimum-wage laws?) But Taylor was a grand huckster who fudged his numbers, as Matthew Stewart proves conclusively in *The Management Myth: Why the Experts Keep Getting It Wrong* (2009).[32] Still, everybody bought his efficiency fable about harmony and abundant wealth for all. Among Taylor's early adherents was one Joseph Stalin, a mass murderer with a penchant for Five-Year Plans. (Hey, Uncle Joe, how'd all that Taylorism and rapid industrialization work out in the Ukraine?)

FIRING EXECUTIVES

Newspapers and blogs are full of stories about long-term employees who turn up one morning or afternoon to find a security guard at their desk demanding their security badge. They're given a few minutes to throw keepsakes in a cardboard box and are escorted from the building. But not all offices are "restructured" so summarily.

Walter Kirn's novel *Up in the Air* (2002)[33] is about a career transition counselor (CTC) called Ryan Bingham. Bingham says he and his fellow CTCs are "smiling undertakers for the still-living"—clever people savvy that "career transition" is corporate-speak for termination. Initially, the CTC industry was marketed as an "ethical revolution" in business, although cynics might suggest its true purpose was to shield executives from unpleasant scenes and minimize law suits. Bingham explained his job to his sister as ferrying "wounded souls across the river of dread and humiliation and self-doubt." CTCs are brought in neither to do the firing nor to find the fired new jobs. Rather, CTCs only offer "shouts of encouragement, 'Keep it up! That's great!'"[34]

In actual fact, CTCs teach their "cases" useless "skill sets" and try to pep them up with bland adages and job-seeking rules. The fired are told it takes a month of cold calling, networking, and mailing résumés by the hundreds for every $10,000 in expected salary. Bingham preaches patience. (How profound and useful!) Also, the terminated must never appear too eager when inquiring about a position. The kicker is that "finding a job is itself a job ... not working is work too ... don't get blue

... forgive yourself. You're only human. But also superhuman. Because you have untapped potential, and it's infinite."[35]

Bingham's first big assignment brought him to a heavy machinery manufacturer in Davenport, Iowa, whose corporate bonds "had been downgraded to scrap paper." From a small office in the back of the company's dilapidated headquarters, Bingham spent two weeks counseling seven middle-aged executives with families who were fired one by one on consecutive days. All but two had asked what they'd done wrong. "Nothing," said Bingham. "Blame interest rates. Blame low commodity prices. This problem's global."[36]

Yes, point to lame generalities—anything but greed and mismanagement at the top. Circumventing plain talk is cruel. Global problems are not acts of nature like hurricanes or droughts. They are caused by the decisions the powerful make for self-gain.

The company gave each of the seven fired executives offices next to Bingham's from which they could make phone calls and take tests that identified their personality types and strengths and weaknesses. Bingham scored and interpreted the tests, turning the results into a five-page "master self-inventory" for each to keep. "One man set his aflame before my eyes, but most of them clung to and studied these documents.... Three of the seven bought the mumbo jumbo. Three others were unreadable. They clammed up. Oddly, these three were the first to find new jobs."[37]

Too cruel. Like offering malaria victims sugared water instead of quinine.

HIRING EXECUTIVES

The Method (2005),[38] Marcelo Piñeyro's dark movie about corporate hiring, takes a reading of postmillennium values and finds that ruthlessness lapsing into cruelty is the make-or-break executive trait. This is conveyed through an executive search that employs a "scientific" technique to find the ideal Dekia "type." Dekia, a multinational corporation based in Madrid, has winnowed its search to seven candidates. Each is seated before a computer at a circular table in the lab-like setting of Dekia's personnel department.

They are told they will be subjected to a screening system from America called the Gronholm method. The candidates represent a mix of desirable professions: economists, lawyers, music studio executives. That they are willing to abandon such good jobs makes it clear that Dekia's salary and perks are stratospheric.

The candidates are alone except for a female "psychologist," Montse, who comes and goes and administers the Gronholm test. Montse, however, is an actor, as is her confederate, Ricardo, who is pretending to be one of the applicants. There is no Gronholm method. Montse and Ricardo make it up as they go along. Their goal is to create an atmosphere of paranoia that turns each candidate into a predator ready to pounce on anyone displaying fear or insecurity. The applicants will gang up upon one another, forming and breaking alliances, until one is left standing.

One of the five male candidates, a yes-man called Enrique, believes he's figured out the game. Enrique has heard that in the United States, they weed out the overly aggressive by locking all the candidates into a room and gauging their interactions. It's a "group dynamic" thing, he says.

The others are incredulous. How? There is no Dekia person in the room.

Hidden cameras and microphones, says Enrique.

Just then, the computers flash congratulatory messages: they've gotten this far owing to the "aptitude" they showed in passing a battery of tests and interviews. Today is the final day for deciding who is most "suitable." The candidates have all signed a Gronholm liability clause; nevertheless, they are given the right to quit at any time.

They are given their first directive, which seems designed to sharpen their claws and increase mistrust: one of the seven is actually a member of Dekia's personnel department; uncover the mole. Enrique pipes up: "I've read about this, they pretend to be candidates so they can observe us up close."

They begin questioning each other. The Mole, Ricardo, sets the tone by refusing to say where he works. He doesn't want his employer to know he's here. He's told withholding information doesn't help group solidarity. Solidarity? What nonsense, says Ricardo. "We're all competing for the same job."

Anna, a recording executive, suspects the economist Carlos.

There is no imposter, declares a woman called Nieves, "I think they're playing with us."

Nevertheless, they are ordered to banish who they suspect is the imposter. They finger Enrique.

Next they are to choose a leader by consensus. They elect someone called Julio by secret vote. Immediately a news article about Julio appears on all computer screens: in 2002, he reported his company for pollution violations. All agree he's a hero except the mole: Wait a minute, you didn't include this on your rèsumè, and because of your disloyalty, didn't 200 employees lose their jobs?

Their next directive is simple: decide whether Julio remains in the selection process.

Nieves says she's sorry about this, but you did "betray" the company you were working for. Julio is eliminated by one vote. He leaves.

Suddenly their screens flash. The test is over. Montes the female shrink says the company has decided to reject all the applicants. It's a false execution. Montes smiles, "I'm joking."

As the day progresses, so does the cruelty. Anna is voted out on the grounds that she's too old, past child-bearing age, and would therefore be useless should the applicants survive a nuclear war—one of the more idiotic scenarios they're given as grounds to weed out another applicant.

The psychological warfare progresses. The Mole toys with Enrique by confiding in him. The Mole is troubled because he's lied on his rèsumè and all other application forms. He never told Dekia that he served as a union agitator in Argentina and opposed what his company called a "structural reformation," a covert way of firing workers. The Mole tells Enrique he's worried about Dekia asking for references. Dekia would never hire an ex-union man as an executive—the two stations are mortal enemies.

The Mole continues to bait Enrique by playing the anticorporate radical. Madrid is hosting a World Bank and an IMF summit and there are antiglobalization riots on the streets. Look at those protestors, says the Mole, don't you agree they're right to protest?

Of course not, says Enrique.

Montse joins the fray. Enrique, is there something you know about this man (the Mole) that the company should know?

"Don't you see what's happening here," says the Mole. "They're asking you to inform on me? . . . and what you know about me is what I told you because I trusted you."

Montse: "Enrique, you know something [Dekia] should know and you won't say what it is? Your idea of company loyalty is a bit strange."

Enrique spits it out: Ricardo worked for a state company in Argentina, "and when it was privatized, he became a union leader and totally screwed management."

Ricardo then admits he's the Mole and asks Enrique if informing on him was right or wrong. It's the old double bind. No matter how he answers, Ricardo and Montse will hammer him from the opposite position.

Apply again when you've clarified your thoughts, Enrique is told.

Ricardo toys with the remaining candidates. All are afraid to contradict him. They don't know what to say when he asks, "We're having fun today, aren't we? Wouldn't you say this is fun?"

Ricardo says the German Army invented selection tests after World War I to better assess their officers—always in the presence of a psychologist. The British and American militaries also adopted these tests, and finally they spread to the corporate world. Ricardo says there is no Gronholm method, he and Montse set up whatever games they like and the candidates' imaginations "project the test."

Where does the name Gronholm come from? someone asks.

Nowhere, says Ricardo, "but it sounds good, doesn't it?"

They are down to two candidates, Nieves and Carlos. Out of earshot, Montse sides with Nieves, the Mole with Carlos. "You've been great all day, you're my favorite," Montse tells Nieves. Montse confides that she and Ricardo are just actors; sometimes they switch roles, and he plays the psychologist.

Elsewhere, Ricardo tells Carlos that Nieves is getting the job because she did better on the tests. But Carlos "fought for him" and the team of psychologists—the candidates have been filmed, recorded, and observed—have agreed to give Carlos one last chance. The job is his if he can make Nieves "go to pieces" within 15 minutes.

How is he to do this? Carlos asks.

Ricardo: "However you think, Carlos. I had to fight for this. Don't let me down."

Meanwhile, Montse is telling Nieves that most of the team prefer Carlos, he's been scoring better. But Nieves has one last chance. If she can persuade Carlos to give up, get him out of the building within 15 minutes, the job is hers. There are no rules, says Montse. Tell him his mother is in the hospital. Anything goes.

In this fashion, executive material is assessed. Like caged rats driven mad with electric shocks, the applicants lose their bearings. They are forced to guess: does the corporation seek loyalty or disloyalty, independence or subservience, honesty or dishonesty? Montse said anything goes. Not quite. Any moral or cooperative approaches most definitely do not go. Neither does the thing most worth fighting for, which is the first thing given up willingly: dignity.

Chapter 8

Scaling the Pyramid: Common Types and Office Games

TYPOLOGIES

Masks and mind games define office life as much as desks and cubicles do. Hierarchical organizations stifle authentic communication. Play-acting hardens into habit. Playing along, sometimes unwittingly, forces a person into playing a supporting role that feels false. The co-optation of the "real" self is particularly insidious when it happens incrementally and imperceptibly; after so many years, it doesn't just wash off. Office life is a guessing game about others' motives. With all the dissembling that occurs, who can tell what's genuine? Guessing wrong can shatter serenity and typecast a person against his or her will. Learning to recognize certain personality types and their ploys early in the game saves psychic wear and tear. The problem is not so much that certain types and their stratagems aren't discernable but that the clues that unlock their games are scattered about and useless unless pieced together. Typologies frame fragmentary bits of knowledge into coherent pictures. The truth about people is sometimes hard to discern because it often stands in plain sight. It's so simple and obvious, it's easy to miss. (This is one advantage of an outsider's perspective.) The perfect metaphor for this is Edgar Allan Poe's short story "The Purloined Letter." When a corrupt minister steals a letter from the Queen's private sitting room, the best police detectives in Paris spend a month combing the minister's apartment. They search behind the wallpaper, under the rugs, and inside cushions and furniture legs but find nothing. Then an amateur detective, Auguste Dupin, walks in and finds the letter in an instant. As Dupin suspected, the letter was "hidden" where no one thought to look: in the open, dangling from a card rack in plain view.

I once encountered a top executive who did absolutely nothing but feast and travel—first class—racking up outlandish expenses at four-star hotels: Rome, Paris, London, New York, Johannesburg. For years, she would disappear for weeks on end while her assistants ran things. The truth was plain and simple but so outrageously blatant, no one dared consider the most obvious explanation. Like other do-nothings I have known, she was a know-it-all. She responded to all briefings the same way, with a musical "yeah, yeah, yeah." Even events she couldn't possibly have known about were met with her slurred cadence, as though she had long foreseen the problem and judged it trivial. Organizations are infested with do-nothings who cultivate a busy-busy, no-time-now persona. Like a funnel cloud, this got-to-run posture buffers questions and keeps people from looking too closely.

Every organization has its goldbrickers. There are, however, just so many types of connivers and cons, just as there are only so many types of people or behaviors. Typologies are the stock in trade of both the social "scientist" and the novelist, whose domain used to be called "psychology" (or human nature) prior to the days of labs and white rats. In his unfinished novel *Confessions of Felix Krull, Confidence Man: The Early Years* (1955), Thomas Mann asserted that all of humanity could be classified under a mere handful of basic types. Account executives at AT&T used to be trained to handle clients by identifying their behavioral tendencies as belonging to one of four essential personality types. Who can say how many discrete types exist? It depends upon the acuity of the perceiver and how finely—or crudely—the lines are drawn. Nevertheless, every fictive or real character is a *type*. Gordon Gekko and Donald Draper are types, just as David Ogilvy and George Lois are.

Naturally, certain types of people are shaped in part by their professions and the kinds of offices they work in. The writers Michael Lewis and Matthew Stewart, for example, offer typologies: Lewis of Wall Street commuters, Stewart of consultants. Anybody who has observed office life says of certain people, "I know that type." The recurrence of certain behaviors I have encountered in offices in the United States and abroad has convinced me that universal types exist. I will offer a typology of three of the more troublesome or even dangerous characters I have encountered as a training consultant, journalist, and account executive. I've labeled the types Ward Boss, Baby Boss, and White Hair.

WARD BOSS

Wards were once the smallest political districts in large American cities. Wards are most indelibly associated with the corrupt political machines of Boss Tweed in New York City and Richard J. Daley's Chicago. Patronage and graft lubricated the great political machines. In return for their votes, ward bosses or district captains doled out jobs, paid medical and burial costs, distributed Christmas turkeys, and generally looked after their constituents, typically poor immigrants.

Like his municipal namesake, the office Ward Boss trades favors for patronage and is corrupt as hell. He's clever at recruiting the corporate downtrodden, those who've taken a beating in a performance evaluation, been passed over for promotion, or are nursing some grievance against the company. As the Ward Boss jockeys for power and material gain, there is no person too vile to serve as an ally. He's a conniver and a climber, but not a typical one. He's an unofficial rather than titled leader. To avoid scrutiny, Ward Bosses prefer to operate in between the lines of organizational charts by using their power and influence to create and gain charge of special projects that may last a year or two. The primary job he's paid to do is always secondary. He's always got something going on the outside, within or without the company. His office is a base of operations from which he can sap the company's resources—phones, supplies, personnel—for his own ends; hence the appeal of running special projects and controlling their budgets and expenditures.

The Ward Boss approaches you smiling, quickening his step as though he can't wait to delight in your company. "How ya doin' buddy?" he exclaims, his head twisting from the force of uncorked joy. Wired on diet Coke, he gets right in your ear and, in a conspiratorial whisper, says: "Look, there's a really important meeting next week and I really need you to support this thing. Because if you don't . . . " With the Ward Boss, it's always good versus evil. He frames everything as "us versus them" and forces you to take sides.

Saying "no" is no simple matter. The Ward Boss knows how to pummel your self-esteem. He acts out his disappointment. Your refusal pains him because *you*, whose moral fortitude he had so admired, won't join the fight to make this company a better place. He must have misjudged your character. Apparently you're one of *them*. His disapproval is instant. His body sags. He sighs, mimicking the inflections of a suffering child. The Ward Boss plays the moral crusader because, darn it, he really cares about the company. In actuality, he mails in his assigned duties and devotes all his energies to recruiting allies to protect or build his fiefdom. The votes he wheedles are only those that affect his interests. Genuine company-wide concerns he curtly disdains by draping a paw across your shoulder and solemnly dispensing his stock retort: "Hey, why should you care? You're still getting your paycheck, aren't you?"

The Ward Boss operates most effectively by stealth. He cajoles others into articulating his issues in meetings. Why doesn't he speak for himself, you ask him. The Ward Boss will say that if it appears he's the only one who cares, the issue will die; a different voice will create the impression that the issue "has legs." A well-placed secretary in a highly polarized organization, where people went out of their way to draw blood, pointed to a Ward Boss type and told me: "This stuff started happening only after he got here. He's the one who really runs the place. He's gotten two presidents fired."

BABY BOSS

Baby Bosses are underlings who want to be bosses—badly. Baby Boss struts and preens and acts like she is a boss. If enough people defer to her, management will think, "She's got the stuff. Look at how people react to her." Ward Bosses slather you in flattery. Baby Bosses do this by playing the supplicant. "Hey, is this a good time to talk?" says Baby Boss. "I'd love to get your take on this because I really respect your mind." To signify that a ponderous problem has her in a chokehold, Baby Boss wears her wrinkled-brow mask. She really lays it on. With your coaching, she can execute a reversal and pin the problem. Of course, the only problem for Baby Boss is how to best manipulate you into accepting a proposal that helps her corporate image and her quest for power. As you speak, Baby Boss bends closer, nodding intently, playing the novice at the feet of the sage. Ostensibly, she questions you to gain clarification. In reality, she's crouched in the tall grass baiting you into articulating *her* position as though it were yours. Her line of questioning beckons you closer: come on, a little more, now turn just a bit. Gottcha! "What a great idea." She spits it back, bending your meaning slightly—the first of many incremental distortions. Then she runs off to sell "your" solution to the problem she created to all the enablers she has cultivated, smitten as they are by this up-and-coming go-getter. Baby Boss wears people down with her incessant, fulsome self-aggrandizement. The gulf between her words and deeds is vast, a purloined-letter point that many seem to miss. Baby Boss complains that she's overworked and underpaid. Yet she lounges about other people's offices, pompous and blustery, acting like she's the boss she so badly wants to be.

This brings me to a real boss and my final type, White Hair, so named because he exudes a grandfatherly air of trust and kindness.

WHITE HAIR

White Hair is an executive who looks and acts like an elder statesman. During heated boardroom exchanges he is stoic, impossible to read. He speaks with deliberate calm, never raising his voice. He is courteous. In private, confronted by a troubled subordinate, he exudes sympathy: "Of course, Chuck . . . there, there, Chuck."

"Is it true," demands Chuck, "that I'm not even in the running for the district job?" White Hair grimaces as if wounded. He shakes his head muttering "no, no, no," as if to himself. His manner conveys the depth of the misunderstanding. Although White Hair never *explicitly* commits to anything, Chuck lights up.

Chuck took the drastic, risky step of going "upstairs" and it paid off. He connected. Chuck now feels understood and valued—even favored. When Chuck leaves, White Hair, for the benefit of his young assistant (none other than me) tilts his head and repeatedly cuffs his ear, affecting to drain his mind of the outpouring he'd been forced to endure. Teasingly he says, "He's not going to get it. I've already picked Jim."

White Hair's empathy shtick can pacify underlings for months. They go about confident that White Hair is in their corner and on the case, all the while completely unaware of how much authority White Hair wields and how little he cares. Because White Hair avoids giving a firm "yes" or "no," subordinates believe that all decisions are subject to convoluted negotiations among senior management. When Chuck follows up and asks how things are progressing, White Hair becomes a father figure, firm, but reassuring: "Yes, yes, these things take time. It will all work out."

Yes, time is the operative word. In time, fervor dies, and in the interim, White Hair is a master of the nonresponse. Those unanswered e-mails? Yes, yes, White Hair has been mulling their contents, but the budget meetings have been brutal and he has to prepare for the board meeting in Washington. Chuck feels ashamed and apologizes for troubling this good, kind man.

Of course, bad news is never White Hair's doing, he's merely the doctor consoling the family. "I'm very sorry, Chuck. But the president insisted on an engineering background for the district slot. You know how he can be. He just wouldn't budge. I'm also sorry you didn't get a raise. But I didn't get one either. Here, I'll lend you this book. Reading it made me feel better."

Thus I offer a composite of personality types drawn from close encounters: The Ward Boss, Baby Boss, and White Hair, each a vicious prevaricator or dissembler. Throughout various organizations, I was always struck by how successfully such characters managed to get over on others. One thing I learned is that responding to certain roles, if only by acting pleasant to get along, can unwittingly trap us into a reciprocal role we don't want to play. By donning a mask to play along, we risk becoming that mask. To paraphrase William James, certain stimuli trigger responses that cut grooves into our neural pathways, which become reflex actions.

Typologies help us understand and negotiate the social world. To say "I know the type," is to recognize that danger lies ahead.

VODAFONE STUDY

In 2006 Vodafone, the British telecommunications behemoth, published a study titled *Changing Faces: How We Adapt Our Identity at Work*.[1] A reasonably happy workforce is a productive workforce; hence the report—subtitled *Working Nation*—surveys employee attitudes across the United Kingdom. The introduction (written by a professor of organizational psychology and health at Lancaster University Management School) elaborates: UK companies' ability to compete in the global economy has been hurt by "identity-stressed" employees, a problem that became particularly acute and pronounced during the 1990s. Three related factors account for identity stress: the incessant pressure to increase efficiency, measuring employee efficiency or performance, and a culture of "presenteeism." This last word can mean several things: reporting to work while ill or working inordinately long days, well past the time that alertness and efficiency start to wane.[2]

Despite its la-la-land prescription, the Vodafone report was well executed, giving methodological rigor to anecdotal knowledge. Half of all bosses said they have "completely adopted their company's values," while the other half have adopted them "within reason." Seventy-nine percent of bosses say they reached their positions by adopting a "work-only" persona; 12 percent said they abandoned their personal values to succeed. And six percent said they lied or "assumed a false identity" to succeed. Turning to all employees, the most widely reported personality change is greater assertiveness (52%); 36 percent of all employees say they become more "sociable" at work, and 26 percent say they become less aggressive. Among the negative personality changes, 29 percent of employees say they become "less true to themselves and less open,"

24 percent become less extroverted, and 10 percent say they are "less honest" in the workplace.

The Vodafone study concludes by calling for workplaces in which employees remain true to their values and differences are "celebrated." For this to occur, workers should be coached in understanding their core personalities, perhaps through personality type indicators. "Once managers are armed with insight into type, they can provide feedback and support that is resonant and makes a real difference to performance because it taps into an individual's world view."

Right. And once hierarchical organizations are civilized, world peace will follow.

The Vodafone study generated several comments of note in response to a Web posting called "Chameleons at Work" (signed by Emma, July 18, 2006).[3] I quote from two of these, which I have edited for grammar and condensed or paraphrased for clarity. Someone identified as Johnny wrote that "the best way to handle your enemy is to become your enemy yourself." If you want to succeed at work, a single work face isn't sufficient. One needs multiple masks to draw in your "targets" before you can take them down. Johnny believes masks are just "tools." And someone identifying herself as "workingal" said she was called to task by higher management because she was deemed less "smiley" than before. She was going through personal problems outside work and made management "nervous" because they claimed she appeared as though she were gritting her teeth and smiling no matter what occurred. In other words, her smile was perceived as fake. She complained that it was exhausting to wear a smiley mask nine hours a day, five days a week. "No wonder waking up in the morning to get to work feels like walking to your own jail."

Leaving the Vodafone study, a blogger called Henry Bingaman posted an entry titled "The Freelance Copywriter's Mask."[4] Technology allows more people to work at home, a type of limbo state in which although physically removed, they still interact with "the office" and are still influenced by its culture. Bingaman makes the excellent point that even if one works at home, one still wears a mask—with an added risk, the danger of never taking the mask off, presumably because office masks are shed automatically upon exiting the office. But absent this physical or geographic stimulus, there is nothing to prompt the mask's removal. Bingaman said he became a freelancer to "enjoy freedom from office buildings and the corporate life. A freelancer that always wears his business mask is like an executive who never leaves the office building. He's trapped in the exact lifestyle that he was trying to avoid." Bingaman explains the necessity of wearing a mask at home. Were he to present himself as the person he truly is, he would never be able to claim to be a "marketer who can take a struggling business and dramatically increase their bottom line" and charge his clients $10,000, rather than $2,000, and claim they're getting a steal at 10 grand—because the mask tells clients they're buying $200,000 for only $10,000. The mask is a marketing ploy, a psychological screen, like wearing a $1,000 suit and putting on an air of success and lack of need when interviewing for an executive position. Would any clients buy or believe the "real" Bingaman, who calls himself a "bald guy that likes to read Harry Potter, watch action movies, and scream at my favorite hockey team through the TV"? The "authentic" Bingaman kicks around his home "in a raggedy t-shirt and gym shorts," while the masked Bingaman wears "a business suit."

SALES TYPES

The Big Short (2010) by Michael Lewis is an account of the machinations that led to the recent unprecedented looting of taxpayer monies: "By early 2009 the risks and losses associated with more than a trillion dollars' worth of bad investments were transferred from big Wall Street firms to the U.S. taxpayer."[5] Lewis tells the story through the eyes of a handful of astute traders and fund managers who caught on to the underlying mortgage fraud several years before Wall Street "officially" crashed the economy in September 2008. One of these traders, the sagacious Danny Moses, offers a typology of the Wall Street commuters he rides the train with every morning from the Connecticut suburbs to Grand Central Station. "To the untrained eye," these "were an undifferentiated mass."[6] Moses, however, picked up on the telling details. Those on their Blackberrys were most likely "hedge fund guys, checking their profits and losses in the Asian markets." Those who slept on the train were probably "sell-side people," that is, brokers who handled only clients' money, investing none of their own. A briefcase indicated the bearer was carrying market research and therefore was not in sales; although brokers write reports, they don't read their own, "at least not in their spare time." Carrying the *New York Times* was another giveaway: if the person does work for a financial firm, it's as an auxiliary, a lawyer or a "back-office" guy. People who dressed casually, as if going to a ball game, were the money people, the "buy-side" guys. For them, results were all that mattered. Thus if a money guy wore a suit, it raised suspicions that he was in trouble (presumably because he was using clothes to signify success, which would be unnecessary if his results were good). A suit might also mean the money guy was in trouble *and* was going to meet with an (unhappy) investor. The buy-side people, however, were generally hard to read from their clothes. But with the sell-side guys, clothes were a dead giveaway: a blazer and khakis signified "a broker at a second-tier firm," while a $3,000 suit and coiffed hair signified an investment banker at J.P. Morgan or some other top-tier firm. Danny Moses could divine where a person worked by where he or she sat on the train. Those in the front were destined for downtown firms such as Goldman Sachs, Deutsche Bank, and Merrill Lynch. But Moses reflected that "few Goldman people actually rode the train anymore. They all had private cars." Hedge fund guys such as himself worked uptown and "exited Grand Central to the north," where they caught cabs to their offices.[7]

Salesmen drive the economy. The old saw that "everybody's selling something" is a fundamental truth. Wall Street's salespeople are the elites of commerce, the polar extreme of door-to-door Bible peddlers. Danny Moses's typology was based on dress and accouterments, the same way police detectives size up suspects at a glance. Of course, appearance reflects the inner person, but not always. The Maysles brothers' documentary *Salesman* (1968) provides a typology of salesmen based on personality that is applicable beyond the world of selling.

FOUR TYPES OF SALESMEN

Paul "the Badger" Brennan is a door-to-door Bible salesman in the throes of a slump. Reflecting on the selling styles and personalities of his colleagues, he explains how three of them acquired their *noms de guerre*: "the Gipper," "the Rabbit," and "the Bull."

The Gipper is unemotional, a "straight man." The Gipper is an extremely effective salesman because he knows how to find and exploit any opening under any circumstances.

The Rabbit is a "very impulsive guy. He sells, he has a lot of energy and he's young." Although he doesn't have "the class" of the other salesmen, perhaps because he lacks their maturity.

The Bull is a "big, powerful man." He lacks the Gipper's "technique" or polish, but makes up for that with stamina.

The Badger, of course, is relentless. Perhaps he presses too much as he digs in and claws for his sales, which puts off customers. Failure to close sales turns to frustration and impatience.

GENERAL RULES AND RANKED TYPES

The truth about pyramid climbing is that the game is rigged. To win, a player needs to keep moving upward. But at rising altitudes, the number of slots decreases exponentially. Those who fail to move to the next rung (by dislodging the current occupant) roll back down. The climbing game is all about masked interactions. In his witty and erudite expose of the consulting industry, *The Management Myth* (2009), Matthew Stewart says that in the end, just about everybody who plays the pyramid game ends up a loser.[8]

Somewhat facetiously, Stewart breaks the game down to a set of ploys governed by one of two basic attitudes, friendliness or hostility. Players belong to one of three ranks: "inferiors," "peers," or "superiors." Following are the basic moves. A player may mentor his inferiors, or "squeeze them like lemons and throw them out." With peers, one may "build partnerships to get things done" or do them in, either through a whispering campaign or by sabotaging or stealing credit for their work. With superiors, one can accept their advice and do good work. (This presumes a kind and competent mentor.) Or, continues Stewart, one can flatter a superior's "self-delusions in order to distract from your own lack of merit." Finally, at the extremity, the subordinate may commit "patricide."[9] Presumably, the new boss whom you've just helped elevate will reward you for your treachery. In addition, it seems to matter not at all whether the old boss deserved betrayal. The prevalence of such odious behavior in putatively civilized corridors of commerce, emblazoned as they are with placards extolling "Trust," "Respect" and such, reiterates that office life is a bizarre mind game.

Whether deserved or not, betrayal is a fact of office life that everybody is likely to experience in some form or another. Betrayal changes eager and idealistic people. After they've been knifed, some victims conclude that villainy is the only path upward and begin sharpening their own blades. The best way to betray someone, says Stewart, is to look them in the eyes and smile while you're doing it. Stewart devised a rough matrix correlating the amount of psychic damage to the amount of time in harness. People who left office life within two to four years usually escaped with "no lasting damage." After six years, however, they accumulated "scars" and "could not pretend it didn't hurt." Finally, of a much different order than the walking wounded are the extreme cases. Stewart recalled a veteran who exuded the impression "that every bone in his body had been shattered into a mass of splinters." The man seemed eaten up "with a desire to exact revenge on the monstrous firm that had done him so much damage."[10]

I can attest that offices are filled with people fixated on getting even. Every utterance exudes resentment. The past is relived, interspersed with daydreams of conquest. However, there are cases in which the grievances are entirely imaginary or are unintended and laughably insignificant. Yet sadly, the fixations become such a part of the person's self-identity, are so entrenched, the person becomes implacable, beyond the reach of reason.

The antidote is old school and very simple: "I see you're unhappy. Get out." Or, "If you're so damn good, you won't have any trouble finding a better job."

The pyramid game reinforces the madness of office life: people move up by stepping on or over others, yet advancement is "officially" based on cooperation, as in the coveted appellation "team player"—perhaps the most vapid sports metaphor ever appropriated by the business world. Thus the schizophrenia of office life has its roots in the yawning chasm between the stated rules of the game—enforced either whimsically or not at all—and the eye gouging and kneecapping that goes on. As Stewart observed, "In more competitive ecosystems, the most desirable trait is the talent for appearing cooperative even while obliterating one's fellows."[11]

The key word is "appearing." In promotions and firings, no matter how heavily real virtues—talent, drive, honesty, decency—sit upon the scales, they rarely outweigh the featherweight pronouncement "not a team player"—at least not while the thumb of deceit tips the scales.

PYRAMID LAWS

Stewart sets down the fundamental, gravity-defying law of pyramids: "the money always flows uphill."[12] Stewart estimated that he and the other consultants who enticed clients, made the pitches and presentations, and closed the deals generated 80 percent of his firm's revenues. All the while, the hierarchy of partners who called the shots got very, very rich. Naturally, the game is to make partner. But the opportunity to do so "typically arises only after eight or so years of youth-destroying labor."[13]

This observation about "youth-destroying labor" corroborates the truth about human pyramids noted by Rudyard Kipling. In the short story "The Education of Otis Yeere" (1895), Kipling examines one of those numberless expendable individuals (stationed in India) whose blood oiled the highly regimented global apparatus called the British Empire:

Fortune had ruled that Otis Yeere should be, for the first part of his service, one of the rank and file who are ground up in the wheels of the Administration;

losing heart and soul, and mind and strength, in the process. Until steam replaces manual power in the working of the Empire, there must always be this percentage—must always be the men who are used up, expended, in the mere mechanical routine. For these promotion is far off and the mill-grind of every day very instant. . . . They are simply the rank and file—the food for fever—sharing with the *ryot* [peasant] and the plough-bullock the honour of being the plinth on which the State rests. The older ones have lost their aspirations; the younger are putting theirs aside with a sigh. Both learn to endure patiently until the end of the day. Twelve years in the rank and file, men say, will sap the hearts of the bravest and dull the wits of the most keen.[14]

Any type of routine, whether riveting a bolt or punching data, saps vitality, creativity, initiative. However, starting at the bottom is presented as equitable and necessary. Great firms all have their stories and legends about how their founders and leaders started as mail clerks. Rags-to-riches stories are one of the great myths of American business—even though such an ascent is less likely than being bitten by a shark. The myths also leave out the maladaptive behavior of those they mythologize, such as mad ambition and ruthlessness. In glorifying the usual virtues and trials as a necessary passage, such you-too-can-make-it myths quell restlessness while the firm wrings dry the talent and enthusiasm from fresh, eager faces. But it doesn't take long for people to figure out that favoritism—who you lunch and play golf with—counts more than skill in choice assignments and promotions. After a time or two around the block, it dawns on the truly talented and ambitious that they're equal if not superior to those who order them about.

This explains why consulting firms and the like, relatively "flat" hierarchies that thrive on *chutzpah*, are constantly spawning spin-offs. Thus Stewart and a group of his peers schemed to secede and start their own firm, stars and dollar signs dancing in their eyes. They decreed hierarchies the source of all evil in the corporate world and planned their new office to be as nonpyramidic as possible: all would be equal partners, endowed with the unalienable "right to pursue profits without having to fill out bullshit reports and show up at pointless staff meetings."[15] One of the rebels even wrote a manifesto. It likened life in an office hierarchy to being imprisoned with a pack of rats and a mountain of cheese. Oblivious to all else, the rats put in their time and climb; two years at the bottom level, two years at the next, and so forth. All the while, in their never-ending quest for "face-time"—that crude-sounding *sine qua non* of getting ahead—they practice servile flattery and wade through all the excrement that tumbles down from the rungs above. "You keep going up until one of the other rats bites your ass off."[16]

Epilogue

THE RISE OF BUSINESS CULTURE

Office life is business culture made visible. Whether the product is hot dogs or collateralized debt obligations, business is all about profiting. Why and how and to whom goods and services are developed, manufactured, and sold is the substance of business culture. Business culture shapes outer and inner office life. Business culture, of course, isn't walled off from the rest of society; each sphere is influenced by and influences the other.

The big corporations, the trusts and conglomerations, have been antagonistic to democratic government throughout American history. In its most primitive, lawless state, big business has proven destructive, for it is used as an instrument of conquest by the few against the many. The regression of modern business into primitivism is not a new impulse but rather the "equilibrium" business has always striven for. This is evidenced in the striking parallels between the Gilded Age and present-day America: different rhetoric, same old scam.

Since the nineteenth century, prominent journalists, public servants, and intellectuals have warned that unregulated business is a savage force that must be held in check. Henry Adams and James A. Garfield, Grover Cleveland, and Harold J. Laski represent three different eras that span 1870 to 1930. Yet each luminary is cautionary in the same way: the narrow-minded propensity to profit by any means harms the nation and is inimical to democracy.

Henry Adams, scion of the presidential family (his great-grandfather and grandfather), wrote political journalism during the Gilded Age. Adams saw the rise of corporations as a "bad omen for democracy." Not unrelated to this was Jay Gould's scheme to manipulate the price of gold during the summer of 1869. Gould wanted to profit from the spread between the price of gold, which was used for international trade, and greenbacks, which were used for domestic trade. (One hundred dollars in gold could purchase anywhere from $135 to $285 in greenbacks—their high during the Civil War.) When gold rose, American commodity prices, such as that of wheat, fell on the world market, spurring sales, and American farmers and the railroads that ferried their crops both prospered. In the summer of 1869, Jay Gould started buying enormous quantities of gold through different brokers to drive up its price. Gould's scheming resulted in Black Friday (September 24, 1870), during which the price of gold plunged from $160 to $138 in moments, setting off panic. Scores of margin traders got burnt. "Fortunes evaporated in minutes; broker-ages failed by the score. The tumult in the gold market spread across the street to the stock market, claiming thousands of victims who had never been tempted by currency speculation." There was such a mess and confusion in record keeping that even Jay Gould "didn't know for months whether he came out ahead or behind in the whole affair."[1] In an article for London's *Westminster Review* titled "The New York Gold Conspiracy," Adams wrote that for the first time since the inception of giant corporations, one of them "has shown its power for mischief, and has proved itself able to override and trample on law, customer, decency, and every restraint known to society, without scruple, and as yet without check." Adams wrote that fear rippled throughout the country that one day corporations far greater than the Erie Railroad, placed in "the hands of mere private citizens," would hold power unprec-edented in world history. And that "single men like Vanderbilt, or by combinations of men like Fisk, Gould, and Lane [Frederick Lane, coun-sel to Fisk and Gould on the Erie]," will have "created a system of quiet but irresistible corruption" that "will ultimately succeed in directing government itself. Under the American form of society, there is now no authority capable of effective resistance."[2]

The Erie Railroad, from its fares to its stock, had been brazenly manip-ulated first by Cornelius Vanderbilt and in turn by his adversaries, the unholy alliance of Daniel Drew, James Fisk Jr., and Jay Gould. Gould, for example, had watered Erie stock, then shorted it, and all parties openly bribed New York state legislators.

Adams correctly insisted that no existing authority had the power to check the giant corporations and trusts. Nonetheless, the U.S.

Congressional Committee on Banking and Currency, toothless in all but rhetoric, investigated the causes of the Gold Panic. Congressman James A. Garfield (Republican, Ohio) wrote the majority report: what Gould and Fisk almost pulled off "is not an unworthy copy of the great conspiracy to lay Rome in ashes and deluge its streets in blood, for the purpose of those who were to apply the torch and wield the dagger." And furthermore,

So long as we have two standards of value recognized by law, which may be made to vary in respect to each other by artificial means, so long will speculation in the price of gold offer temptations too great to be resisted, and so long may capital continue to be diverted from enterprises which add to the national wealth, and be used in this reckless gambling which ruins the great majority of those who engage in it, and endangers the business of the whole country.[3]

THE AMERICAN CHARACTER IN PERIL

Grover Cleveland, the only president to serve two nonconsecutive terms (1885–1889 and 1893–1897), led the Democratic Party's probusiness wing. He was a fiscal conservative who opposed high tariffs and took the railroad's side during the Pullman strike of 1894. Antibusiness he was not. In 1905, Cleveland wrote an article for *Harper's Monthly Magazine* titled "The Integrity of American Character." Cleveland worried that Americans were beginning to mold themselves around the more reckless business values—a sure sign of impending decadence:

In business and social circles the pursuit of money has become heartless and rapacious; the deference to those who have won great fortunes has grown in many quarters to be so unquestioning and so obsequious as to amount to scandalous servility . . . In politics there is far too often concealed behind a pretence of devotion to the public weal the sly promotion of disreputably selfish and personal advantages . . .[4]

Cleveland does not begrudge wealth. But he condemns those who grovel before wealth, and its acquisition by such ignoble means as buying off politicians. Politicians who filch public funds or lend themselves to the "pilfering schemes of others" belong behind "prison bars" and deserve the "irredeemable disgrace" of justice-loving, honest Americans. Cleveland singled out the scandal-ridden life insurance industry as exemplifying the worst business practices: it engaged in "overt acts of wrong-doing" and was astonishingly heedless in disregarding its "duties of trusteeship."

Cleveland viewed the public censure of "tainted money" as a vital sign of the American character's health. But if the American character was to remain stout, it must express its righteous indignation in political action. However, "Thousands in the mad pursuit of riches see no profitable relationship between good government and their intents and designs." And even worse, too many citizens "superciliously regard politics as an unclean thing." There is still time to save our "institutions," said Cleveland. But that time will pass if the American character's "moral fibre is . . . further weakened by the creeping corrosion of greed or wicked neglect." Therefore, the American people must be forever watchful and "in all things patriotic."[5]

CIVILIZING BUSINESS?

In the immediate aftermath of the stock market crash of 1929, the British historian Harold J. Laski wrote a piece for *Harper's Monthly Magazine* titled "Can Business Be Civilized?" Laski, who had lectured at Harvard, Yale, and the London School of Economics, pointed out that the recent prominence and influence of the "business man" was a new social development:

Until the nineteenth century there is hardly a period in which the business man defines in any significant way the character of his time. We know, of course, that he was there, but he was an anonymous presence. We did not build our character, our hopes, our institutions upon the things he held as necessary or desirable.

The "evils" Laski fingered in 1930 are today's norms. The business chieftain operates with the unchecked autonomy to fire employees at will, issue stock at will, "appoint fellow-directors without regard to competence," and "issue balance sheets from which no real insight into his business can be obtained." Consequently, immense wealth accrues to those whose pursuits are "unrelated to true service."[6] Business standards have become social standards. Thus those who accumulate the most, regardless of character, are assured of "social idolatry in the measure of their wealth."[7] Businessmen have elbowed artists, philosophers, statesmen, and the like off of center stage, thus completing their "control over the process of civilization. They can buy courts and legislatures, make war and peace . . . " In fact, certain business moguls are as powerful as sovereign states: "Mr. [J. P.] Morgan and his partners, the Governor and Company of the Bank of England, Standard Oil . . . "[8]

Business has become a faith, a religion blanketing the globe. Its principal tenet is that making money without regard to public well-being or how it is made is the most desirable end. Business people have propagated the idea that the more intensely, the more efficiently money is pursued, the better for society. Thus, business has demanded that all barriers, all limitations, all laws that hinder ever higher profits be eradicated.

Today, this old snake oil is peddled as "deregulation." What used to pass for insider trading is now "legal" or simply overlooked, unless, of course, the transgression involves really big money—forty grand—and someone truly dangerous—Martha Stewart.

A FINAL WORD ABOUT POP CULTURE

Pop culture continues to command more and more scholarly respect. But, compared to "real" history books, history told through popular and everyday culture is just slag. It lacks validity because it's fictive, fun, or appears in mass-circulation newspapers and magazines or best-selling books. But paradoxically, many excellent history books use everyday culture—newspapers, letters, and the like—as primary source material. Nor is method-laden historiography necessarily any truer than "unschooled" unsanctioned accounts, especially when professional historians impute motives to persons long dead or lace their accounts with fictional dialogues.

This is not meant as an attack on historians or their books, which I have cited admiringly throughout this book. However, a recent book review argues that pop culture is the most influential force in shaping attitudes and is primary to people's comprehension of the social world. In his review of Steve F. Anderson's *Technologies of History*, Peter Monaghan cites an interview given by the author: "It is very likely not the book by the Harvard historian that 300 people in the world read that gives us a historical sensibility and becomes part of how we behave in the world. . . . It's *The X-Files.*"[9] Anderson argues that everyday people—fans, geeks, teenagers, and others—who don't view themselves as creators of historical discourse do just that. They make the past their own by remixing, reimagining, and retelling it in highly individualistic and compelling ways. Monaghan makes the excellent point that "academic history has not yet developed ways to handle the kinds of approaches to history-telling found in many media forms. Whether or not academically credentialed historians like it, they are far from the only ones telling history and defining how it can be conveyed."[10]

Much earlier, Ray B. Browne (1922–2009) propagated a similar argument. Browne, a specialist in literature and folklore, muscled pop culture into academia by beginning to offer courses in popular culture at Bowling Green University in 1967; and in 1972, he founded the first Department of Popular Culture. Browne once said he wished he'd called the discipline something more serious sounding—perhaps "everyday culture." The term "pop," of course, was and is an instant turn-off to some.

Browne called popular culture "democracy speaking and acting," and

the seedbed in which democracy grows. It is the everyday world around us: the mass media, entertainments and diversions. It is our heroes, icons, rituals, everyday actions, psychology and religion—our total life picture. It is the way of living we inherit, practice and modify as we please. It is the dreams we dream while we sleep.[11]

I have shown how pop culture transmits and preserves the values and ideas (such as rugged individualism) that create—or once created—a sense of national identity. Just as the expansion west produced archetypical American characters based on frontier prowess, industrial and financial expansion in the east produced archetypes who battled in boardrooms and legislative chambers. The propagation of business values reshaped the American character; hence, the centrality of office life. Transcending physical location, "the office" is an outcropping of business culture or the culture of acquisition—the dominant ideology of our day.

Notes

CHAPTER 1

1. *Wall Street*, DVD. Directed by Oliver Stone. 20th Century Fox Film Corporation, Chameleons at Work, 1987.

2. *Always Tomorrow*, Film. 1941, Always Tomorrow: Free Download & Streaming: Internet Archive. Internet Archive: Digital Library of Free Books, Movies, Music & Wayback Machine, accessed October 8, 2011, http://www.archive.org/details/always_tomorrow.

3. Ibid.

4. *The Jetsons*, DVD. The Complete First Season, Disc 1, Episode 1, "Rosie the Robot." Story by Larry Markes, Teleplay by Tony Benedict. Produced and directed by William Hanna and Joseph Barbera. Hanna-Barbera Productions, 2004. (Originally broadcast Sept. 23, 1962.)

5. *Bewitched*, DVD, Season 1, Disc 1, Episode 7, "The Witches Are Out." Story by Bernard Slade, directed by William Asher, Sony Pictures Home Entertainment, 2005. (Originally broadcast October 29, 1964.)

6. "Extortion," *This is Your FBI*, ABC Radio. Original broadcast, August 3, 1945.

7. "Night School," *The Life of Riley*, ABC Radio. Original broadcast December 10, 1944.

8. Gordon Childe, *Man Makes Himself* (New York: New American Library, 1951), 149.

9. Ibid.

10. Dale Carnegie, *How to Stop Worrying and Start Living* (New York: Simon and Schuster, 1948), 201.

11. Tracee Hamilton, "A Minicamp Becomes a Major Issue Between Mike Shanahan and Albert Haynesworth." *Washington Post*, sec. D1, April 11, 2010.

12. Ernest Hemingway, "Big Two-Hearted River: Part 1," *The Complete Short Stories* (New York: Scribner, 2003), 164.

13. Tennessee Williams, "Sweet Bird of Youth," in *Plays 1957–1980* (New York: The Library of America, 2000), 214.

14. Walter Kirn, *Up in the Air* (New York: Anchor Books, 2002), 222.

15. Kirn, 43.

16. Kirn, 221–22.

17. I wish to thank Frithjof Bergmann, my philosophy professor at the University of Michigan, for suggesting this interpretation.

CHAPTER 2

1. "Preservation Basics," National Firm Preservation Foundation, accessed September 30, 2011 http://www.filmpreservation.org/preservation-basics.html.

2. Lawrence W. Levine, *Highbrow/Lowbrow: The Emergence of Cultural Hierarchy in America* (Cambridge, MA: Harvard University Press, 1988), 221.

3. Ibid., 223.

4. Ibid., 202.

5. Ibid., 203.

6. Ibid.

7. Ibid., 239.

8. Ibid., pp. 236–37

9. Ibid., 224.

10. Ibid., 18–19.

11. Ibid., 88.

12. Stuart Ewen's *PR! A Social History of Spin* (New York: Basic Books, 1996) offers a wonderfully detailed account of the CPI.

13. Aravind Adiga, *The White Tiger* (New York: Free Press, 2008), 8.

14. Ibid., 33.

15. John Durham Peters and Peter Simonson, eds., *Mass Communication and American Social Thought: Key Texts 1919–1968* (Lanham, MD: Rowman & Littlefield Publishers, Inc., 2004), 471.

16. Ibid., 467.

CHAPTER 3

1. Charles Dickens, *The Pickwick Papers* (New York: Heritage Press, 1938), 274.

2. Ibid., 413.

3. Ibid., 415.

4. Ibid., 417.

5. Ibid., 419.

6. Ibid., 263.

7. Ibid., 265.

8. Ibid., 261.

9. Ibid., 406.

10. Herman Melville, *Bartleby the Scrivener: A Story of Wall Street* (New York: Simon & Schuster, 1997), xi.

11. Ibid., xviii.

12. Ibid., 20.

13. Ibid., 25.

14. Fred Kaplan, *Lincoln: The Biography of a Writer* (New York: Harper, 2008), 146.

15. Mark Twain, "The Office Bore," in *Sketches: New and Old* (New York: Harper Brothers, 1917), 119.

16. Rudyard Kipling, *Collected Stories* (London: David Campbell Publishers Ltd., 1994), 27.

17. Ibid., 28.

18. Ibid., 29.

19. Ibid., 30.

20. Kipling, 31.

21. Tom Peters, *The Little Big Things: 163 Ways to Pursue Excellence* (New York: Harper Studio, 2010), 77–87.

22. O. Henry, "The Romance of a Busy Broker," in *The Worker and His Work*, ed. Stella Stewart Center (Philadelphia: J.B. Lippincott, 1920), 77–80.

23. Ibid.

24. Ibid.

25. Carl Sandburg, "Skyscraper," in *Chicago Poems* (Mineola, NY: Dover Publications, Inc., 1994), 29–32.

26. Ibid.

27. Ibid.

28. Arnold Bennett, "The American Telephone," in *The Worker and His Work*, ed. Stella Stewart Center (Philadelphia: J. B. Lippincott, 1920), 49.

29. Ibid.

30. Ibid.

31. Ibid.

32. Willa Cather, "Ardessa," *The Century Illustrated Monthly Magazine* 96 (May 1918): 105–116.

33. Ibid., 105.

34. Ibid., 106.

35. Ibid., 110.

36. Elizabeth Sears, "Business Women and Women in Business," *Harper's Monthly Magazine* (January 1917): 274–280.

37. *Success: A Magazine for Future Executives—Both Young Men and Young Women.* Battle Creek: Michigan Business & Normal College, March, vol. IV, no. 2 (1922).

38. Ibid., 2.

39. Ibid., 3.

40. Ibid., 4.

41. Ibid., 6.

42. Ibid., 9–10.

43. Ibid., 19.

44. Edna Ferber, "Fanny Herself," in *The Worker and His Work*, ed. Stella Stewart Center (Philadelphia: J. B. Lippincott, 1920), 64–77.

45. Ibid., 67.

46. Ibid., 70–71.

CHAPTER 4

1. Rick Prelinger, "Eccentricity, Education and the Evolution of Corporate Speech," in *Films that Work: Industrial Film and Productivity of Media*, ed. Vinzenz Hediger and Patrick Vonderau (Amsterdam: Amsterdam University Press, 2009), 211–220.

2. Patrick Vonderau, "Vernacular Archiving: an Interview with Rick Prelinger," in *Films that Work: Industrial Film and Productivity of Media*, ed. Vinzenz Hediger and Patrick Vonderau (Amsterdam: Amsterdam University Press, 2009), 51–61.

3. Ibid., 60.

4. Ibid., 213.

5. "Profile: Jamison Handy (Part I): WWJ-TV (Detroit): Free Download & Streaming: Internet Archive," Internet Archive: Digital Library of Free Books, Movies, Music & Wayback Machine, accessed September 30, 2011, http://www.archive.org/details/ProfileJ26.

6. Patrick Vonderau, "Vernacular Archiving: an Interview with Rick Prelinger," in *Films that Work: Industrial Film and Productivity of Media*, ed. Vinzenz Hediger and Patrick Vonderau (Amsterdam: Amsterdam University Press, 2009), 213.

7. "Profile: Jamison Handy," accessed October 9, 2011, http://www.archive.org/details/ProfileJ26.

8. "Open Door: The Story of Foreman Jim Baxter and His Family, The (Part I): Handy (Jam) Organization: Free Download & Streaming: Internet Archive," Internet Archive: Digital Library of Free Books, Movies, Music & Wayback Machine, accessed September 30, 2011, http://www.archive.org/details/OpenDoor1945; "Open Door: The Story of Foreman Jim Baxter and His Family" accessed September 30, 2011, http://www.archive.org/details/OpenDoor1945_2.

9. "Success in Business: Unknown: Free Download & Streaming: Internet Archive," Internet Archive: Digital Library of Free Books, Movies, Music & Wayback Machine, accessed September 30, 2011, http://www.archive.org/details/Successi1928.

10. "Office Etiquette: Encyclopaedia Britannica Films: Free Download & Streaming: Internet Archive," Internet Archive: Digital Library of Free Books, Movies, Music & Wayback Machine, accessed September 30, 2011, http://www.archive.org/details/OfficeEt1950.

11. "The Bright Young Newcomer: Calvin Productions: Free Download & Streaming: Internet Archive," Internet Archive: Digital Library of Free Books, Movies, Music & Wayback Machine, accessed September 30, 2011, http://www.archive.org/details/BrightYo1958.

CHAPTER 5

1. William H. Whyte Jr., *The Organization Man* (Garden City, NY: Anchor Books, 1957).

2. Stephen Rhodes, "At the Top of His Game," in *Wall Street Noir*, ed. Peter Spiegelman (New York: Akashic Books, 2007), 34.

3. Ibid., 270

4. Ibid., 271.

5. Ibid., 272.

6. Ibid., 183.

7. Ibid., 185.

8. Ibid., 186.

9. Ibid., 11.

10. Ibid., 11.

11. Ibid., 14.

12. "Open Door: The Story of Foreman Jim Baxter and His Family, The (Part I): Handy (Jam) Organization: Free Download & Streaming: Internet Archive," Internet Archive: Digital Library of Free Books, Movies, Music & Wayback Machine, accessed September 30, 2011, http://www.archive.org/details/OpenDoor1945 and "Open Door: The Story of Foreman Jim Baxter and His Family, The (Part I): Handy (Jam) Organization: Free Download & Streaming: Internet Archive." Internet Archive: Digital Library of Free Books, Movies, Music & Wayback Machine, accessed September 30, 2011, http://www.archive.org/details/OpenDoor1945_2.

13. New Old Time Chautauqua, "History," accessed September 30, 2011, http://www.chautauqua.org/history.html.

14. Russell, H. Conwell, *Acres of Diamonds* (Westwood, NJ: Fleming H. Revell Company, 1960), 24.

15. Ibid., 14.

16. Ibid.

17. Ibid., 22.

18. Ibid., 24.

19. Ibid., 24–25.

20. Ibid., 27.

21. Ibid., 30.

22. Ibid., 37.

23. Warren I. Susman, *Culture as History: The Transformation of American Society in the Twentieth Century* (New York: Pantheon Books, 1984), 123–26.

24. Bruce Barton, *The Man Nobody Knows* (New York: Collier Books, 1987), 68.

25. Ibid., vi.

26. Ibid.

27. Ibid., vii.

28. Susman, 130.

29. Ibid., 136.

30. John Arlidge, "I'm doing 'God's work'. Meet Mr Goldman Sachs—*Times Online*," *The Times* | UK News, World News and Opinion, accessed October 11, 2011, http://www.timesonline.co.uk/tol/news/world/us_and_americas/arti cle6907681.ece.

31. Goldman Sachs' pernicious influence on the nation has been thoroughly documented by *Rolling Stone*'s Matt Taibbi. Since the so-called "bailouts" of 2008, no journalist has done better reporting on the Wall Street debacle than Taibbi.

32. Ibid., 131.

33. Ibid.

34. Zig Ziglar, *Zig Ziglar's Secrets of Closing the Sale* (New York: Berkley Books, 1984), 116.

35. Ibid., 117–19.

36. Whyte, 125.

37. Ibid., 126.

38. Ibid.

39. Ibid. 126–27.

40. Ibid., 127.

41. Ibid.

42. Ibid., 128–29.

43. Ibid., 130–31.

44. Ibid.

45. Ibid., 132.

46. Harold, F. Willard, *Insurance Ripoffs and Dirty Tricks: The Sucker's Dilemma* (Kirkland, WA: Thumbsdown Books, 1987), 143.

47. Ibid., 144–45.

48. Ibid., 147.

49. Ibid., 149–50.

50. Ibid., 154.
51. Ibid., 155.
52. Wilson, 156.
53. Ibid., 162.
54. Baldwin stated this in a special-features interview for *Glengarry Glenn Ross* on DVD, 1992.
55. Ibid.

CHAPTER 6

1. *Executive Suite*, directed by Robert Wise (2007, Burbank, CA: MGM), DVD,
2. *Desk Set*, directed by Walter Lang (1957, Burbank, CA: Twentieth Century Fox), motion picture.
3. The film's credits thank IBM for its "cooperation."
4. Frederick W. Taylor, *The Principles of Scientific Management* (New York: Harper & Brothers), 1911.
5. Ibid., 6.
6. Ibid., 13.
7. Ibid.
8. Larry Markes, teleplay by Tony Benedict, "Rosie the Robot," *The Jetsons*, The Complete First Season, disc 1, episode 1, produced and directed by William Hanna and Joseph Barbera, originally broadcast Sept. 23, 1962 (2004, Hanna-Barbera Productions), DVD.
9. Chris Provenzano, "Hobo Code," *Mad Men*, season one, disc 3, episode 8, directed by Phil Abraham (2007, Lions Gate Television Inc.), DVD.
10. David Ogilvy, *Confessions of an Advertising Man* (New York: Athenaeum), 1988.
11. George Lois (with Bill Pitts), *What's the Big Idea?* (New York: Doubleday), 1991.
12. Bernard Slade, "The Witches Are Out," *Bewitched*, season 1, disc 1, episode 7, directed by William Asher, originally broadcast October 29, 1964 (2005, Sony Pictures Home Entertainment), DVD.

CHAPTER 7

1. *Glengarry Glen Ross*, directed by James Foley (2002, New Line Cinema), DVD.
2. Michael Lewis, *Liar's Poke*
3. Tom Wolfe, *The Bonfire of the Vanities* (New York: Farrar, Straus, Giroux, 1990), 58–59.

4. Ibid.

5. Stephen Rhodes, "At the Top of His Game," in *Wall Street Noir*, ed. Peter Spiegelman (New York: Akashic Books, 2007), 21–48.

6. Michael Lewis, *The Big Short* (New York: W.W. Norton & Co., 2010).

7. Ibid., xiv–vi.

8. Wolfe, 59.

9. Lewis, 104.

10. Ibid., 105.

11. Ibid., 68.

12. Ibid., 51.

13. Wolfe, 56–57.

14. Ibid.

15. Ibid., 61.

16. Ibid., 309.

17. Ibid., 12.

18. Lewis, 69.

19. Rhodes, 47.

20. Ibid.

21. Ibid., 48.

22. Lewis, 247–248.

23. Rhodes, 35.

24. Edwin Lefevre, "The Woman and Her Bonds," in *The Worker and His Work*, ed. Stella Stewart Center (Philadelphia: J.B. Lippincott, 1920), 81–95.

25. Lewis, 81.

26. *Wall Street*, Directed by Oliver Stone (1987, Twentieth Century Fox Film Corporation, Chameleons at Work), DVD.

27. Theodore Louis Trost, "The *Pan Am Quipper* as Site of Anxiety; or Negotiating Identity in an Era of Corporate Decline." Lecture, Popular Culture Association Conference, St. Louis, Missouri, April 2, 2010.

28. I wish to thank Professor Theodore Louis Trost of the University of Alabama for giving me 10 editions of the *Quipper*, including the first and last. Professor Trost worked as a flight attendant and purser for Pan Am for nine years, which included the *Quipper* era.

29. *Pan Am Quipper: Layoff Edition*. No. 3, Oct. '81, 2–3.

30. Ibid., 3.

31. Lewis, 216.

32. Matthew Stewart, *The Management Myth: Why the Experts Keep Getting It Wrong* (New York: W.W. Norton & Company, 2009), 27–38.

33. Walter Kirn, *Up in the Air* (New York: Anchor Books), 2002.

34. Ibid., 202.

35. Ibid.

36. Ibid., 205.

37. Ibid., 204–205.

38. *The Method (El Metodo)*, directed by Marcelo Piñeyro (2005, Los Angeles: Palm Pictures), DVD.

CHAPTER 8

1. Vodafone Limited, *Changing Faces: How We Adapt Our Identity at Work*, Corporate Sponsored Study, July 2006.

2. This reminds me of a very intelligent and prescient edict delivered by the chairman of AT&T, John D. deButts, while I worked there. He admonished those who practiced—and pressured others to do the same—that bizarre type of machismo expressed by staying in the office as late as possible. If you can't execute your daily responsibilities within seven-and-one-half hours, deButts said, then *you* are incompetent. Furthermore, working on weekends was foolish and unnecessary. He himself, deButts said, never worked on weekends. He golfed. One ironic piece of history. When the government ordered AT&T's breakup in 1984, Pacific Telephone became Pacific Bell, which became Pacific Telesis, which spun off AirTouch, which merged with Vodafone in 1999. Here's a cheap shot: 20 years after deButts's warning, Vodafone, with its surveys, in-depth interviews, industrial psychologists, and other "experts," in a 54-page booklet is essentially saying what deButts said from his gut in a few sentences. However, deButts never addressed phoniness head on, which the Vodafone study does.

3. Leon Gettler, *"Chameleons at work,"* Management Line (blog), The Age.com.au, July 18, 2006, accessed September 30, 2011, http://blogs.theage.com.au/executivestyle/managementline/2006/07/18/chameleonsatwork.html.

4. Henry Bingaman, *"The Freelance Copywriter's Mask,"* Home of Ascension Marketing Systems (blog), accessed March 19, 2009, http://www.henrybingaman.com/freelance-copywriters-mask.

5. Michael Lewis, *The Big Short* (New York: W.W. Norton & Co., 2010), 261.

6. Ibid., 235.

7. Ibid., 236.

8. Matthew Stewart, *The Management Myth: Why the Experts Keep Getting It Wrong* (New York: W.W. Norton & Company, 2009).

9. Ibid., 144.

10. Ibid., 146.

11. Ibid., 144.

12. Ibid., 124.

13. Ibid., 125.

14. Rudyard Kipling, "The Education of Otis Yeere," in *Collected Stories* (London: David Campbell Publishers Ltd., 1994), 19–20.

15. Stewart, 89.

16. Ibid.

EPILOGUE

1. H. W. Brands, *American Colossus: The Triumph of Capitalism 1865–1900* (New York: Doubleday, 2010), 36.

2. Henry Adams quoted in H. W. Brands, *American Colossus: The Triumph of Capitalism 1865–1900* (New York: Doubleday, 2010), 39.

3. Ibid., 37.

4. Grover Cleveland, "The Integrity of American Character," *Harper's Monthly Magazine*, December, 1905, 67.

5. Ibid., 70.

6. Harold J. Laski, "Can Business Be Civilized?" *Harper's Monthly Magazine*, January 1930, 173.

7. Ibid., 170.

8. Ibid., 170–71.

9. Steven F. Anderson, quoted in Peter Monaghan, "What do Rocky and Bullwinkle have to do with History?" Review of *Technologies of History: Visual Media and the Eccentricity of the Past*, by Steven F. Anderson, *Chronicle of Higher Education Chronicle Review*, April 22, 2011, B15.

10. Ibid.

11. "Conversation with Professor Ray B. Browne ‖ Americana: The Journal Of American Popular Culture 1900-Present." American Popular Culture. http://www.americanpopularculture.com/journal/articles/fall_2002/browne.htm (accessed January 22, 2012).

Bibliography

Abrams, Nathan. "From Madness to Dysentery: *Mad*'s Other New York Intellectuals." *Journal of American Studies* 37 (2003): 435–451.

Adams, Scott. *Dogbert's Top Secret Management Handbook*. New York: HarperBusiness, 1996.

Adams, Scott. *The Joy of Work: Dilbert's Guide to Finding Happiness at the Expense of Your Co-Workers*. New York: HarperBusiness, 1998.

Adiga, Aravind. *The White Tiger*. New York: Free Press, 2008.

Aikman, Duncan. "The New Decadents: Babbitt Starts To Reform." *Harper's Monthly Magazine* September (1926): 449–456.

Always Tomorrow. Film. 1941, *Always Tomorrow*: Free Download & Streaming: Internet Archive. Internet Archive: Digital Library of Free Books, Movies, Music & Wayback Machine, accessed October 8, 2011, http://www.archive.org/details/always_tomorrow.

Anonymous. "Is Big Business A Career?" *Harper's Monthly Magazine* January (1926): 211–218.

Arlidge, John. "I'm doing 'God's work'. Meet Mr Goldman Sachs—*Times Online*." *The Times* | UK News, World News and Opinion, accessed October 11, 2011, http://www.timesonline.co.uk/tol/news/world/us_and_americas/article6907681.ece.

Austen, Ben. "End of the Road." *Harper's Magazine* August (2009): 26–26.

Barton, Bruce. *The Man Nobody Knows*. New York: Collier Books, 1987.

Bennett, Arnold. "The American Telephone." In *The Worker and His Work*, edited by Stella Stewart Center, 46–49. Philadelphia: J.B. Lippincott, 1920.

Bewitched, DVD. Season 1, Disc 1, Episode 7, "The Witches Are Out." Story by Bernard Slade, directed by William Asher, Sony Pictures Home Entertainment, 2005. (Originally broadcast October 29, 1964.)

Bing, Stanley. *Throwing the Elephant: Zen and the Art of Managing Up*. New York: HarperBusiness, 2002.

Bingaman, Henry. *The Freelance Copywriter's Mask*. Home of Ascension Marketing Systems (blog), accessed March 19, 2009, http://www.henrybingaman .com/freelance-copywriters-mask.

Brands H. W. *American Colossus: The Triumph of Capitalism 1865–1900*. New York: Doubleday, 2010.

The Bright Young Newcomer. Calvin Productions. Internet Archive: Digital Library of Free Books, Movies, Music & Wayback Machine, accessed September 30, 2011, http://www.archive.org/details/BrightYo1958.

Carnegie, Dale. *How to Stop Worrying and Start Living*. New York: Simon and Schuster, 1948.

Cather, Willa. "Ardessa." *The Century Illustrated Monthly Magazine* 96 (May 1918): 105–116.

Cavaiola, Alan A. and Neil J. Lavender. *Toxic Coworkers: How to Deal with Dysfunctional People on the Job*. Oakland, CA: New Harbinger Publications, Inc., 2000.

Chase, Stuart. "The Luxury of Integrity." *Harper's Magazine* August (1930): 336–344.

Childe V. Gordon. *Man Makes Himself*. New York: New American Library, 1951.

Cleveland, Grover. "The Integrity of American Character." *Harper's Monthly Magazine* December (1905): 67–70.

Collins, Jim. *Good to Great*. New York: HarperCollins, 2001.

"Conversation with Professor Ray B. Browne || Americana: The Journal Of American Popular Culture 1900-Present." American Popular Culture. http://www .americanpopularculture.com/journal/articles/fall_2002/browne.htm (accessed January 22, 2012).

Conwell, Russell H. *Acres of Diamonds*. Westwood, New Jersey: Fleming H. Revell Company, 1960.

Cooke, Alistair. "Frank Lloyd Wright." In *Memories of the Great and the Good*. Thorndike, ME: Thorndike Press, 2000.

de Botton, Alain. *The Pleasures and Sorrows of Work*. New York: Pantheon Books, 2009.

Desk Set. Directed by Walter Lang. Twentieth Century Fox, 1957.

Dickens, Charles. *The Pickwick Papers*. New York: Heritage Press. 1938.

Drew, John M. L. *Dickens the Journalist*. New York: Palgrave Macmillan, 2003.

Epstein, Joseph. "The Virtues of Ambition." *Harper's Magazine* October (1980): 41–56.

Executive Suite. DVD. Directed by Robert Wise. MGM, 2007.

"Extortion." *This is Your FBI*. ABC Radio. Original broadcast, August 3, 1945.

Ferber, Edna. "Fanny Herself." In *The Worker and His Work*, edited by Stella Stewart Center, 64–77. Philadelphia: J.B. Lippincott, 1920.

Ferber, Edna, "The Man Within Him." In *The Worker and His Work*, edited by Stella Stewart Center, 108–123. Philadelphia: J.B. Lippincott, 1920.

Gettler, Leon. *Chameleons at work.* Management Line (blog), The Age.com.au, July 18, 2006, accessed September 30, 2011, http://blogs.theage.com.au/executive-style/managementline/2006/07/18/chameleonsatwork.html.

Glengarry Glen Ross. DVD. Directed by James Foley. New Line Cinema, 2002.

Hamilton, Tracee. "A minicamp becomes a major issue between Mike Shanahan and Albert Haynesworth." *Washington Post*, April 11, 2010, page D1.

Hediger, Vinzenz and Vonderau, Patrick (Eds.). *Films that Work: Industrial Film and Productivity of Media.* Amsterdam: Amsterdam University Press, 2009.

Hemingway, Ernest. "The Battler." In *The Complete Short Stories*. New York: Scribner, 2003.

Hemingway, Ernest. "Big Two-Hearted River: Part 1." In *The Complete Short Stories*. New York: Scribner, 2003.

Henry O. "The Romance of a Busy Broker." In *The Worker and His Work*, edited by Stella Stewart Center, 77–80. Philadelphia: J.B. Lippincott, 1920.

Herold, Robert. "Leaking Laissez Faire." *The Pacific Northwest Inlander* May 20 (2010): 6.

Internet Archive: Digital Library of Free Books, Movies, Music & Wayback Machine, accessed September 30, 2011, http://www.archive.org/.

The Jetsons. DVD. The Complete First Season, Disc 1, Episode 1, "Rosie the Robot." Story by Larry Markes, Teleplay by Tony Benedict. Produced and directed by William Hanna and Joseph Barbera. Hanna-Barbera Productions, 2004. (Originally broadcast Sept. 23, 1962.)

Kaplan, Fred. *Lincoln: The Biography of a Writer.* New York: Harper, 2008.

Kelly, Kate. *Street Fighters: The Last 72 Hours of Bear Stearns, the Toughest Firm on Wall Street.* New York: Portfolio, 2009.

Kipling, Rudyard. "A Bank Fraud." In *Collected Stories*. London: David Campbell Publishers Ltd., 1994.

Kipling, Rudyard. *Collected Stories*. London: David Campbell Publishers Ltd., 1994.

Kipling, Rudyard. "The Education of Otis Yeere." In *Collected Stories*. London: David Campbell Publishers Ltd., 1994.

Kirn, Walter. *Up in the Air*. New York: Anchor Books, 2002.

Lapham, Lewis H. "Notebook: Compass bearings." *Harper's Magazine* September (2002): 9–11.

Lapham, Lewis, H. "Notebook: Elephant Act." *Harper's Magazine* August (1998): 7–10.

Laski, Harold J. "Can Business Be Civilized?" *Harper's Monthly Magazine* January (1930): 170–179.

Leach, William. *Land of Desire: Merchants, Power, and the Rise of a New American Culture.* New York: Vintage Books, 1994.

LeFevre, Edwin. "A Woman and Her Bonds." In *The Worker and His Work*, edited by Stella Stewart Center, 81–95. Philadelphia: J.B. Lippincott, 1920.

Levine, Lawrence W. *Highbrow/Lowbrow: The Emergence of Cultural Hierarchy in America.* Cambridge, MA: Harvard University Press, 1988.

Lewis, Michael. *The Big Short.* New York: W.W. Norton & Co., 2010.

Lewis, Michael. *Liar's Poker.* New York: Penguin Books, 1990.

Lois, George (with Bill Pitts). *What's the Big Idea?* New York: Doubleday, 1991.

Mad Men, DVD. Season One, Disc 3, Episode 8, "Hobo Code." Directed by Phil Abraham, written by Chris Provenzano. Lions Gate Television Inc., 2007.

Mad Men, DVD. Season Three, Disc 1, Episode 1, "Out of Town." Directed by Phil Abraham, written by Matthew Weiner. Lions Gate Television Inc., 2009.

The Man in the Gray Flannel Suit. DVD. Directed by Nunnally Johnson. Twentieth Century Fox Home Entertainment, LLC, 2005.

Melville, Herman. *Bartleby the Scrivener: A Story of Wall Street.* New York, NY: Simon & Schuster, 1997.

Melville, Herman. *The Complete Shorter Fiction.* London: David Campbell Publishers, Ltd., 1997.

The Method (El Metodo). DVD. Directed by Marcelo Piñeyro. Los Angeles: Palm Pictures, 2005.

Monaghan, Peter, "What do Rocky and Bullwinkle have to do with History?" Review of *Technologies of History: Visual Media and the Eccentricity of the Past*, by Steven F. Anderson, *Chronicle of Higher Education Chronicle Review*, April 22, 2011.

Murphy, John Allen. "Can the Small Business Man Survive?" *Harper's Magazine* June (1937): 1–7.

Nader, Ralph. *Only the Super-Rich Can Save Us!* New York: Seven Stories Press, 2009.

National Film Preservation Foundation. "Why Preserve Film?" 2011. http://www .filmpreservation.org/preservation-basics.

New Old Time Chautauqua. "History," 2011. http://www.chautauqua.org/ history.html.

"Night School." *The Life of Riley.* ABC Radio. Original broadcast December 10, 1944.

Office Etiquette. Encyclopaedia Britannica Films. Internet Archive: Digital Library of Free Books, Movies, Music & Wayback Machine, accessed September 30, 2011, http://www.archive.org/details/OfficeEt1950.

Ogilvy, David. *Confessions of an Advertising Man.* New York: Athenaeum, 1988.

Open Door: The Story of Foreman Jim Baxter and His Family (Part 1): Handy (Jam) Organization: Free Download & Streaming: Internet Archive. Internet Archive: Digital Library of Free Books, Movies, Music & Wayback Machine, accessed September 30, 2011, http://www.archive.org/details/ OpenDoor1945_2.

O'Toole, Caitlin. "Upbeat office culture fake and creepy, says Alain de Botton." www.news.com.au, April 23, 2009.

Outsourced. DVD. Directed by John Jeffcoat. Shadowcatcher Entertainment, LLC, 2006.

Peters, John Durham and Peter Simonson (Eds.). *Mass Communication and American Social Thought: Key Texts 1919–1968*. Lanham, MD: Rowman & Littlefield Publishers, Inc., 2004.

Peters, Tom. *The Little Big Things: 163 Ways to Pursue Excellence*. New York: HarperStudio, 2010.

Prelinger Archives, Internet Archive: Digital Library of Free Books, Movies, Music & Wayback Machine, accessed September 30, 2011, http://www .archive.org/details/prelinger.

"Profile: Jamison Handy (Part I): WWJ-TV (Detroit): Free Download & Streaming: Internet Archive." Internet Archive: Digital Library of Free Books, Movies, Music & Wayback Machine, accessed October 9, 2011, http:// www.archive.org/details/ProfileJ26.

Rhodes, Stephen. "At the Top of His Game." In *Wall Street Noir*, edited by Peter Spiegelman, 21–48. New York: Akashic Books, 2007.

Rich, Frank. "Goldman Can Spare You a Dime." *New York Times*, October 18, 2009, WK8, New York edition.

Rogers, Agnes. "Is It Anyone We Know?" *Harper's Magazine* June (1946): 496–501.

Salesman. DVD. Directed by David Maysles, Albert Maysles, Charlotte Zwerin. The Criterion Collection, 2001.

Sandburg, Carl. "Skyscraper." In *Chicago Poems*. Mineola, NY: Dover Publications, Inc., 1994.

Schlicke, Paul. *Dickens and Popular Entertainment*. London: Allen & Unwin, 1985.

Schudson, Michael. *Discovering the News: A Social History of American Newspapers*. USA: Basic Books, 1978.

Sears, Elizabeth. "Business Women and Women in Business." *Harpers Monthly Magazine* January (1917): 274–280.

Servin, Jaques and Igor Vamos. "Congress Went After ACORN. Big Business Must Be Next." *Washington Post*, September 27, 2009, Outlook section.

Snow, C. P. *Variety of Men*. New York: Charles Scribner's Sons, 1967.

Sondheim, Stephen. *Finishing the Hat: Collected Lyrics (1954–1981) with Attendant Comments, Principles, Heresies, Grudges, Whines and Anecdotes*. New York: Alfred A. Knopf, 2010.

Stewart, Matthew. *The Management Myth: Why the Experts Keep Getting It Wrong*. New York: W.W. Norton & Company, 2009.

Stiles T. J. *The First Tycoon: The Epic Life of Cornelius Vanderbilt*. New York: Vintage Books, 2010.

Success: A Magazine for Future Executives—Both Young Men and Young Women. Battle Creek: Michigan Business & Normal College, March, 1922, Vol. IV, No. 2.

Success in Business. Unknown. Internet Archive: Digital Library of Free Books, Movies, Music & Wayback Machine, accessed September 30, 2011, http://www.archive.org/details/Successi1928.

Susman, Warren, I. *Culture as History: The Transformation of American Society in the Twentieth Century.* New York: Pantheon Books, 1984.

Taibbi, Matt. "Sick and Wrong." *Rolling Stone* 3 September (2009): 58–65.

Taibbi, Matt. "Wall Street's Naked Swindle." *Rolling Stone* 15 October (2009): 50–59.

Taylor, Frederick W. *The Principles of Scientific Management.* New York: Harper & Brothers, 1911.

Terrace, Vincent. *The Complete Encyclopedia of Television Programs 1947–1979, Volume 1, A–L.* Cranbury, NJ: A.S. Barnes and Co., Inc., 1979.

Thorndike, Edward, L. "The Psychology of the Profit Motive." *Harper's Magazine* September (1936): 431–437.

Townsend, Robert. "Up the Organization." *Harper's Magazine* March (1970): 73–90.

Trost, Theodore Louis. "The *Pan Am Quipper* as Site of Anxiety; or Negotiating Identity in an Era of Corporate Decline." Lecture, Popular Culture Association Conference, St. Louis, Missouri, April 2, 2010.

Twain, Mark. *Life on the Mississippi.* New York: Quality Paperback Book Club, 1993.

Twain, Mark. "The Office Bore." In *Sketches: New and Old,* 117–119. New York: Harper Brothers, 1917.

Vodafone Limited. *Changing Faces: How We Adapt Our Identity at Work.* Corporate Sponsored Study, July 2006.

Vonderau, Patrick. "Vernacular Archiving: An Interview with Rick Prelinger." In *Films That Work: Industrial Film and Productivity of Media,* edited by Vinzenz Hediger and Patrick Vonderau, 51–61. Amsterdam: Amsterdam University Press, 2009.

Wall Street. DVD. Directed by Oliver Stone. Twentieth Century Fox Film Corporation, 1987.

Whyte, William H., Jr. *The Organization Man.* Garden City, NY: Anchor Books, 1957.

Willard, Harold, F. *Insurance Ripoffs and Dirty Tricks: The Sucker's Dilemma.* Kirkland, WA: Thumbsdown Books, 1987.

Williams, Tennessee. "Sweet Bird of Youth." In *Plays 1957–1980.* New York: The Library of America, 2000.

Wilson, Sloan. *The Man in the Gray Flannel Suit.* New York: Four Walls Eight Windows, 2002.

Wilson, Sloan. *The Man in the Gray Flannel Suit II.* New York: Arbor House, 1984.

Wolfe, Tom. *The Bonfire of the Vanities.* New York: Farrar, Straus, Giroux, 1990.

Wouk, Herman. *The Caine Mutiny.* New York: Back Bay Books, 2003.

Yellin, Emily. *Your Call Is (not that) Important to Us: Customer Service and What It Reveals About Our World and Our Lives.* New York: Free Press, 2009.

Ziglar, Zig. *Zig Ziglar's Secrets of Closing the Sale.* New York: Berkley Books, 1984.

Index

About the Author

TONY OSBORNE, PhD, teaches courses in rhetoric, leadership, and mass communication at Gonzaga University, Spokane, Washington, and writes and speaks about art and popular culture. He has worked as an investigative reporter and feature writer for a daily newspaper, an account executive and speech writer for AT&T Communications, and an independent business consultant and trainer. Osborne received his doctorate from Ohio State University, a master's degree from Columbia University's School of Journalism, and a bachelor's degree from the University of Michigan.